Capital Punishment, Clemency and Colonialism in Papua New Guinea, 1954–65

Capital Punishment, Clemency and Colonialism in Papua New Guinea, 1954–65

Murray Chisholm

ANU PRESS

PACIFIC SERIES

ANU PRESS

Published by ANU Press
The Australian National University
Canberra ACT 2600, Australia
Email: anupress@anu.edu.au

Available to download for free at press.anu.edu.au

ISBN (print): 9781760466459
ISBN (online): 9781760466466

WorldCat (print): 1430729664
WorldCat (online): 1430729221

DOI: 10.22459/CPCCPNG.2024

This title is published under a Creative Commons Attribution-NonCommercial-NoDerivatives 4.0 International (CC BY-NC-ND 4.0) licence.

The full licence terms are available at creativecommons.org/licenses/by-nc-nd/4.0/legalcode

Cover design and layout by ANU Press. Cover photograph: 'The valley floor—where once they were afraid to live (2) Wahgi Valley, Papua New Guinea, 1970'. Source: Terence E.T. Spencer and Margaret Spencer, National Library of Australia, nla.gov.au/nla.obj-145573965.

This book is published under the aegis of the Pacific editorial board of ANU Press.

This edition © 2024 ANU Press

Contents

Abstract	vii
List of figures and tables	ix
Abbreviations	xi
Introduction	1
1. Meet our friend, Papua New Guinea	17
2. 'Why should the government want to fight us when we refuse to chip grass off the roads': The Telefomin killings of 1954	49
3. 'Mentally upset and a nymphomaniac': *R. v. Kita Tunguan, 1954*	93
4. The limits of mercy in Australian PNG: *R. v. Usamando, 1954*	127
5. 'The Crown as the fount of justice': *R. v. Ako Ove, 1956* and *R. v. Sunambus, 1956*	153
6. 'We do not think this is a sufficient deterrent': *R. v. Aro of Rupamanda, 1957*	181
7. The end of mandatory sentencing	215
Bibliography	253

Abstract

'What factors affected the decision by the Australian Government to grant clemency to offenders condemned to death in the territories of Papua and New Guinea (PNG) between 1954 and 1965 and by what process did Australian officials make their decision?' This book attempts to answer this question. It provides a close examination of an archive of files that advised the executive on Papua New Guineans found guilty of capital offences in PNG between 1954 and 1965. The files provide insight into conceptions held by officials at different stages of the process into justice, savagery, civilisation, colonialism and Australia's role in the world. Interrogated as a sequence, the files reveal three main domains of discussion between those interested in the fate of offenders and highlight change over time in the ideas and relations between the levels of the process. First, there were different ideas about what punishments would be appropriate to the particular context of the crime to be just and to maintain and extend Australian colonial control. Second, officials debated whether justice was best achieved by policies that accommodated cultural differences or strictly adhered to the Australian rule of law. Third, decisions were affected by the changing demands of protecting Australia's hold on PNG by representing Australian colonialism as benevolent, effective and temporary. In explaining the impact of these factors, the particular combination of idealism and self-interest, liberalism and paternalism, and justice and authoritarianism axiomatic to Australian colonialism becomes apparent and enables insight and analysis of Australia's administration of PNG in the lead-up to the acceptance of independence as an immediate policy goal. In answer to the second part of the question, the archive of clemency submissions reveals three elements of the process by which Australian officials and politicians enacted clemency. First, clemency was a discretionary, political process common to English-based jurisdictions and involved officials gathering information, evaluating it, and making political and administrative calculations in coming to a decision. Second, officials and politicians took into account information gained from both the official advisers and informal networks. Finally, as the colonial administration changed with changes in personnel, the files show Australia gathering the authority to grant mercy into the hands of the Commonwealth before devolving it back to the territories. In these transitions, the lens of the capital case review shows the trajectory of Australian colonialism during a period when Australia was unsure of the duration and nature of its future relationship with PNG.

List of figures and tables

Figures

Figure 0.1: Numbers and types of sentences of death under different capital offences, 1949–66.   7

Figure 1.1: Topography of New Guinea.   18

Figure 1.2: 'Educated in Australia, of course!'   40

Figure 3.1: Ela Beach Native Hospital, Port Moresby, Papua New Guinea, 1953.   95

Figure 3.2: Offences against women in Papua.   102

Figure 3.3: Offences against women in New Guinea.   102

Figure 4.1: Native prisoners weaving house walls, Minj Station, Wahgi Valley, Papua New Guinea, 1954.   129

Figure 5.1: Native village, Port Moresby, 1955 or 1956.   154

Figure 5.2: 'His Excellency the Governor-General of Australia, Field Marshal Sir William Slim, inspects a guard of honour of the Pacific Islands Regiment at Port Moresby', 1956.   163

Figure 7.1: 'The valley floor—where once they were afraid to live (2) Wahgi Valley, Papua New Guinea, 1970'.   220

Figure 7.2: 'Detainees working on the Corrective Institution farm at Bomana near Port Moresby'.   228

Tables

Table 4.1: Supreme Court prosecutions for sodomy.   140

Table 6.1: Tabulation of PNG Supreme Court judges' sentencing records, 1954–59.   195

Abbreviations

ACT	Australian Capital Territory
ALP	Australian Labor Party
ANGAU	Australian New Guinea Administrative Unit
APO	assistant patrol officers
ASOPA	Australian School of Pacific Administration
CPA	Communist Party of Australia
CT	*Canberra Times*
CWA	Country Women's Association
MHA	Member of the House Assembly
NSW	New South Wales
PO	patrol officer
SMH	*Sydney Morning Herald*
SPP	*South Pacific Post*
UN	United Nations
UNTC	UN Trusteeship Council
US	United States
USSR	Union of Soviet Socialist Republics
VTHC	Victorian Trades Hall Council
WW	*Women's Weekly*
WWPO	White Women's Protection Ordinance

Introduction

On 30 November 1961, Acting Justice Selby of the Supreme Court of the Territory of Papua and New Guinea (PNG)[1] sentenced to death Sakul, son of Sakaili, for the murder of his lover Akua's husband, the village *luluai*[2] Lukas Aisepal. Yet that was not the end of Sakul's story, as between 1954 and 1965 all capital sentences handed down in the Australian-administered territories were subject to a review by the governor-general of Australia. That legal arrangement set up a system by which Papua New Guineans who committed crimes in homes and gardens across PNG became entangled in the prejudices and problems of colonial management, their fates determined amid the politics of Australia's control of the remarkable diversity of indigenous peoples there. It meant that Australian politicians, far removed from the facts on the ground, had to decide what was fair punishment in cultural situations that were unfamiliar to them using their own notions of justice, race and gender, as well as their political acumen.

To support decision-making in Canberra, the first step in the sentence review process was for the trial judge to provide recommendations to the administrator of PNG on whether to confirm the death penalty, or to propose an alternate punishment. In this case, Selby recommended that Sakul's sentence be commuted from death to five years of hard labour in prison. The administrator then conveyed those recommendations to the Australian federal minister for territories, and, in some cases, provided accompanying reports and recommendations from other authorities. In Sakul's case, the administrator endorsed the judge's reasoning. In explaining this, they engaged with the sorts of ideas that they and their colleagues struggled with

---

1   The initialism PNG, usually associated with Papua New Guinea, is used to describe the Territory of Papua and New Guinea for ease of readability.
2   *Luluai*—a government appointed liaison in the village who might also have independent status in the community sufficient to influence people in the community. Sometimes translated as 'headman', but not as powerful as that might suggest.

in each clemency review, though the relative significance of issues changed over time. They interpreted unfamiliar cultural contexts, explored the implications for colonial control, parsed questions of justice and considered the characters of the accused, the witnesses and the victim. In this case, Acting Justice Selby provided reasons for his proposed alternate sentence, and for granting clemency, in terms of colonial control, acculturation, gender and race. With a literary flourish, Selby wrote:

> Sakul appears to be about thirty years of age. He had been married but divorced his wife when she left him. He had had no education but worked as a plantation labourer near Talasea for two years and later worked at a sawmill near Rabaul for one year. His village, Walwalpua, is in a comparatively isolated part of the North Coast of New Britain between Talasea and Cape Gloucester, but the district has long been under Administration influence which, since the establishment of the Cape Gloucester Patrol Post in 1958, has been considerable. There is an Anglican mission Station about two hours walk from the village; Sakul has been confirmed as an Anglican and is an intermittent churchgoer. The people in the area are well aware of the prohibition against murder and have shown some resentment against this particular killing. Sakul has been in custody awaiting trial for the inordinately lengthy period of eleven months. Despite the callous nature of the murder, I am of the opinion that great consideration should be given to the provocation aroused by Akua in her role as Lady Macbeth. The type of taunt which she employed is one which is indulged in from time to time by natives of New Guinea and is almost invariably effective. The New Guinea male is extremely sensitive to any aspersions on his manhood and can frequently be driven to violence by such attacks. Male and Female natives seem to be well aware of this, and it is not uncommon for them to use this method of inciting a man to violence and lawlessness. In the circumstances, I consider it proper to recommend that His Excellency, should he be pleased to, commute the Sentence of Death, which was recorded, and in its place impose a term of imprisonment with hard labour. If asked to recommend a suitable period, I would respectfully suggest a term of five years imprisonment with hard labour. In suggesting this term, I am taking into account the fact that Sakul has already spent eleven months in custody.[3]

---

3   David M. Selby to administrator, 6 December 1961, *Commutation of Death Sentence on New Guinea Native—Sakul, Commonwealth Department of Territories*, NAA: A452, 1961/7632.

With evidence and argumentation of this nature from PNG officials, the governor-general, advised by the Executive Council, and, in particular, by the minister for territories, then determined whether the sentence of death would be upheld or commuted. In this way, Sakul's personal life and punishment and how to make colonialism work at the level of his small community were considered at the highest levels of Australia's government as a significant policy decision. Sakul's sentence was commuted to the recommended five years despite the nominal sentence of death for having committed a particularly brutal and premeditated murder. In fact, mercy was the most likely outcome for a capital crime in Australian-administered PNG. This book explains why such an outcome was the most likely result.

This book is, in part, a legal history of PNG while under Australian law and Australian control. It examines when and why Australia used capital punishment and clemency, illuminating a key aspect of how Papua New Guineans experienced the law, and also what Australia intended and performed as a purveyor of law and justice to indigenous people in a colonial setting. As the historian of punishment in colonial Africa Stacey Hynd wrote, 'the death penalty was a crucial element of a colonial state's coercive capabilities, but it was also a potential marker of its violence and inefficiency'.[4] In examining why and how the death penalty was used, this book uses capital punishment and clemency to measure the extent of violence and inefficiency used to control Papua New Guineans in colonial PNG. It illuminates the context of capital punishment as a point of debate and contention in the history of an independent PNG. The death penalty was initially abolished with independence in 1976; however, it was reinstated in 1984 and its reach was expanded in 1991 and 2013. It was brought to prominence again with its abolition in January 2022.

This book also aims to understand Australian colonialism and the experiences of Papua New Guineans through the lens of law and punishment. The exercise of colonial control in PNG is a topic little mentioned in Australian histories and mythologies. Australians, while they celebrated an egalitarian ethic for themselves, determinedly controlled a complex array of political entities across the archipelago of PNG. The Australian officials who engaged in the absolute control of people—in a profoundly undemocratic fashion— did not like to think of themselves as colonists, but, rather, as friends and helpers: as missionaries of modernity. This book explores that peculiar

---

4   Stacey Hynd, 'Killing the Condemned: The Practice and Process of Capital Punishment in British Africa, 1900–1950s', *Journal of African History* 49, no. 3 (2008): 403–18.

and ongoing ambivalence. The journalist Sean Dorney wrote recently that Australians were 'embarrassed colonialists'.[5] He called upon Australians to know themselves and PNG better. This book is a step in that direction. It asks: what factors affected the Australian government's decisions to grant clemency or not to offenders condemned to death in PNG between 1954 and 1965, and by what process did Australian officials make those decisions?

Between 1954 and 1965, a multilayered process of judicial and official evaluation determined who of those condemned to death in PNG courts would be executed and who would be granted the mercy of the Crown. In that eleven-year period, only two men, out of an average of fifty-five Papua New Guineans per year condemned for the capital crimes of murder or rape, were executed, which suggests a legacy of clemency well in excess of some other colonial enterprises in the 1950s.[6] This apparent leniency was often the product of careful, and sometimes contentious, debate within and beyond government, particularly after 1954. After that date, a process previously superintended by PNG officials then became one controlled by Canberra and subject to the political calculations of the Commonwealth and the international climate. It was then devolved back to PNG in 1965 as the territory prepared for independence.

Determining whether to hang or spare people found guilty of often violent and terrible crimes engaged decision-makers in questions fundamental to the experience and practice of colonialism, such as appropriate punishment, how to express authority, and broader considerations of the role of justice and the legitimacy of the colonial state in PNG. These questions assumed particular importance during the years in which Australian practice moved from the paternalism of the immediate post–Second World War period to the acceptance of a more immediate path to self-determination for the territories.

The 822 capital case reviews arising during the decade under review (1954–65) present a large archive from which aggregated trends might be deduced. Yet this book does not use a statistical approach, as it is the

---

5   Sean Dorney, *The Embarrassed Colonialist* (Sydney: Lowy Institute Papers, 2016), Kindle edition, final paragraph of introduction.
6   Australia, Department of Territories, *Territory of Papua: Annual Report for the Period 1949–1950* (Canberra: Government Printer, 1951); Australia, Department of Territories, *Report to the General Assembly of the United Nations on the Administration of the Territory of New Guinea from 1st July, 1948, to 30th June, 1949* (Canberra: Government Printer, 1950); Stacey Hynd, '"The Extreme Penalty of the Law": Mercy and the Death Penalty as Aspects of State Power on Colonial Nyasaland, c. 1903–47', *Journal of East African Studies* 4, no. 3 (2010): 542–59.

processes by which, in each case, a decision was made amid shifting relations between PNG villagers, lawyers, judges and officials in Port Moresby and Canberra, and more general national and international interest, that the story and history of this place and time emerges in a manner that retains the particularity of thoughts, feelings and experiences of those involved. Accordingly, the method adopted in this book has been to work with a selection of specific cases that illuminate these transitions. More specifically, each case is reconstructed and contextualised through the file that was assembled to inform the decision of the governor-general-in-council on whether clemency should be exercised. These files, now held by the National Archives of Australia, are in themselves a rich archive of colonial practice, as notes prepared for prosecution, the verdicts of judges, reactions of Papua New Guineans, the commentary of PNG and Canberra-based bureaucrats, the PNG administrator, and the minister for territories were assembled in an extended exercise in colonial justice and accountability. Each file records, at varying depths, reflections, opinions and often debates around conceptions of civilisation, criminality, gender and violence, and the contributions these factors made to individual culpability amid the challenge of Australian officials managing a people that they did not really understand. Each case generated its own archive of evidence, inquiry, advocacy, judgement, review and punishment. Rather than draw general conclusions from a statistical analysis of a mass of files, the approach used here offers a detailed, immersive analysis of these processes in specific cases. This approach not only brings us closer to the crimes, the criminals and the court, but also to the people who, with limited resources to hand, made the decisions, weighed the factors and set the 'markers' to which Stacey Hynd referred.

In each capital case review file selected, the process of review involved testimony and argument from a consistent range of figures and was managed in terms of set procedures. Before 1954, the administrator of PNG had enacted the royal prerogative of mercy; subsequently, the governor-general of Australia, as the head of state and the Queen's representative, was required to determine the use of the royal prerogative of mercy. While the judge was bound by a mandatory sentence of death for those found guilty of capital crimes—wilful murder, piracy, treason and, until 1958, rape, or attempted rape of a white woman—two options existed for the guidance of the governor-general. If a judge thought that the matter concerned was an egregious crime deserving of capital punishment, they could 'pronounce a sentence of death'. If they held reservations regarding such a severe sentence, either in terms of the crime and the accused, or the impact of the punishment on Australian control of the colony, they would 'record a sentence of death' and recommend the use of the royal prerogative of mercy.[7] Once such a sentence was recorded, it was accepted custom and practice in PNG that a hanging could not occur and the sentence could not be increased beyond that recommended by the judge and minister. This firm distinction was unlike other jurisdictions that retained the practice of recorded or pronounced sentences of death.[8] It was at this point of executive discretion that each case presented its own complexity as a microcosm of colonial governance.

Figure 0.1 summarises the use of the death penalty by PNG Supreme Court justices and the final outcome of capital case reviews. It shows that all recorded and most pronounced sentences of death were commuted. There was an execution in 1954 and another in 1957. The higher figures for sentences for wilful murder in some years are due largely to mass arrests, up to thirty at a time, for killings of a political nature related to inter-group warfare and killings of officials, rather than individual murders.[9] My analysis is primarily focussed on cases selected from the pronounced group, as it is in the consideration of those crimes that colonial officials and Australian politicians tested the limits of mercy. Similar to other Australian jurisdictions, such as the state of Victoria, PNG made little use of execution to punish crimes. Between 1952 and 1958 in Victoria, there were eighteen sentences of death with no executions, and the next execution was in 1967, the last ever in Australia.[10]

---

7   'The Criminal Code (Queensland, Adopted) 1903', section 652, NAA: A432, 1958/3143, item 7801743.
8   Murray Tyrell, interview by Mel Pratt for the Mel Pratt collection [sound recording], 1974, transcript, 45–6, National Library of Australia. This was a different application of the British *Judgement of Death Act*, 1823 (UK 4 Geo. 4, c.48) than other British colonies and dominions and, according to the Attorney-General's Department, that was partially due to the wording of the PNG Criminal Code. See NAA: A432, 1958/3143, item 7801743; Hynd, 'Killing the Condemned'; Andrew Novak, 'Capital Sentencing Discretion in Southern Africa: A Human Rights Perspective on the Doctrine of Extenuating Circumstances in Death Penalty Cases', *African Human Rights Law Journal* 14, no. 1 (2014): 24–42; Carolyn Strange, 'Discretionary Justice: Political Culture and Death Penalty in New South Wales and Ontario, 1890–1920', in *Qualities of Mercy: Justice, Punishment and Discretion*, ed. Carolyn Strange (University of British Columbia Press, 1996), 130–65.
9   See, for example, Editor, 'New Guinea Death Sentences', *Sydney Morning Herald*, 12 February 1957, 2; '16 Cannibals Sentenced to Gallows', *St Joseph News-Press*, 22 May 1960, 6.
10 Jo Lennan and George Williams, 'The Death Penalty in Australian Law', *Sydney Law Review* 34 (2012): 659–94, 674; Barry Jones, 'The Decline and Fall of the Death Penalty', in *The Penalty is Death: Capital Punishment in the Twentieth Century*, ed. Barry Jones (Melbourne: Sun Books, 1968), 257–71.

INTRODUCTION

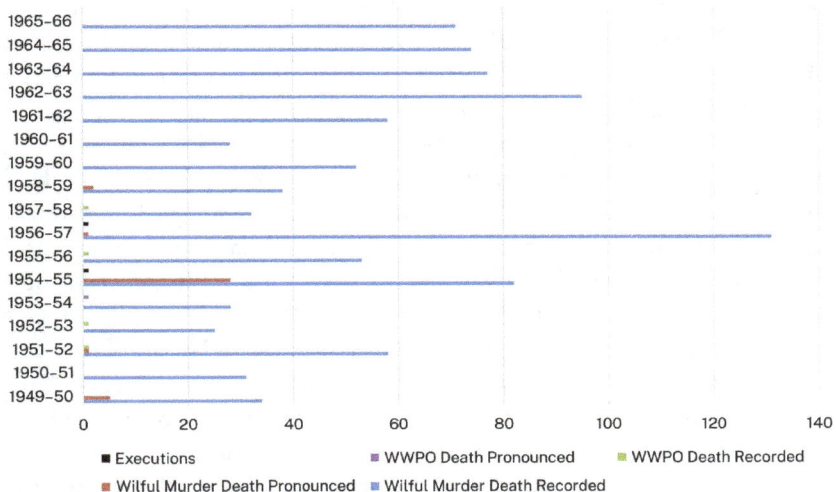

Figure 0.1: Numbers and types of sentences of death under different capital offences, 1949–66.

Note: *WWPO: White Women's Protection Ordinance.*

Sources: Australia, Department of Territories, *Territory of Papua: Annual Report for the Period [1949–1965]* (Canberra: Government Printer, [1949–66]); Australia, Department of Territories, *Report to the General Assembly of the United Nations on the Administration of the Territory of New Guinea [1946–1966]* (Canberra: Commonwealth Government Printer [1947–1967]).

In answer to the first question—why decisions were made—this book shows that the Australian officials who reviewed capital sentences were influenced by policy concerns, notions of justice and the demands of international accountability. In answer to the second question—how decisions were made—this book shows that the processes involved in weighing those influences reflected a shifting alignment of interests and ideologies within the ranks of the politicians, judges, lawyers, officials, expatriates, journalists and commentators who shaped Australia's governance of PNG.

Among those ideologies, the most prevalent and contested was that relating to 'advancement'. The term was much used by the most prominent figure directing PNG policy for much of the period covered by this book: Paul Hasluck, the first minister for territories from shortly after his election to parliament in 1951 until 1963. A dominant personality, Hasluck brought experience and commitment to this portfolio. Before entering politics, he had researched the history of Western Australia's Aboriginal policy, particularly regarding law and justice. Later, after joining the public service, he served as a diplomat and was closely associated with, and soon disenchanted by,

Australia's role in the United Nations (UN). In PNG, Hasluck sought to manage what he described as 'the advancement of the natives … towards a civilized mode of life'.[11] His vision of 'civilised' was essentially defined by a Westernised, capitalist, democratic and Christian paradigm.[12] Further, it ran parallel to the ways the term 'advancement' was used in the charter of the UN Trusteeship Council (UNTC), under whose aegis Australia held New Guinea, but not its Crown colony of Papua, as a project through which 'to promote the political, economic, social, and educational advancement of the inhabitants of the trust territories'.[13] In between these models, Australian colonial officials, in day-to-day practice, believed they had to maintain control of the people, both in terms of law and order and cultural change.[14] After the Second World War, Australia invested large sums of money to gradually extend more than nominal control over all parts of PNG, including its more than 800 culturally distinct language groups, seeking to translate pragmatic advancement, as well as uniform practice and observance, into comprehensible forms across a diverse range of settings. While elsewhere the course of postwar colonialism tended to be moving towards exercising less direct control, Australia was extending its authority over PNG with these mixed concepts of advancement.

One of the primary means by which this aim of advancing Papua New Guineans was affected was through law and punishment. By imposing an Australian legal order on peoples with diverse social control practices, colonial officials sought to indicate how people in a 'modern' state should conduct themselves.[15] Such priorities were often explicitly expressed in clemency files, as capital crimes were seen as instances in which the need to redefine understandings of justice were most pressing. For example, officials expressed the intention to direct people away from cultures of vendetta or

---

11 Paul Hasluck, *A Time for Building: Australian Administration in Papua and New Guinea 1951–1963* (Carlton: Melbourne University Press, 1976), 94–5.
12 Ibid., 94–7.
13 Ibid., 5, 45–9; United Nations, *United Nations Charter*, chapter XII, article 76b, www.un.org/en/about-us/un-charter; Oxford English Dictionary Online, 'Advancement', www.oed.com/view/Entry/2887?redirectedFrom=advancement#eid.
14 Edward P. Wolfers, *Race Relations and Colonial Rule in Papua and New Guinea* (Brookvale: Australian and New Zealand Book Company, 1975), 5, 127; John Dademo Waiko, *A Short History of Papua New Guinea*, 2nd ed. (Melbourne: Oxford University Press, 2007), 114.
15 Bruce L. Ottley, and Jean G. Zorn, 'Criminal Law in Papua New Guinea: Code, Custom and the Courts in Conflict', *American Journal of Comparative Law* 31, no. 2 (1983): 251–300.

from perceived customs of gendered violence.[16] As well as messages directed towards the colonised, officials were equally aware of messages that needed to be sent to critics of Australian colonialism, whether in the metropole or internationally. Throughout this period, the Australian government was required to report annually to the UNTC, submit to triennial inspections by council members, and navigate the postcolonial and Cold War scrutiny of its administration of PNG. Like the concept of 'advancement', there were mixed messages about the role of punishment depending on the intended audience. The case files discussed in this book reveal the complexities of these tasks and the multiple messages intended by punishment.

'Advancement' not only had several audiences but also reflected a range of ideological investments. At least four ideologies of justice intersected as each case file made its way from the crime to the Executive Council. First, some officials continued to hold onto prewar colonial practices that favoured ad hoc dispute resolution determined by local knowledge, paternalistic discretion and an implicit scepticism regarding the prospects for significant indigenous self-determination. Generational change in the ranks of expatriate officials, judges and commentators tested this outlook during the period under review but never completely displaced it. The files examined here capture its influence—in assumptions, turns of phrase and rhetorical gestures as much as formal articulation. Second, there was an existing 'old' colonialism that was not so much local as imported through experience and example in other British colonies, and which seemed to acquire greater salience with more systematic attention to the postwar future of 'subject peoples'. As governor-general from 1953 to 1960, Sir William Slim, having had a career in the Indian Army, emphasised deterrence and coercion as the tools of responsible colonialism. His influence was felt in his unprecedented intervention in several clemency determinations. Third, there was a contrasting postwar liberal ideology of justice that valued due process before the law, on Australian models, and the equal treatment of races, leading to the eventual autonomy of populations within an ostensibly Western model of the nation, state and law. Paul Hasluck, an official with considerable power over policy and the culture of institutions, exemplified this perspective. Finally, there was an emerging, progressive ideology that

---

16 John Greenwell, *The Introduction of Western Law into Papua New Guinea*, unpublished manuscript given to author by John Greenwell, former first assistant secretary and director of Papua New Guinea Office Government and Legal Affairs Division, Department of External Territories, 1970–75; Sinclair Dinnen, 'Sentencing, Custom and the Rule of Law in Papua and New Guinea', *Journal of Legal Pluralism* 20, no. 27 (1988): 19–54.

valued Papuan and New Guinean cultures and peoples as they were and envisaged an integration of traditional and Western legal practices. By 1964, a synthesis of prewar colonial notions and more progressive notions had occurred that saw significant authority invested in the discretion of judges to make determinations about the meaning of traditional practices and conceptions of justice, rather than the Executive Council. This synthesis presented a solution both to international scrutiny, which was forcing the pace of political autonomy for PNG, and to opposition to the death penalty in Australia, which was becoming a prominent social cause. In pursuit of justice, the holders of these ideological positions maintained different assumptions about appropriate social controls, conflict resolution systems and punishments for Papua New Guineans. Those assumptions informed their decision-making and arguments in the clemency case files.

While it would be easy to see the processes revealed in the clemency files as confirming an already-familiar chronology of Australian colonial administration in PNG; the value of the detailed record they offer is that the progression in these concepts, ideals and policy was rarely neat. The files capture the logic, calculation, anxieties and, sometimes, simple prejudice that shaped not only individual life-or-death decisions but also the management of wider processes, including the efficiency of policing and imprisonment systems, of gender relationships between Papua New Guineans and between Papua New Guineans and non–Papua New Guineans. They show officials drawing on formal briefings and legal precedents and principles, as well as informal information—sometimes gossip and often the confidences of close-knit, insular and under-resourced networks. Equally, these files capture not only the imposition of colonial authority but also the terms in which the place of justice was conceptualised within transitional Papua New Guinean societies, in which execution was seen to have its own role in maintaining the credibility of authority and the cohesion of communities. And they reflect sensitivity to a wider public debate, already well attuned to the tensions of a decolonising world and the moral collapse of other colonial regimes through harsh enforcement of power and authority. Here, too, the messages of advancement were complex.

These files cannot be read in isolation. They are puzzles, the significance of which to their moment in time, we must try to solve. The ciphers that help to reveal the motivations, anxieties and policies behind decisions include the histories of discretionary justice in both metropole and colonial jurisdictions that drew on British legal traditions. There are also previous histories of Australian colonialism in PNG. Finally, there is a wealth of primary documentation about the people, place and period related to the events and decisions.

The first context that assists in interpreting the capital case files is the scholarship dealing with questions of crime and discretionary justice, especially as they intersect with colonialism. Historians have discussed the role and impact of executive clemency on nations and colonies, and have concluded that clemency promoted political and policy goals as well as the legitimacy of the government, domestic or colonial.[17] At these moments of professional, personal and political choice, officials and politicians took into account information gained through formal, legislated systems of consultation, such as the submission process, and information gained through informal social networks of influence that came from living and working in colonial communities. The selected cases show each of these elements in operation.

Historians of law and governance have highlighted mismatches between Australian policy statements and actual colonial practice on the mainland and in PNG, and the extent to which legal principles mattered at all in calculations of political or strategic priorities.[18] Berger, Foster and Buck have asked: 'How much sham was involved in the law of colonial enterprises?'[19] The capital case files offer an opportunity to test the level of 'sham' in the claims of officials, such as Hasluck, that Australia's relationship with PNG was 'the experimental stage of something which the world has not yet seen … an attempt at cooperation and mutual service between two peoples'.[20] In analysing legal practice and punishment, this book casts into relief the nature of Australian colonialism and the ways in which discretionary justice

---

17 Tina Loo, 'Savage Mercy: Native Culture and Modification of Capital Punishment in Nineteenth Century British Columbia', in *Qualities of Mercy: Justice Punishment and Discretion*, ed. Carolyn Strange (Vancouver: University of British Columbia Press, 1996); Douglas Hay, 'Property, Authority and the Criminal Law', in *Albion's Fatal Tree*, ed. Douglas Hay (London: A. Lane, 1975), 41; Hynd, 'The Extreme Penalty of the Law', 552; Stacey Hynd, 'Murder and Mercy: Capital Punishment in Colonial Kenya, ca. 1909–1956', *International Journal of African Historical Studies* 45, no. 1 (2012): 92.
18 Allan M. Healy, 'Monocultural Administration in a Multicultural Environment: The Australians in Papua New Guinea', in *From Colony to Coloniser: Studies in Australian Administrative History*, ed. J. J. Eddy and J. R. Nethercote (Sydney: Hale and Iremonger, 1987), 224; Wolfers, *Race Relations and Colonial Rule*, 3–4.
19 Benjamin Berger, Hamar Foster and A. R. Buck, 'Introduction: Does Law Matter? The New Colonial Legal History?', in *The Grand Experiment: Law and Legal Culture in British Settler Societies*, ed. Hamar Foster, Benjamin L. Berger and A. R. Buck (Vancouver: University of British Columbia Press, 2008), 11.
20 Paul Hasluck quoted in Nicholas Brown, *Governing Prosperity: Social Change and Social Analysis in Australia in the 1950s* (Melbourne: Cambridge University Press, 1995), 74.

was used to serve other objectives. A clear evidentiary trail of changing ideas about, and representations of, Papua New Guineans and the relationship between Australia and PNG from 1954 to 1965 can be seen in the capital case review files examined here.

The second context is the extensive literature on Australia's history in PNG. Historical scholarship provides insight into Australia's relationship with PNG, though many studies focus on the transition to independence. Further, many were written decades ago and, therefore, reflect the preoccupations of those times. This book reflects today's questions and investigates Australia as a willing colonialist. It focuses on Australian colonialism at a time before its practitioners knew clearly when, or if, it would end, and policy was formulated largely to support its continuance. By examining this period, this book primarily seeks to understand the ways in which the handling of capital cases reflected tensions within colonialism rather than those emerging from its perceived ending. Following on from studies by Hank Nelson and Amirah Inglis that made valuable contributions to our understanding of the place of capital punishment in Australian colonialism prior to and during the Second World War, this book extends our understanding into the postwar period and the continued use of executive clemency, although the terms had changed.[21]

A diverse range of primary sources provided the third context for interpreting the capital case files and the 'markers' associated with each decision. The cases were discussed in contemporary newspapers, magazines and memoirs, providing different perspectives and helping to explain the arguments and silences in the files. Further, the PNG newspaper, the *South Pacific Post*, the widely circulated *Pacific Island Monthly*, PNG parliamentary debates, memoirs, other archival files, ephemera and literature on PNG in a broader sense provide a cultural and political context in which the references and assumptions made in the files can be understood. By placing the files and the participants within a network of people and interests, the decisions can be interpreted more readily.

---

21 Hank Nelson, 'The Swinging Index: Capital Punishment and British and Australian Administration in Papua and New Guinea 1888–1945', *Journal of Pacific History* 13, no. 3 (1978): 130–52; Amirah Inglis, *The White Women's Protection Ordinance: Sexual Anxiety and Politics in Papua* (London: Sussex University Press, 1975). On a new standard for colonialism, see Hank Nelson, 'From Kanaka to Fuzzy Wuzzy Angel', *Labour History*, no. 35 (1978): 172–88.

INTRODUCTION

Six cases that the executive found particularly difficult to resolve are examined in this book. In the process, general claims made by Australia at the time and subsequently about its benevolence, as well as subsequent scholarly analyses of Australian colonialism in the postwar period, are tested against the particular experiences of ordinary Papua New Guineans and the actions of the colonial officials who punished them. Using a similar methodology, Martin J. Wiener argued that 'large, indeed global, questions were worked through in small, specific contexts'.[22] Of course, case files are a particular genre of writing that utilises, as Valverde suggests, 'highly formatted resolutions'; nevertheless, they reveal the thoughts and priorities of the bureaucrats and politicians who developed them and made decisions using them.[23] Through their layered documentation, the cases unveil core concepts that decision-makers considered or held to be axiomatic to their discussions, ranging from ideas of 'primitive' to 'advanced' Papua New Guineans, ordinary to extreme violence, unprovoked to provoked violence, unmanly to manly behaviour, immoral to moral conduct, and customs to be acknowledged and those to be eradicated.

This book begins with an orienting chapter that briefly outlines the most relevant aspects of the Australian colonial project in PNG up to 1954 and provides background for the following chapters, each of which is based around one or two cases that were problematic in some way for the decision-makers.

Chapter 2 focuses on the Telefomin killings of 1954 in which patrol officers and Papua New Guinean police constables were killed in an attempt to defy Australian colonialism. The killers were not executed—despite pronounced sentences of death being handed down, despite extended public discussion, despite the seriousness of the crimes and despite the fact that similar crimes earlier in the century had led to deadly official reprisals.[24] The decision on clemency recognised the extent of dissatisfaction with Australian governance within that district, the need to enhance Australia's international reputation and the need to shore up Australia's continued control of the territories.

---

22 Martin J. Wiener, *Empire on Trial: Race, Murder, and Justice under British Rule, 1870–1935* (New York: Cambridge University Press, 2009), ix.
23 Mariana Valverde et al., 'On the Case: Explorations in Social History: A Roundtable Discussion', *Canadian Historical Review* 8, no. 1 (2000): 269.
24 Hank Nelson, *Papua New Guinea: Black Unity or Black Chaos?* (Pelican Penguin, 1972), 66–7.

Chapter 3, also from 1954, analyses the prosecution of Joseph Kita Tunguan for the rape of his European employer, Dr Blanka Nesbit. Kita Tunguan's crime was a capital offence under section 3 of the *White Women's Protection Ordinance, 1926–1934*[25] and he received a pronounced sentence of death. That he was granted clemency reveals the disorderly nature of the administration of discretionary justice in 1954 and the role of informal networks of knowledge in influencing legal processes. This case also highlights an increasing focus on the welfare of the colonised, exchanges between Australian and PNG debates over crimes of sexual violence and the highly gendered terms in which the tasks of 'advancement' were being defined.

The third case study is *R. v. Usamando, 1954*. Usamando was hanged after killing five people over a period of some thirty years. The decision to hang Usamando was an attempt to manage the disorder of Papua New Guinean prisons and the expectations of Papua New Guineans regarding Australia and customary justice, and to frame the idea of 'advanced' Papua New Guineans that the colonial project was seeking to create. In handling this case, officials and politicians explicitly considered ways to maintain the sentencing precedent for the sanction of the death penalty while seeking to present a positive image of Australian colonialism to a range of audiences.

In Chapter 5, I compare and contrast the cases of *R. v. Ako Ove, 1956* and *R. v. Sunambus, 1956*, which were paired in a critique of PNG justice written by the then governor-general, Field Marshall Sir William Slim. Slim argued that both men should be hanged, despite their receiving recorded sentences. Together, these cases highlight the extent of intervention possible in discretionary processes. A test of public and procedural thresholds to the use of execution, they expose the tension between the ideological frameworks within Australian practice.

The fifth case study looks at *R. v. Aro of Rupamanda, 1957*. Aro brutally killed his two wives and received a pronounced sentence of death, becoming the last person executed by Australian authorities in PNG, and, indeed, the last person ever executed in PNG to date. Capital punishment was abolished in PNG in 1976; although it was reintroduced in 1984, no one was hanged prior to its abolition in January 2022. The moral and political reasoning in this case reveals evolving views on how public order and gender boundaries should be enforced, and provides insight into the relationship between administrative priorities, international scrutiny and contending ideologies.

---

25   *White Women's Protection Ordinance, 1926–1934*, Pacific Island Legal Information Institute, www.paclii.org/pg/legis/papua_annotated/wwpo19261934342/.

Chapter 7 assesses the factors leading to the cessation of the legal framework underpinning the clemency process examined in this book. In 1959, there was a perception that this increasingly centralised review process was functioning smoothly. In 1960, however, prime minister Robert Menzies announced his government's intention to more rapidly bring PNG to independence, thereby effectively altering the calculus of decision-making in capital cases and favouring the devolution of final authority back to judges in PNG. By 1964, mandatory sentencing was abolished, giving judges more discretion in finalising punishment. With the freedom to set their own sentences, judges ceased condemning offenders to death, even though the death penalty itself was not abolished until 1976. This chapter assesses the significance of this return to localised discretion as a further reframing of ideas of 'advancement'.

Each chapter, except the last, begins with a narrative constructed from the basic facts of the crime, trial and administrative process of preparing a file for presentation to the governor-general-in-council. They then outline the main contextual factors shaping assessments of the place of the case in the matrix of colonial concerns and track the influence of these considerations on how the arguments mounted related to the exercise of discretionary justice for each individual. The files under consideration vary in completeness: wherever possible, the analysis utilises the file as the primary artefact of the issues under consideration; however, where appropriate, evidence is inferred from other sources, such as reports of public statements in newspapers and passing references in official and personal correspondence. As noted above, each chapter then summarises the contemporary issues influencing the case and any existing scholarship in building an assessment of its significance. Presented chronologically, each case is assessed as a point of transition, testing or challenging the Australian colonial project.

In his extensive memoir of his time as minister for territories, Hasluck wrote that Australia was attempting to replace an old Papua New Guinean system of what he called 'government by jabber'—that is, by consensus building and discussion—with fair and even-handed Australian justice.[26] Ironically, in the case of capital punishment, 'government by jabber' was what Papua New Guineans obtained as Australian officials 'jabbered' to reach their own view of what was just and good.

---

26 Hasluck, *A Time for Building*, 167.

1

Meet our friend, Papua New Guinea

On 6 May 1955 in Madang, PNG, seven men, Iarumagin, Oregom, Kaman, Kubunda, Maiamandi, Mui-e and Umia, killed a family of three, husband, wife and daughter, Gigira, Mui-An and Murom, with arrows and spears as the family worked at their farm. Justice Kelly of the PNG Supreme Court wrote to Donald Cleland, administrator of PNG that:

> All seven accused maintained that Gigira had been practicing sorcery and was responsible for the deaths of their fellow men and they were entitled to kill him … All seven denied any knowledge, at the time of the killing, of Administration teachings against killing.[1]

The men testified that Gigira's father had been a famous sorcerer as well. They regretted the death of Murom who had been struck accidentally and whose life they had tried to save. Justice Kelly concluded that:

> If Your Honour desires my suggestion as to any proposed sentence then, because all the accused have been in custody for some six months, and because of their honest but wrongful belief that they were more or less obliged to kill Gigira, I respectfully suggest that justice will be done if all seven accused be sentenced to 21 months' imprisonment with hard labour.[2]

---

1 Justice A. Kelly to administrator, 20 June 1955, NAA: A518, CQ840/1/3_PART1, item 3252669.
2 Ibid.

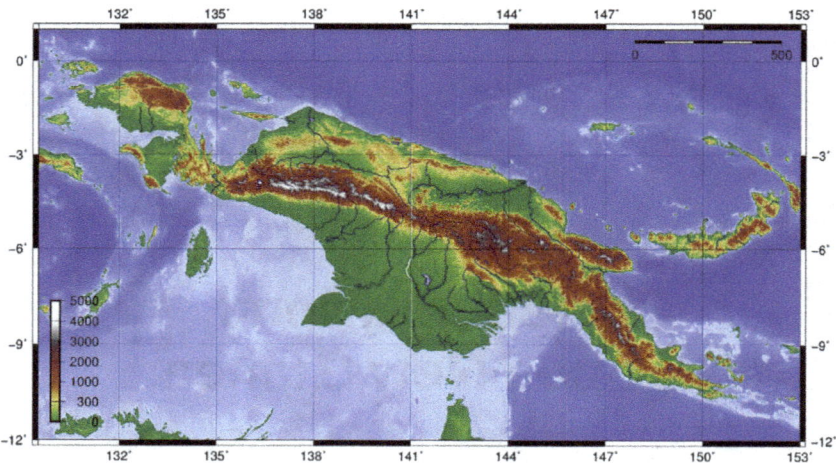

Figure 1.1: Topography of New Guinea.
Note: Papua and New Guinea comprise the Eastern half of the main island and its neighbouring archipelago.
Source: commons.wikimedia.org/w/index.php?curid=47308148.

Justice Kelly and Cleland, as a part of the colonial project, were attempting to impose Australian law in a foreign land that had its own beliefs and practices. Neither the Criminal Code in PNG nor the Australian common law had scope for addressing sincere belief in witchcraft as a provocation to murder. The discretion permitted to the executive during the clemency process was the means they used to address that mismatch in worldviews.

By 1955, Australia's colonial project in PNG was fifty years old. Australia had retained its hold over Papua and New Guinea out of a belief in its geopolitical importance—a belief proved by the events of the Second World War. However, its possession had not resulted in large-scale economic and political development prior to the war, which left Australia with a large task to fulfil in terms of its role and responsibilities to Papua New Guineans and the UN Trusteeship Council (UNTC) after the war, resulting in reassessments of colonialism, paternalism and 'advancement' by Australia and its colonial administration. Despite bipartisan support for the geopolitical strategy of possessing PNG, and for the sense of duty to Papua New Guineans as wartime allies, Australia's desire to hold and develop PNG ran counter to the decolonisation movement taking place around the world. Equally, and in response to this decolonisation movement, there was also widespread support within PNG and Australia for the territories to remain under Australian control for the longer term.

In the 1950s and 1960s, policy in relation to PNG was formed within the context of these tensions—that is, between staying and going. While that discussion unfolded, the administration of PNG, including its political and legal systems, remained predicated on Australian practices, even when the very different cultures and geography of PNG strained the capacities of the bureaucracy and the very concepts on which those systems were founded. See Figure 1.1 to understand the rugged, mountainous topography and the difficult nature of internal movement and communications. This chapter sketches the dimensions of Australian practices as they shaped the contexts for the cases examined in this book.

An underdeveloped colony

A pattern of protection for Papuans and, consequently, limited export-oriented economic development for both expatriates and Papuans, was systematised from 1906 to 1942 under the direction of the long-serving lieutenant-governor of Papua, Hubert Murray, which became known as the 'Murray system'. New Guinea had been subject to a more commercially oriented regime prior to the Second World War, first as a German colony and then, after the First World War, through an Australian mandate under the aegis of the League of Nations. The difference between the levels of advancement in Papua and New Guinea should not, however, be overstated, as both were rather nominal and rudimentary colonial administrations. Further, both were brought under sudden and intense pressure and scrutiny with the coming of the Second World War.

Many people who supported what I have termed an 'old' colonial ideology of law drew on the Murray system as their guide. After the war, B4s—'befores', as they were colloquially known, that is, 'lived in Papua *before* the war'— from Papua also administered New Guinea as a part of their responsibilities across all of PNG. As such, the Murray system was used by many officials as a reference point in mapping out future possibilities and for assessing the value of policy in the 1950s and 1960s, including questions raised in the commentary on clemency cases. An outline of that system, then, is helpful in understanding the parameters of clemency.

While Murray, on his appointment as lieutenant-governor in 1906, was interested in the development of mining, exploitation of oil reserves and prospects for agriculture, his determinative priority remained social stability for Papuans and New Guineans. Over time, this emphasis came to rest, in particular, on the continuation of village and family social and economic structures, both as a way of minimising the disruption to populations who were, thus, brought slowly into economic 'contact' with the wider world, and of managing those populations within the constraints of tiny budgets from the Commonwealth and low levels of commercial investment.[3] Under Murray, in 1924, Port Moresby had a population of about 400 expatriates and 3,000 Papuans. Labour contracts were limited in scope and extent and only leasehold title on land was allowed to settlers to prevent speculation, all of which was designed to keep Papuans enmeshed in traditional socio-economic obligation and support systems. Colonial and federal bureaucrat and writer Francis West has argued that Murray's system, in part, was aimed at preventing a landless proletariat, with the associated social disruption and degradation of urban poverty, and that Murray preferred subsistence agriculturalists to the landless unemployed who could be found in the towns and on the margins of plantations or mines.[4] Though hoping to encourage cash cropping in commodities, such as copra, that would not disrupt the social order, Murray's regulations extended from labour controls to a comprehensive strategy that attempted to maintain and preserve Papuan culture, including regulations banning Papuans from drinking alcohol, watching fictional cinema and wearing shirts. Papuans also had to follow curfews and restrict themselves to certain parts of the towns.[5] The segregation of space and culture maintained a social gulf between the expatriate and the indigenous communities in the scattering of small towns established by expatriates, such as Port Moresby, despite the use of Papuan commercial and domestic labour by expatriates.[6] By way of justification, Murray claimed that such distinctions helped Papuans to become 'better brown men' and not some sort of 'racial' and cultural hybrid, which he presumed to be implicitly inferior.[7] Seemingly, Murray subscribed somewhat to eugenicist principles, which were popular at that time. Under him, Papuans were subject to what he and his officials regarded as protection from an unkind world.[8] Along with Australia's tariff barriers to

---

3   Clive Moore, *New Guinea: Crossing Boundaries and History* (Honolulu: University of Hawaii Press, 2003), 185–6.
4   Francis West, *Hubert Murray: The Australian Pro-Consul* (Melbourne: Oxford University Press, 1968), 122–7, 129.
5   Edward P. Wolfers, *Race Relations and Colonial Rule in Papua and New Guinea* (Brookvale: Australian and New Zealand Book Company, 1975), 31, 36; Moore, *New Guinea*, 185–6.
6   Wolfers, *Race Relations*, 122; Owen Genty, *The Planter* (Wellington: Geebar Enterprises, 2006), 111.
7   Hubert Murray, cited in West, *Hubert Murray*, 274.
8   Hank Nelson, 'The View from the Sub-district', in *The Defining Years: Pacific Islands, 1945–65*, ed. Brij V. Lal (Canberra: Division of Pacific and Asian History, The Australian National University, 2005), 34–5.

products from Papua and New Guinea, pervasive global protectionism, and the Australian government's resistance to cheap plantation labour meant that there was little outside economic interest in the colony and few markets for its produce.[9] An economic climate of low investment and low returns, coupled with minimal interracial engagement, provided few resources and little incentive to expand direct Australian control.[10]

Another reason for the limited extent of development in Papua by 1954 was the difficulty of establishing a legal regime that would support commerce and personal security on an island with extreme cultural and legal diversity. Australians understood the different peoples of Papua and New Guinea to possess few constant, hierarchical, judicial or legal structures capable of being adapted to protecting and regulating capital and business interests on the part of, or on behalf of, the indigenous population. Neither, it was thought, could the many and varied local and personalised dispute resolution systems provide personal security. Further, there was certainly no system that was consistent across the complicated cultural and political patchwork of the territories. These assumptions led to recourse to Australian law as the uniform code to which Papua New Guineans had to adhere.[11] Therefore, establishing an Australian legal and administrative regime was a long-term project under Hubert Murray and one that he saw as a necessary prelude to real economic development.[12] Another consequence of small budgets was that Australian law prior to 1942 effectively covered only part of the territories. The goal of gradually establishing an overarching system of law and governance was at the heart of the 'old' colonial legal ideology whose practitioners, in 1954, saw themselves as training Papua New Guineans in a system that was alien to them and that they would only gradually come to understand over time. Aspiring to an eventual incorporation of the population into Australian law, there was also a recognition that prevailing circumstances required ad hoc adaptation by Australian officials, which took account of what they perceived as the capacity of local people to encompass

---

9 C. D. Rowley, *The New Guinea Villager: The Impact of Colonial Rule on Primitive Society and Economy* (London: Pall Mall Press, 1966), 12–3.
10 West, *Hubert Murray*, 140–1, 145–7; Hank Nelson, *Papua New Guinea: Black Unity or Black Chaos?* (Pelican Penguin, 1972), 22–3.
11 John Dademo Waiko, *A Short History of Papua New Guinea*, 2nd ed. (Melbourne: Oxford University Press, 2007), 30; John Greenwell, *The Introduction of Western Law into Papua New Guinea*, unpublished manuscript given to author by John Greenwell, former first assistant secretary and director of Papua New Guinea Office Government and Legal Affairs Division, Department of External Territories, 1970–75, 2.
12 H. N. Nelson, 'Murray, Sir John Hubert Plunkett (1861–1940)', *Australian Dictionary of Biography*, adb.anu.edu.au/biography/murray-sir-john-hubert-plunkett-7711; 'Australia in Papua', *Papuan Courier* (Port Moresby), 5 March 1920, 2.

foreign practices, and a perception of their needs, while being circumscribed by the imperative of maintaining Australian control and authority. It was a complicated balancing act that played out in the everyday work and decisions of colonial officials.

Many people who supported the 'old' colonial ideology of law drew on the Murray system as their guide. After the Second World War, B4s from Papua also administered New Guinea. As such, the Murray system was used by many officials as a reference point in mapping out future possibilities and for assessing the value of policy in the 1950s and 1960s, including questions raised in clemency cases.

Whereas Australia had acquired Papua in 1906 from the United Kingdom as a colonial territory, Australian forces had seized German New Guinea during the First World War. At the completion of hostilities, and after intense lobbying by Prime Minister of Australia Billy Hughes at the Paris Peace Conference, Australia gained a League of Nations Class C mandate over New Guinea.[13] This classification followed the judgement that New Guinea was largely undeveloped economically, culturally and politically, and was 'best administered under the laws of the mandatory power as integral portions of its territory'.[14] This did not mean annexation, as a mandate did not grant sovereign rights; however, in practice, the League had little control over mandated territories, particularly at the Class C level.[15] Such mandates were predicated on the principle of eventual independence, 'tutelage' being expected until the territories were 'able to stand by themselves under the strenuous conditions of the modern world'—a test more explicit than Australia's indefinite possession of Papua, but still far from a specific timetable.[16] German New Guinea had seen traders and business people practising aggressive plantation agriculture, seizing land from local people and using spurious sales practices. Recognising the benefits of such practices for export development, the Australian administration allowed looser labour and land regulation in New Guinea than in Papua during the interwar years.[17] Equally significant, as Nelson has shown, Western law was enforced

---

13   Anuerin Hughes, *Billy Hughes: Prime Minister and the Controversial Founding Father of the Australian Labor Party* (Milton: John Wiley & Sons, 2005).
14   *The Versailles Treaty June 28, 1919: Part I*, article 22, The Avalon Project: Documents in Law, History and Diplomacy, Yale University, avalon.law.yale.edu/imt/parti.asp.
15   W. J. Hudson, *Australia and the Colonial Question at the United Nations* (Honolulu: East-West Centre Press, 1970), 12–3.
16   *The Versailles Treaty June 28, 1919: Part I*, article 22.
17   Moore, *New Guinea*, 186.

more violently in New Guinea than in Papua. The commercial interests at stake seemingly resulted in the colonists being less forgiving of local resistance and violence, and more determined to their maintain authority.[18]

The two territories were administered separately until 1942, during which time New Guinea adopted the Queensland Criminal Code among other regulations and laws then in use in Papua. Certain variations to the code introduced in Papua, such as labour ordinances, were not introduced in New Guinea; for example, labour recruiters in New Guinea were not restricted on the length of time and value of contracts as they were in Papua.[19] Rejecting those aspects of Murray's regime that inhibited business, commercial interests in New Guinea lobbied hard to prevent the administrative amalgamation of the territories in the 1920s. It nevertheless remained the case that, beyond relatively small areas of development and significant levels of Australian control, much of New Guinea remained under traditional systems of control and was little visited by Westerners, even in those areas formally patrolled by Australian officials. Many Papuans and New Guineans travelled widely during the war as conscripts and labourers; consequently, knowledge among Papuans and New Guineans of Australian governance, the territories and the world was greater after the war.

In areas outside Australian control, social and economic activities were regulated by customs and consensus-based systems that varied across the island. In many cultures, in the event of a disruption of communal harmony or violation of a community member's property rights or honour, discussion among kinship groupings determined workable solutions to return the community to peace. For example, among the Abelam people of Papua, consensus building by prominent people produced a balance between competing forces to settle disputes and expiate offences.[20] If consensus could

---

18   Hank Nelson, 'The Swinging Index: Capital Punishment and British and Australian Administration in Papua and New Guinea 1888–1945', *Journal of Pacific History* 13, no. 3 (1978): 130–52, 152.
19   *Criminal Code (Queensland, Adopted) in Its Application to the Territory of New Guinea*, Pacific Islands Legal Information Institute, www.paclii.org/pg/legis/newguinea_annotated/cca254/. See also *Criminal Code Amendment Ordinance 1923–1939*, Pacific Islands Legal Information Institute, www.paclii.org/pg/legis/newguinea_annotated/ccao19231939248/; *Natives' Contracts Protection Ordinance 1921–1936*, Pacific Islands Legal Information Institute, www.paclii.org/pg/legis/newguinea_annotated/ncpo19211936386/; *Native Labour Ordinance, 1911–1927*, Pacific Islands Legal Information Institute, www.paclii.org/pg/legis/PG-papua_num_act/nlo19111927202/.
20   Richard Scaglion, 'Kiaps as Kings: Abelam Legal Change in Historical Perspective', in *Customary Law in Papua New Guinea: A Melanesian View*, ed. D. Gewertz and E. L. Schieffelin (Port Moresby: The Law Reform Commission of Papua New Guinea, 1983), 78.

not be reached, then vendetta or violence might result. In practice, this threat of violence, loss of property and social pressure produced obedience to custom and communal consensus.

In 1954, this diverse range of customs and practices across more than 800 language groups in PNG posed numerous challenges for policies aimed at uniform development. Policymakers, police and the courts found it difficult to account for cultural obligations that might lead a Papua New Guinean to violate Australian law. As a result, Papua New Guinean cultural norms and obligations received limited recognition from Australians, except within a framework of judicial discretion to encompass diverse systems of property tenure, domestic arrangements and obligations to enact violence.[21] Ultimately, customary law could be overruled by Australian decision-makers using Australian policing, courts, principles and codes as deemed appropriate by colonial officials. Mediating between these systems, including the decisions of superior courts in Australia, were the examinations and judgements made by PNG Department of Native Affairs officials, and, in particular, patrol officers.

In the absence of economic interests or political devolution, law was the primary means of colonial control and acculturation for colonial officials.[22] With that understanding, and hoping to extend the reach of acculturation, Australian authorities continued the policy of the first British lieutenant-governor, Dr William McGregor, in developing the Royal Papuan Constabulary, a police force staffed by Papua New Guineans that was tasked with imposing order in the limited areas under Australian control from 1896 and throughout the colonial period.[23] Embodying the acculturation of Papua New Guineans to Australian ways, members of the constabulary saw themselves as agents of change for the people around them.[24] Australian officials who superintended assigned districts and subdistricts directed the work of the constables. The areas under formal and actual Australian control during the 1950s and 1960s remained loosely administered. This control was devolved through district officers (DO) within the Department of Native Affairs who directed patrol officers (PO) and assistant patrol

---

21 Greenwell, *The Introduction of Western Law*, 19–21.
22 Rick Sarre, 'Sentencing in Customary or Tribal Settings: An Australian Perspective', *Federal Sentencing Reporter* 13, no. 2 (2000): 74–8; Heather Douglas and Mark Finnane, *Indigenous Crime and Settler Law: White Sovereignty and Empire* (Basingstoke: Palgrave Macmillan, 2012), 5, 8.
23 Brian Essai, *Papua and New Guinea: A Contemporary Survey* (Melbourne: Oxford University Press, 1961), 6–7.
24 August Ibrum Kituai, *My Gun, My Brother: The World of the Papua New Guinea Colonial Police, 1920–1960* (Honolulu: University of Hawaii Press, 1998), 129.

officers (APO), also known as police masters, in their work. In the more remote locations, DOs, POs and APOs acted as magistrates, lawyers, health officials, economic advisers and generally as promoters of Westernisation. Given their direct contact with the people, they also wrote reports about the administration's progress in the regions that could be used to formulate and monitor policy.[25] This direct system of contact had been designed by Murray to build confidence and gradually introduce Papua New Guineans to Australian laws and systems. Under postwar pressures of development, such chains of control could also expose gaps in accountability and highlight the capacity for eventual autonomy and independence.

In addition to the constabulary, the Department of Native Affairs appointed respected locals as 'headmen', called *luluai*, with deputies called *tultul*, to act as liaisons and advocates for colonial policy and law.[26] That structure had some success in extending Australian influence and control over Papua New Guineans, encouraging some compliance with regulating village hygiene and law and order. Even here, however, there were complexities regarding the direction of influence and control. Local people subverted Australian intentions to their own ends, as Papua New Guinean villagers expected *luluais* to prevent most problems from coming to the attention of Australian authorities whose response would be to impose Western law.[27] In most cases, they preferred their own solutions.

Nevertheless, arguably the most influential officials in villages were the constables who had more effective power over locals than *luluais* and were often more present than the POs and APOs. Their salary and outsider status gave them relative wealth, and their position gave them more independent, coercive power than *luluais* or *tultuls*.[28] Rarely posted in their home areas, they were less entangled in local obligations and so could bring legal sanctions against people, or not, with fewer social consequences. Yet, the constables were also an itinerant presence in smaller hamlets, far from patrol stations. Under such circumstances, traditional systems continued to deal with most issues of social order within communities. Only the most intractable of situations, such as inter-group or transgressive murders, came to the

---

25   For extended descriptions of kiap duties, see Kituai, *My Gun, My Brother*, ch. 1; Hank Nelson, *Taim Bilong Masta: The Australian Involvement with Papua New Guinea* (Sydney: Australian Broadcasting Commission, 1982), ch. 21.
26   Waiko, *A Short History of Papua New Guinea*, 42–3, 106.
27   Kenneth Read, 'Native Attitudes to European Law', Kenneth Read Papers Relating to Teaching Australian School of Pacific Administration (ASOPA) Courses, Australian National University Archives, ANUA444, box 1, folder 7, 1–4.
28   Kituai, *My Gun, My Brother*, 19.

attention of Australian officials for much of the colonial period. Indeed, until the Second World War, much of PNG remained beyond the precise, constant control of the Australian administration.[29] Thus, the constabulary, although one of the more successful apparatuses of Australian colonialism, policing and law, still had a limited effect on development.

The world order after the Second World War and the administration of PNG

From 1942 to 1945, PNG was a Second World War battlefield and vital to Australia's defence. The Japanese bombing attacks on Australian territory seemingly proved the geopolitical value of holding PNG to protect the Australian mainland from the north. During that emergency, for the first time, the territories were administered as one through the Australian New Guinea Administrative Unit (ANGAU). Military personnel took over civil functions that could be continued during the war, such as health and policing. The war resulted in massive destruction; however, after 1942, the United States provided large investments in infrastructure, as well as some disbursement of consumer goods to Papua New Guineans to cultivate their support in the conflict. The war and US investment gave Papua New Guineans and Australians a sense of the possibilities of greater engagement in the territories.[30] Ultimately, then, the war changed Australian notions of its role in PNG.

After returning to civilian administration in 1946, the administrative union of the two territories continued, although the foundation of the UNTC changed the regulations under which Australia held the territories. New Guinea was converted from a League of Nations mandate into a UN trust territory. Similar to the mandate, trusteeship presupposed a pathway to independence for New Guinea, although the terms of that pathway were subject to more stringent review by the UNTC, which was a more powerful and influential body than the League of Nations. After the Second World War, in the context of the Cold War, and with former colonies taking up places in the UNTC, the Eastern Bloc and newly independent states moved against the retention of colonial possessions by Western powers.[31]

---

29 Bill Gammage, *The Sky Travellers: Journeys in New Guinea 1938–1939* (Carlton: Melbourne University Press, 1998), 6.
30 Waiko, *A Short History of Papua New Guinea*, 91–2.
31 Christopher Waters, 'The Last of Australian Imperial Dreams for the Southwest Pacific: Paul Hasluck, the Department of Territories and a Greater Melanesia in 1960', *Journal of Pacific History* 51, no. 2 (2016): 169–85.

PNG newspapers regularly reported criticisms of Australian policy from the Eastern Bloc and non-aligned nations, particularly India, through UNTC discussions and public commentary on Australian administrative decisions.[32] The colonial relationship complicated Australian foreign policy significantly.[33] As such, the retention of New Guinea and Papua required careful management of policy and external perceptions.

Amid suspicion that Australia would annex rather than free New Guinea, Australia experienced more scrutiny of its actions from the UNTC than it had from the League of Nations. Anti-colonial members of the Trusteeship Council were suspicious enough of Australian policy goals to oppose, if unsuccessfully, the ongoing administrative union of the two territories. Australia used the support of its Western allies in the UNTC to gain permission to formally unify the administration of both territories, resulting in the Commonwealth *Papua and New Guinea Act, 1949*.[34] In administering New Guinea and Papua together, Australia proposed that both territories would progress to independence as one nation at some point in the future.[35] Nevertheless, due to the disapproval of other nations, Australia faced the moral and political problem of holding PNG at all.

While anti-colonial critics were generally unsure of Australia's plans for PNG, it is also true that such plans remained unclear to most Australians and Papua New Guineans. Different groups in PNG and Australia had different medium- and long-term visions for PNG. Whether administrative unification signalled a movement towards self-determination in the near term, annexation by Australia as a state or an extended period of domination by Australia under the existing terms, was cause for debate.[36] Some expatriates and Australians coveted PNG for its potential wealth while others felt that Papua New Guineans were better off governed by Australia for their own protection from the world. According to some Australian officials, many Papua New Guineans wanted Australia to remain in control, as Australia's trusteeship brought benefits to them.[37]

---

32 See, for example, 'Minister Hits Back at Indian Critics', *South Pacific Post*, 7 July 1954, 3.
33 Rowley, *The New Guinea Villager*, 1.
34 J. K. Murray, 'The Provisional Administration of the Territory of Papua New Guinea: Its Policy and Problems', Lecture, University of Queensland, Brisbane, 1949, in *Education and Colonial Control in Papua New Guinea: A Documentary History*, ed. Peter Smith (Melbourne: Longman Cheshire, 1987), 161.
35 NAA: A518, A846/6/45 PART 1, item 3272356; NAA: A518, A846/6/21, item 3272255.
36 Hudson, *Australia and the Colonial Question*, 28–30, 147, 151–3.
37 Nelson, *Taim Bilong Masta*, 211.

Australian officials tended to assume that the international community and the UNTC were hostile to Australian colonialism; therefore, they presumed the need to assuage a critical audience when making significant decisions, such as on clemency and execution. The formal oversight of the UNTC rendered policy decisions on New Guinea, and, to a lesser extent, Papua, visible to the world community, including anti-colonial critics. A feature of oversight meant that the UNTC sent triennial delegations to review progress in New Guinea. Australia was anxious about how policy decisions would reflect on its administration in UNTC reports.[38] Further, newspaper articles in the *South Pacific Post* (*SPP*), PNG's only newspaper for some decades after the war, kept attention focussed on the possibility of international scrutiny by providing regular articles about overseas commentary and the attitudes of UN delegations and officials. This concern influenced administrative practice; for example, in 1949, the then administrator, Jack Murray, gave an official direction to current and future PNG officials to be cautious of the UN's reception of policy in PNG.[39]

Paul Hasluck, minister for territories from 1951 to 1963, shared PNG's cautious attitude to the UN and the level of scrutiny when forming policy. Before becoming a politician, the Western Australian had been one of the diplomats working for the Australian minister for external affairs, Dr Evatt, when the UN was established. Hasluck knew a great deal about UN institutions, both their weaknesses and possibilities.[40] As such, he had strategies for maintaining a positive image of Australian colonialism in New York. For example, he encouraged public diplomacy to depict Australian colonialism in a positive light, such as educational films, exhibitions and information booklets.[41] Despite having concerns about the UN, he used its authority to justify his policy choices to administration officials, such as citing UN Charter provisions as a basis for policy development in

---

38   On the reception of such delegations, see discussion in Ian Downs, *The Australian Trusteeship Papua New Guinea 1945–75* (Canberra: AGPS, 1980), ch. 7.
39   Murray, 'The Provisional Administration of the Territory of Papua New Guinea', 160–1. No relation to Hubert Murray.
40   Carl Bridge, 'Diplomat', in *Paul Hasluck in Australian History: Civic Personality and Public Life,* ed. Tom Stannage, Kay Saunders and Richard Nile (St Lucia: University of Queensland Press, 1999).
41   Jane Landman, 'Visualising the Subject of Development: 1950s Government Film Making in the Territories of Papua and New Guinea', *Journal of Pacific History* 45, no. 1 (2010): 71–88. For an example of public diplomacy, see Australia, Department of Territories, *Territory of Papua and New Guinea: An Information Folder Prepared by the Department of Territories* (Canberra: Department of Territories, 1961). For a discussion of such diplomacy, see Nicholas Brown, *Governing Prosperity: Social Change and Social Analysis in Australia in the 1950s* (Melbourne: Cambridge University Press, 1995), 54.

education.⁴² He saw the UN as an obstacle that had to be appeased when necessary to achieve Australia's geopolitical and moral aims, but also as a tool to overcome opposition to new policy directions within PNG. This approach was sometimes noted, and resented, by the expatriate community, which, overall, preferred to see PNG's future as bound to Australia.⁴³

While the UNTC had imposed a duty on Australia, the Second World War had also caused a sense of obligation to PNG, particularly to the auxiliaries who had supported Australian troops—the Papua New Guinean men that Australian wartime reporters termed 'fuzzy-wuzzy angels'.⁴⁴ This sense of duty played itself out in many policy areas, including clemency and capital punishment. This new focus was evident in a highly influential Commonwealth report of 1944 on PNG's future by the war hero General Sir Thomas Blamey. Blamey argued both that PNG was vital to the defence of Australia and that Australia owed it a duty: 'It may be that we are confronted with one of those rare moments in history when morality coincides with expediency.'⁴⁵ Blamey proposed that Australia could use PNG for its defence, as a barrier to the north, while also helping its people to advance. In 1946, Australia's Labor government concurred with Blamey's assessment. Minister for External Affairs Eddie Ward described his dissatisfaction with previous Australian efforts in PNG:

> The government is not satisfied that sufficient interest has been taken in the territories prior to the Japanese invasion, or that adequate funds had been provided for their development and the advancement of the native inhabitants.⁴⁶

Ward promised significant investment in the wellbeing of Papua New Guineans as defined in UNTC provisions: 'to promote the political, economic, social, and educational advancement of the inhabitants of the trust territories'.⁴⁷

---

42 Paul Hasluck, *A Time for Building: Australian Administration in Papua and New Guinea 1951–1963* (Carlton: Melbourne University Press, 1976), 5, 94.
43 See, for example, 'Less Bureaucracy and More Development: Fighting Speech before Rabaul Chamber of Commerce', *Pacific Islands Monthly* 24, no. 10 (1954): 85–6.
44 Scott MacWilliam, 'Papua New Guinea in the 1940s: Empire and Legend', in *Australia and the End of Empires: The Impact of Decolonisation in Australia's Near North, 1945–65*, ed. David Lowe (Geelong: Deakin University Press, 1996), 32–70.
45 Thomas Blamey, cited in ibid., 33.
46 Eddie Ward, cited in Downs, *The Australian Trusteeship*, 13–4.
47 United Nations, *United Nations Charter*, chapter XII, article 76b, www.un.org/en/about-us/un-charter.

Labor increased the funding for the territory to address the UNTC's requirement for 'advancement', using Australian institutions as the means for that development, while still ensuring control.[48] For example, Labor abolished indentured labour and introduced a legal framework in which Papua New Guineans might negotiate their work conditions, but these measures also sought to limit the growth of a collective labour movement that might have challenged colonial authority.[49] Also, changes to the titles of those in charge reflected a change in vision; Colonel Jack Murray arrived in Port Moresby as the first administrator of the territory, not its lieutenant-governor, the new designation signalling supervision rather than ownership.[50] Advancement policies were also aimed at producing a bulwark to the north, thereby justifying Australia's strategic possession of PNG.[51] Policymakers waxed lyrical on the benefits of Australian occupation, including promising to greatly increase the budget for development in PNG.[52] Proof of the wisdom of Blamey's strategy of a northern bulwark in PNG, combined with assistance to the people, was provided with the expansion of communism in Asia and the Malayan emergency. Subsequently, South-East Asia became 'the primary focus of Australian strategic thinking'.[53] The reformation of the Pacific Islands Regiment in 1951, which recruited from Papua New Guinean communities and was led by Australian officers, was indicative of such thinking.[54]

---

48 Downs, *The Australian Trusteeship*, 14.
49 Michael Hess, 'In the Long Run …' Australian Colonial Labour Policy in the Territory of Papua and New Guinea', *Journal of Industrial Relations* 25, no. 1 (1983): 51–67, 58; Allan M. Healy, 'Monocultural Administration in a Multicultural Environment: The Australians in Papua New Guinea', in *From Colony to Coloniser: Studies in Australian Administrative History*, ed. J. J. Eddy and J. R. Nethercote (Sydney: Hale and Iremonger, 1987), 222–3.
50 Essai, *Papua and New Guinea*, 57.
51 Downs, *The Australian Trusteeship*, xviii; Essai, *Papua and New Guinea*, 57; Waters, 'The Last of Australian Imperial Dreams', 171. See also Hudson, *Australia and the Colonial Question*, 174; Sally Percival Wood, '"Chou Gags Critics in Bandoeng" or How the Media Framed Premier Zhou Enlai at the Bandung Conference, 1955', *Modern Asian Studies* 44, no. 5 (2010): 225–52. See also, David Lee, *Search for Security: The Political Economy of Australia's Post-war Foreign and Defence Policy* (St Leonards: Allen & Unwin, 1995), 130–1; David McLean, 'Australia in the Cold War: A Historiographical Review', *International History Review* 23, no. 2 (2001): 299–321; Stuart Doran, 'Toeing the Line: Australia's Abandonment of "Traditional" West New Guinea Policy', *Journal of Pacific History* 36, no. 1 (2001): 5–18; T. B. Millar, *Australia in Peace and War: External Relations since 1788* (Canberra: Australian National University Press, 1991); David Goldsworthy, *Losing the Blanket: Australia and the End of Britain's Empire* (Carlton: Melbourne University Press, 2002), 51; E. W. Tipping, 'Australians in the Near North', in *Near North*, ed. Robert J. Gilmore and Denis Warner (Sydney: Angus and Robertson, 1948), 1; David Lowe, *Menzies and the 'Great World Struggle': Australia's Cold War 1948–1954* (Sydney: UNSW Press, 1999), 54.
52 Downs, *The Australian Trusteeship*, 13.
53 Tristan Moss, *Guarding the Periphery: The Australian Army in Papua New Guinea, 1951–75* (Cambridge: Cambridge University Press, 2017), 23.
54 Ibid.

Having been cast as a great battle for freedom against imperialist aggression, the Second World War left Western, democratic, colonial powers morally compromised due to the contrast between their support for self-determination and control of subject people. The climate of suspicion against conventional justifications for colonialism was such that even major colonial powers, such as Britain and France, felt intense pressure to translate their imperial practice into developmental policies, rather than merely enriching themselves.[55] That contrast was a substantial problem for Australian colonial officials well into the 1970s, including in UNTC and UN General Assembly debates.[56]

In short, with its colonialism on display to the world, Australia had to be a benign influence rather than an exploitative presence in PNG. If Australia wished to have a strategic presence in PNG, it also needed to have UN approval of its plans for development, advancement and autonomy. In addition, due to the legacy of the Second World War, Australians were motivated by gratitude to do more for PNG than just pursue strategic necessities.[57] That obvious tension between benevolence and expediency played out in the actions of officials responsible for making discretionary decisions in capital cases. They were aware of wider geopolitical concerns as they discussed the possible effects of clemency or execution on advancement, law and order, and perceptions of Australian colonialism.

Bipartisanship for advancement policies in the 1950s and early 1960s

Following the change from a Labor to a Liberal–Country Party coalition government in 1949, Australia's new prime minister, R. G. Menzies, supported a policy of increased investment of funds and labour in PNG to fulfil Australia's international obligations and a sense of duty. A bipartisan approach prevailed on most policy issues until the 1960s, although, according to historian Ian Downs, a former PNG official, farmer and politician, and historian of the trusteeship, the new Liberal–Country Party government

---

55   Frederick Cooper and Ann L. Stoler, 'Tensions of Empire: Colonial Control and Visions of Rule', *American Ethnologist* 16, no. 4 (1989): 609–21, 616; Martin J. Wiener, *Empire on Trial: Race, Murder, and Justice under British Rule, 1870–1935* (New York: Cambridge University Press, 2009), 231–3.
56   Hudson, *Australia and the Colonial Question*, 151.
57   Hank Nelson, 'From Kanaka to Fuzzy Wuzzy Angel', *Labour History*, no. 35 (1978): 172–88.

wanted more private enterprise than Labor had planned.[58] In reality, with more money to spend, the first and new minister for territories, Paul Hasluck, hoped to do more for economic development in the early 1950s than had been done before the war. In his 1976 memoir of his work in PNG, *A Time for Building*, Hasluck recalled that his intention in assuming the portfolio was to encourage business, with the proviso that Papua New Guineans had to be heavily involved in any enterprises. He believed that economic development had to start with improving food production in subsistence farms to produce a surplus that would allow a transition to a cash economy. However, in keeping with the Murray system, he also wanted to prevent any 'harsh disruption of the indigenous social organisation and any sudden breakdown of social cohesion and discipline'.[59] Yet, due to his much larger budget and staff, Hasluck could be more ambitious than Murray. Signalling the new government's intention of being consistent with Labor in terms of investment and effort in PNG, Menzies separated the Department of Territories from External Affairs to allow more focus on PNG by the minister.

Hasluck, in 1951, spoke of a new kind of relationship between PNG and Australia—'an attempt at cooperation and mutual service between two peoples'.[60] This type of governance, rather than colonial, would be a product of Australia's gratitude. Placing Hasluck's sentiments and plans in a wider context, Peter Fitzpatrick argues that his claim of a 'new relationship' should be read with caution, as colonialists had adopted such benevolent postures before, but had not fulfilled their promises:

> As for ideology, Australia as a colonist claimed a particular humanitarian virtue. As a colonial power, Australia was, of course, far from unique in a belief in its superior benevolence. Indeed, the exploitative relations of any colonialism was so manifestly at odds with the egalitarian nature of Australia's self-image, that they appear to have to deny that they were colonists at all.[61]

Nevertheless, Hasluck's language was consistent with Blamey's, Ward's and H. Murray's; all believed that self-interest and altruism could coincide in Australian colonial practice.[62] The capital case review files provide an

---

58   Downs, *The Australian Trusteeship*, 71.
59   Hasluck, *A Time for Building*, 128–9.
60   Brown, *Governing Prosperity*, 74.
61   Peter Fitzpatrick, *Law and State in Papua New Guinea* (London: Academic Press, 1980), 68.
62   Hubert Murray served as lieutenant-governor of Papua. Jack Murray was the first administrator of PNG. They were not related.

opportunity to examine these seemingly opposing priorities at work in a significant area of policy, demonstrating attempts to bring them together in decision-making. Fitzpatrick is right to suggest that Australians did not see themselves as colonialists. It is also the case that significant attempts were made for the betterment of Papua New Guineans at Australia's considerable expense. Yet, the process of advancement had mixed success. Constrained by sometimes ill-informed policymaking, the implementation of reformist policy was further marred by deeply ingrained, racist paternalism that showed minimal regard for the will of the people.

Hasluck's policies were based on his appraisal of Papua New Guineans' capacity for advancement, in particular, their capacity to sustain a democratic nation-state. The minister's judgement is vital in understanding this period, as he held tremendous discretionary power, as he observed: 'for in a country of two million people I was virtually the Premier and the whole of a state Cabinet'.[63] He pictured advancement as Papua New Guineans 'taking a share in their government … over a number of generations'.[64] Hasluck would be minister for territories for twelve years and his plans and policies had an enormous impact on the territories, so his intentions and view of the work of Australia in PNG are highly significant. For this reason, his statements and recollections are given value in this book, notwithstanding the evidentiary weaknesses inherent in a memoir, even one written by a historian, as Hasluck's first career was as an Australian historian. Hasluck represented himself as the primary mover to alter prewar practices, pushing those ideas and practices that I term 'liberal colonial' ideology. Whereas prior to the Second World War, Papua New Guineans had been soldiers, police and *luluai*, but not candidates, politicians and bureaucrats, Hasluck wanted the gradual introduction of democracy, beginning with local shire councils on the Australian model and a gradual expansion of Papua New Guinean representation in the legislature. When the PNG Legislative Council first opened in 1951, in addition to appointed expatriate members, there were three appointed non-official Papua New Guinean members. Hasluck's intention to build Papua New Guineans' capacity for autonomy helps to frame an understanding of his policy decisions as minister in charge of PNG from 1951 to 1963, including in clemency.

---

63   Hasluck, *A Time for Building*, 6; Downs, *The Australian Trusteeship*, 93.
64   Hasluck, *A Time for Building*, 69–73.

Nevertheless, as with Ward, Hasluck's views were contested. Old colonialists saw the bipartisan consensus as a threat to the economic interests of Australian capitalists. Some members of the McGregor Club, a group that advocated in Australia for PNG and PNG expatriates, called Hasluck a 'kanaka lover'. Hasluck overheard himself being called this after he gave a speech to the group in Sydney. He took pride in what these prewar, old colonialists regarded as an insult. Rejecting such criticisms, he maintained that there were real prospects for the development of Papua New Guineans—socially, politically and economically—as leaders, rather than merely as workers and servants, with a distant hope of self-determination.

A major source of tension between Australian policymakers and international observers was that the timetables envisioned for independence for PNG were wildly different, in some cases by a century or so. This disparity tends to explain why, despite Australian party-political consensus about the altruism of trusteeship, Australia's benevolence, was not universally accepted. To critics of colonialism, Australia's actions did not seem to signal a pathway to independence, but rather, considering the attenuated timeframe, excuses and obfuscation.

Despite the intention to be altruistic and to advance PNG, as a range of scholars have noted, Australian colonialism in PNG *was* paternalistic and predicated on a racist conception of Papua New Guineans as needing guidance and protection because they were 'unsophisticated', or, as Justice Ralph Gore of the PNG Supreme Court put it in 1965, 'infants in history'. Such paternalistic colonialism could only be sustained politically and diplomatically in the 1950s and 1960s—a period characterised by decolonisation and a radical critique of imperialism—if it was represented as a liberal project, that is, as benevolent and, most of all, temporary, as Peter Gibbon, Benoit Daviron and Stephanie Barral have argued in relation to Africa.[65] Gibbon, Daviron and Barral's propositions about colonialism in the postwar period help to explain why paternalistic colonialism continued to be present in PNG, despite its repackaging as a liberal project by the Labor and Liberal–Country parties. Such differences between officials outline the difficulties of policy implementation and the fault lines of contention in decision-making.

---

65 Peter Gibbon, Benoit Daviron and Stephanie Barral, 'Lineages of Paternalism: An Introduction', *Journal of Agrarian Change* 14, no. 2 (2014): 165–89, 188.

PNG historians, in examining the paternalistic nature of Australian colonialism, have observed that Australia's direct rule in PNG was paternalistic because it was unasked for and because it was presumed that Papua New Guineans were 'not sophisticated' and needed protection and guidance.[66] Indeed, as August Ibrum Kituai noted, ironically, Australian paternalism actually rendered people too dependent on 'advice and guidance' and, as such, generated the conditions it was supposed to ameliorate. Therefore, despite the explicit purpose of postwar control—being, as Hasluck asserted, to give PNG 'a measure of independence'—it was not entirely successful.[67] Due to the perception of Papua New Guinean cultures and peoples as being too 'unsophisticated' to comprehend and engage with the 'modern' world, despite advancement policies, the timeframe for independence stretched well into the future, thus enabling more protective and paternalistic policies.

Like Kituai, Regis Tove Stella has argued that Australian literature, fiction and non-fiction, of PNG represented the colonised as uncivilised, as savages, to justify Australia's continued control, regardless of Papua New Guinean wishes.[68] The primary material explored in this book supports these propositions about paternalism. For example, Hasluck wrote of the care he took in guiding and protecting 'native' people from themselves; in relation to clemency, he noted that authorities considered the 'compulsion of native custom'.[69] The exercise of discretionary justice explored in this book provides evidence to support these contentions, as mercy was used in the belief that many Papua New Guineans were too unsophisticated to understand capital punishment, and thus required Australian mercy to protect them from themselves.

As reflected in his policies, including those on the law, Hasluck was a proponent of guardianship. Yet, at the same time, he expressed opposition to colonial attitudes that he described of being reminiscent of the Raj. In decrying colonialism while also commenting on the backwardness of the people and their need for guidance, he was paternalistic and liberal in Gibbon et al.'s definition: it was temporary. His approach was controlling and colonial, but also helpful, educative and temporary. That such language

---

66 Kituai, *My Gun, My Brother*, 2–8; secretary for law, PNG administration, to administrator, 1 October 1956, NAA: A432, 1956/3371, 7801327.
67 Hasluck, *A Time for Building*, 194–7. On 'a measure of independence', see Hank Nelson, 'Papua and New Guinea', in Stannage, Saunders and Nile, *Paul Hasluck in Australian History*, 160.
68 Regis Tove Stella, *Imagining the Other: Representation of the Papua New Guinean Subject* (Honolulu: University of Hawaii Press, 2007), 206–7.
69 Hasluck, *A Time for Building*, 70, 81.

and ideas permeated much of the policy and argumentation of the period suggests that they were both genuinely held and also the means of justifying Australian occupation to the world. The case studies examined in this book demonstrate the notional and actual pursuit of this liberal paternalism through the high-profile life-and-death decisions of capital punishment and clemency.

Countercurrents to change: The 'B4s' and their resistance to change

Opposition to the bipartisan commitment to liberalise Australia's relationship with PNG continued well into the 1960s. Ideas other than Hasluck's about how to pursue policies for advancement were discussed, and significant press and public interest was shown about how best to fulfil Australia's obligations to advance and repay its allies.[70]

The B4s—the businesspeople, farmers and colonial officials who had been in PNG before the war—came into conflict with the Liberal–Country and Labor parties' bipartisan liberal approach to colonialism. They had prewar ideas about working with Papua New Guineans, which Moore called 'deep-seated arrogant racism'.[71] Dame Rachel Cleland, whose husband was the administrator of PNG from 1951 to 1967, illustrated her understanding of the difference between liberals and old colonialists in an anecdote in her memoir.[72] When the Clelands first arrived in Port Moresby, they held a reception and invited Papua New Guinean members of the new legislature. However, the Papua Hotel in Port Moresby did not allow Papua New Guineans inside. This was due both to unofficial segregation and an ordinance that prohibited Papua New Guineans from drinking alcohol 'for their own good'. The Clelands had to insist that the owner of the hotel allow entry to invited Papua New Guinean legislators. Evidently, as this incident shows, during the 1950s and early 1960s there was a tension between established patterns of relations in PNG and Commonwealth policies for change.

---

70 Brown, *Governing Prosperity*, 55.
71 Moore, *New Guinea*, 185.
72 This very long tenure allowed him to put a stamp on the territory's bureaucracy and culture. As a Liberal Party appointee with experience in the territory from the war, Hasluck listened to him, particularly in the initial stages of Hasluck's tenure.

Hasluck and his officials in Canberra were aware of these philosophical differences among Australians living and working in PNG. Such differences made Canberra cautious about accepting recommendations on clemency from expatriates in PNG who were perceived to be tainted by racism and colonialism. As Hasluck noted in his memoir:

> I came away from that first trip [1951] revolted at the imitation of British colonial modes and manners by some Australians who were there to serve the Australian Government … never before in my life had I come across so many Australians who had lost so quickly any capacity to clean their own shoes, or pour themselves another drink without the attention of a 'boy'.[73]

Hasluck saw a connection between the relationships that Australians formed with Papua New Guinean workers and the wider attitude of officials to the future of PNG:

> Looking back I see now that what I said was very heavily influenced by my distress at the signs of colonialism in the part of both officials and private persons on my first visit to Papua and New Guinea and by the impression I had formed, from the present backwardness of the native people and the absence of any real participation by them in daily affairs that the present progress towards self-government would be likely to take several generations.[74]

Hasluck configured a segment of the expatriates in opposition to himself as illegitimately paternalistic—as having no vision for the end of paternalism and little recognition of essential equality. He saw them as lacking in Australian values and as standing in the way of more rapid advancement. He saw Papua New Guineans as equals who could aspire to eventual self-rule but in a potential rather than an existing capacity. Even though only some expatriates demonstrated these tendencies, they dominated the minister's understanding of the general culture of expatriates in PNG. The prejudice Hasluck perceived in old colonists was one reason he did not always rely on the advice that came out of PNG during clemency deliberations.

The racism of the B4s expressed itself in several ways, one of which was that they favoured the protective aspect of the Murray system. As will be shown in the case studies examined in this book, another aspect of unequal treatment was that Australian officials believed that Papua New Guineans

---

73   Hasluck, *A Time for Building*, 14–5.
74   Ibid., 70.

did not properly understand Australian laws or punishments. Thus, it was established practice to grant clemency to Papua New Guinean murderers if it could be shown that they were too 'unsophisticated' to comprehend the law and the meaning of state-sanctioned capital punishment—that is, that it was distinct from vengeance or vendetta. In their desire to be just, Australians of the old colonial school were wary of executing Papua New Guineans—partly because they did not fully understand them, or the calculus of their actions, and partly because they wanted to protect them. While some critics suspected that Australia was too paternalistic and colonial in its approach to PNG, the old colonials wanted this situation to continue.

Punishment as education: Enforcing the law and prison reform in PNG

Despite sixty years of British and Australian colonialism, advancing Papua New Guineans meant dealing directly and forcefully with customary practices that were serious enough to become conspicuous even with the limited extent of Australian control. Often, law enforcement related to ending the widespread practice of vendetta—or redeeming honour through reciprocal killing. In many Papua New Guinean cultures, honour required that the killing of a member of a given group be avenged by killing a member of the group to which the killer belonged. Hasluck wrote: 'the basic first lesson however was that of law and order'.[75] Justifying his position, Hasluck wrote of the gratitude of Papua New Guinean people who attributed the relative prosperity and security they experienced during his administration to the repression of vendettas—to his 'lesson'. Reshaping responses to violence was a key part of advancement; however, it required considerable changes in personal and social beliefs by Papua New Guineans. Under the Murray system and immediately after the war, this entailed officials and judges making ad hoc judgements about which parts of the law to enforce and how to modify its implementation to suit local problems.

Hasluck worried that this ad hoc approach, and the different treatment Papua New Guineans and expatriates experienced under the law, was a barrier to using punishment and the law to advance people. In 1951, Hasluck believed that many of the administration's ordinances and some practices by patrol officers and police in PNG undermined the principles of

---

75 Ibid., 80.

Australian law. Unequal treatment could not support Australia's claims to be a benevolent administration. Yet, there was agreement between liberals, such as Hasluck, and old colonial PNG officials on the centrality of maintaining law and order. Despite this overlap in priorities, there was still tension. The old colonial legal practice of controlling people to prevent crime was, in many ways, autocratic.[76] For example, some patrol officers acted outside Australian legal norms to imprison people for reasons that included pre-empting violence; witnesses and/or perpetrators were sometimes removed from the community to calm situations while passions were hot but also to ensure they were available for testimony and did not disappear into the wilderness. While not in keeping with the rule of law, pre-emptive arrest and detention of witnesses was effective in keeping order in the short term. Hasluck was content enough with the result that he did not dispute the utility of such measures, especially at the beginning of his tenure as minister. Yet he came to insist on more equitable practices over time to ensure the rule of law. This was because the legal and penal regime served an educative function in PNG in instructing Papua New Guineans in what behaviour was acceptable so that they would learn to function in a Western world. However, the aim and the practice were not always or entirely consistent. This conflict between paternalistic old colonialism and the efforts of liberals to 'Australianise' the legal system and treat people more equally can be seen in the case studies explored in this book, including instances in which PNG convictions were overturned by the High Court of Australia on points fundamental to the fair and impartial rule of law.

Questions of discretion and unequal treatment were complicated by the fact that, despite the goal of 'uniform development', not all areas of PNG were the same in terms of their level of advancement.[77] Advancement was producing urban workers who were actively engaged with the colonial project and who seemed to be growing weary of being pacified (see Figure 1.2). 'Advanced' Papua New Guineans were living and working with expatriates in urban communities, yet some still committed crimes of shame and vendetta similar to those who had not been acculturated. It was difficult to accommodate disparate groups of Papua New Guineans using the same legal calculus designed to understand the violence of less advanced people of the hills and valleys. Indeed, as Rachael Cleland observed, many urbanised Papua New Guineans resented being treated in

---

76 Healy, 'Monocultural Administration', 224.
77 For a thorough analysis of the policy, see Downs, *The Australian Trusteeship*, ch. 7.

the same way as less Westernised people.[78] Similarly, Papua New Guinean and Australian scholars have pointed to increasing objections to paternalism among urban Papua New Guineans across the 1950s, while rural Papua New Guineans resisted policies of equality, such as local shire councils.[79] Such dissonance made understanding the cultural context and justice issues of offences committed by urban Papua New Guineans in contrast to rural offenders a struggle. This struggle can clearly be seen in the deliberations on clemency when administration officials and the Executive Council strove to understand what might have motivated an urbanised Papua New Guinean to violence and what lessons to the community would result from mercy.

"Educated in Australia, of course!"

Figure 1.2: 'Educated in Australia, of course!'
Notes: Expatriates were unsure how to deal with newly educated Papua New Guineans.
Source: *South Pacific Post*, 6 January 1954, 12.

---

78 Rachel Cleland, *Pathways to Independence: Story of Official and Family Life in Papua New Guinea from 1951–1975* (Cottesloe: Singapore National Printer, 1985), 200–4.
79 See, for example, Waiko, *A Short History of Papua New Guinea*, 96–8; Nelson, *Papua New Guinea*, 168–9; Wolfers, *Race Relations*, 129–30; Sinaka Vakai Goava and Patrick Howley, *Crossroads to Justice: Colonial Justice and a Native Papuan* (Madang: Divine Word University Press, 2007), 19–21.

While some Papua New Guineans, to differing extents, sought to become part of a capitalist, urban society as intended by Australia, expatriates of the old colonialist school were anxious about the migration of increasing numbers of Papua New Guineans to urban areas. During the 1950s and 1960s, such migration put added pressure on the courts and police, as evident in the case files and newspaper reports, to enforce law and order and to promote laws that might serve to prevent crime. That anxiety overlaid existing anxieties about the prevalence of Papua New Guineans in the towns from before the war.[80] For example, legislation was introduced in 1952 and 1954 to control the movement and presence of Papua New Guineans in urban areas. On the one hand, there was a desire to restrict and control Papua New Guineans among some parts of the administration, but on the other, there was an official policy to liberate and modernise Papua New Guineans. These two approaches were clearly in conflict. The case studies in this book will suggest that, in some cases, discretionary justice allowed administrators the freedom to make public statements to resolve that conflict.

Punishment and prison played a role in advancement policies. Prisons were seen as a useful alternative to capital punishment because the administration hoped that Papua New Guineans would become accustomed to Australian ways in prison and then become agents for change upon their release. This belief was held in spite of the fact that the purpose, conduct and quality of PNG prisons had been a problem for Canberra since before the war.[81] Before and after the war, prisons pooled together prisoners who had committed minor and major offences to use them as a labour force for government infrastructure projects. During the period 1949–65, ongoing discussions were held about the benefits and financial costs of reforming the PNG prison system to turn prisons into schools of Westernisation and advancement. That such discussions were ongoing highlights the PNG administration's limited capacity to make and implement policy changes.[82]

---

80 Amirah Inglis, *The White Women's Protection Ordinance: Sexual Anxiety and Politics in Papua* (Sussex University Press, 1975), 147.
81 Prime minister to the Territory of New Guinea, 5 July 1935, NAA: A518, A846/1/12, item 107135.
82 Hasluck, *A Time for Building*, 175–84; Bruce L. Ottley, and Jean G. Zorn, 'Criminal Law in Papua New Guinea: Code, Custom and the Courts in Conflict', *American Journal of Comparative Law* 31, no. 2 (1983): 251–300; C. J. Buttsworth, extract of classification report, 26 February 1947, and extract of minutes of meeting no. 19 of the Executive Council of PNG, 12 July 1950, NAA: A452/1959/4611, item 533996; C. R. Lambert, secretary, Department of External Territories, to administrator, 12 August 1952, NAA: A452/1959/4611, item 533996; D. M. Cleland, administrator, to secretary, External Territories, 30 October 1952, NAA: A452/1959/4611, item 533996.

Nevertheless, belief in the educational and acculturating function of prisons continued. In 1963, the Department of Territories argued in a submission to the UNTC that PNG prisons not only successfully rehabilitated people but also drew them into the economic and social system of the nascent PNG state.[83] In claiming, to world audiences, that prisons advanced Papua New Guineans as capitalists and Westernised citizens, Australian authorities expressed faith in PNG prisons as educational institutions. Such claims meant that the Commonwealth saw clemency as a clear alternative to execution, as it believed it would assist with the goals of advancement policies.

In contrast, some Papua New Guineans were dissatisfied with a punishment system that left offenders fatter, happier and more educated than when they entered prison. Some Papua New Guinean critics of Australian prisons complained that offenders got to learn Tok Pisin, the lingua franca, in prison and thus gained better jobs upon leaving prison. While Papua New Guineans sometimes doubted the efficacy of punishing with imprisonment, they recognised how the experience might change people.[84] Thus, to an extent, Papua New Guinean perspectives on prison experiences indicate that prison did contribute to Westernisation. It is worth remembering that the prison experience also included heavy labour, and sometimes murder and rape, so prison was not a jolly boarding school in the 1950s.

Staying in step with mainland lawyers

The signals and lessons to Papua New Guineans were products of the culture of the law in which judges and lawyers in PNG were immersed. There was a particular jurisprudence of the PNG Supreme Court bench, but, despite that distinctiveness, in the postwar period, PNG's place in the wider Australian legal system limited the extent of inequity, paternalism and ad hoc decision-making. Australian legal trends and precedents provided limits to punishment and policing practices, and, several times in this period, the High Court of Australia enforced those limits by quashing

---

83 'Observations of the Administering Authority on Petitions', NAA: A452, 1961/4256, 3500477; C. R. Lambert, secretary, Department of Territories, to secretary, Department of External Affairs, 6 June 1962, NAA: A452, 1961/4256, 3500477.
84 Hasluck, *A Time for Building*, 179; 'Luxury Life for Killers Criticised', *Age* (Melbourne), 21 January 1965, NAA: A432, 1956/3371, item 7801327.

PNG Supreme Court judgements to protect the rule of law.[85] There was a shared culture among legal practitioners across Australian jurisdictions, including PNG—a necessity if PNG was to be advanced using Australian-style institutions and systems. Consequently, in attempting to replicate those systems for the project of advancement, the Australians who ran the territories participated in the same cultural, legal and ethical debates as on the mainland, and these debates, particularly those on capital punishment, affected clemency decisions.

Legal practitioners in PNG took their lead from mainland jurisdictions such as Queensland, New South Wales and Victoria, and the broader British common law, with some local adaptations. For example, while PNG adopted the Queensland Criminal Code, it made several changes to suit local circumstances. Such adaptations of metropolitan systems in colonial contexts were not unusual.[86] One such adaptation significant to understanding PNG criminal cases was that trial by jury was not used for indigenous offenders, instead judges acted as jury and judge.[87] Further, there was seldom a trial by jury for Europeans because the expatriate community was so small that an impartial juror was thought impossible to find, and Papua New Guineans were not considered peers.[88] In practice, the PNG Criminal Code drew on Griffith Code prescriptions, and PNG, Australian and common law precedents.[89]

The expatriate community that administered the law in PNG and made judgements about the quality and character of offenders were educated in Australia and culturally Australian. They read Australian newspapers, holidayed in Australia, retired to Australia and thought of themselves as Australians. The influence of Australian norms on PNG's legal system was particularly noticeable in the prevalence of capital punishment before, during and after the Second World War. Hank Nelson has demonstrated

---

85 For example, *Smith v. R. [1957] HCA 3; (1957) 97 CLR 100 (21 January 1957)*, Australian Legal Information Institute, University of Technology Sydney and University of New South Wales, www5.austlii.edu.au/au/cases/cth/HCA/1957/3.html.
86 Wiener, *Empire on Trial*, 3.
87 Hasluck, *A Time for Building*, 175. The *Criminal Code (Queensland, Adopted) in Its Application to the Territory of New Guinea,* sections 590–612, goes to the use of juries. There were subsequent amendments, such as *Jury Ordinance of 1907—Jury Ordinance Amendment Ordinance of 1909*, Pacific Island Legal Information Institute, www.paclii.org/pg/legis/papua_annotated/joo1907joao01909480/.
88 Hasluck, *A Time for Building*, 175; Nelson, *Papua New Guinea*, 71; Greenwell, *The Introduction of Western Law*, see rules of evidence, 16; J. V. Barry, G. W. Paton and G. Sawer, *An Introduction to the Criminal Law in Australia* (London: McMillian and Co., 1948), 6.
89 Barry, Paton and Sawer, *An Introduction to the Criminal Law*, 6–7. Also, the trial transcripts show the application of precedents from Australian and other British common law jurisdictions.

that PNG largely reflected Australian practice prior to the Second World War.[90] The emergencies and exigencies of the war saw a spike in the number of people executed, as, during the war, PNG was run by the military. According to Nelson, temporary military judicial officers made limited reference to the existing legal regimes and precedents in Australia, New Guinea and Papua. Thirty-four men were hanged in 1943 and 1944 due to this altered legal culture.[91] After the war, civilian judges regained control and PNG returned to an average sentencing rate of less than one execution per year, which was more or less consistent with the various jurisdictions on the mainland.[92] Nelson makes it clear that capital punishment was used more extensively during the war than in the years preceding it; this book discusses the postwar years.[93] When Australian lawyers were in charge, the results were normatively Australian. This became more pronounced as more Australian expatriates took on short-term public sector jobs. The intensification of Australian culture over the period under review provides additional parameters for understanding the legal and moral decisions regarding clemency.

Similar to civilian PNG, Australia used capital punishment sparingly in the various state jurisdictions. Indeed, Queensland had abolished the death penalty in 1922 and the most populous states were mostly clement.[94] New South Wales hanged no one after 1940 and abolished the death penalty for all but treason and piracy in 1955, abolishing it entirely in 1985.[95] Victoria did not hang anyone between 1951 and 1967, when the last person was hanged in Australia in 1967. No one was ever executed under Commonwealth and Australian Capital Territory criminal law. Tasmania held what was to be its last hanging in 1946. The Northern Territory hanged two people, both in 1952. Somewhat contrary to this trend, South Australia hanged six people between 1939 and 1964 and then abolished the practice in 1976. Similarly, Western Australia hanged five people between 1939 and 1964, before

---

90   Nelson, 'The Swinging Index', 150–2.
91   Ibid., 149.
92   Jo Lennan and George Williams, 'The Death Penalty in Australian Law', *Sydney Law Review* 34 (2012): 659–94, 678.
93   Nelson, 'The Swinging Index', 149.
94   R. N. Barber, 'The Labor Party and the Abolition of Capital Punishment in Queensland, 1899–1922', *Queensland Heritage* 1, no. 9 (1968): 3–12.
95   Barry Jones, 'The Decline and Fall of the Death Penalty', in *The Penalty is Death: Capital Punishment in the Twentieth Century*, ed. Barry Jones (Melbourne: Sun Books, 1968), 257; Lennan and Williams, 'The Death Penalty in Australian Law', 680.

abolishing the death penalty in 1984.[96] I will argue that this limited use of capital punishment in Australia was one of the reasons for the lack of resort to it in PNG. Despite a large number of death sentences in PNG—Hasluck commuted ninety-five sentences in just one year[97]—Australian authorities hanged only two men in the postwar period (see Figure 0.1). In PNG, as in Australia, clemency was the most common outcome of a capital conviction and that tendency increased over time.

There was an increasing alignment between PNG and the Australian bureaucracy from the 1950s because of Hasluck's expansion of the public service in PNG and improvements in communication technology linking PNG to Canberra.[98] New, and more progressive, attitudes were apparent as the new recruits had not been fully socialised into prewar colonial attitudes.[99] Further, new officials, such as POs, received more extensive formal training than before the war.[100] At the new Australian School of Pacific Administration, they undertook courses in anthropology and the law and learned a range of practical skills and administrative procedures. Thus, they had a more systematic understanding of the law and of PNG upon their arrival than many of their predecessors, such as Errol Flynn's haphazard entry into the New Guinea service.[101] This 'Australianisation' resulted in more openness to change. Many new recruits were keenly aware of Australia's debt and duty to PNG—a consequence of the celebration of the 'fuzzy-wuzzy angels' of the battlefields of the Second World War.[102] Most were junior employees with a limited ability to effect policy and practice, but during this period Canberra-based officials exercised more influence than previously.

The generational change was limited by the fact that most of the key figures of the administration had worked in the territories prior to the war, such as Chief Justice Phillips and his most senior judge, former chief justice of

---

96   Lennan and Williams, 'The Death Penalty in Australian Law', 670–8; A. R. G. Griffiths, 'Capital Punishment in South Australia, 1836–1964', *Australian and New Zealand Journal of Criminology* 3, no. 4 (1970): 214–6; Jones, 'The Decline and Fall of the Death Penalty'.
97   Hasluck, *A Time for Building*, 81.
98   Downs, *The Australian Trusteeship*, 77–98.
99   Donald Denoon, Philippa Mein-Smith and Marivic Wyndham, *A History of Australia, New Zealand and the Pacific* (Oxford: Blackwell, 2000), 328–9; Downs, *The Australian Trusteeship*, 98.
100 Brown, *Governing Prosperity*, 65; Kenneth Read Papers Relating to Teaching Australian School of Pacific Administration (ASOPA) Courses, box 1.
101 Brown, *Governing Prosperity*, 65; Errol Flynn, *My Wicked, Wicked Ways* (New York: Dell Publishing Co., 1961).
102 Nelson, 'From Kanaka to Fuzzy Wuzzy Angels', 10.

Papua, Ralph Gore. New patrol officers and company employees usually worked under experienced B4s; thus, they were indoctrinated to varying degrees into the old colonial perspective, despite the public statements of Cleland and Hasluck in support of advancement.[103] Nevertheless, some new arrivals were selective in taking on the ideas of the previous generation, rejecting some of their racial and sexual mores, as described in memoirs such as Owen Genty's and Gloria Chalmers's.[104]

The officials charged with enforcing the law were a mix of old and new colonialists and important decisions were made in the context of changing attitudes and disagreements over how the law and punishment might best contribute to the betterment of Papua New Guineans. The broader context for all this legal and moral reasoning was Australian mores, standards, attitudes and worldviews, which were brought to PNG by Australian expatriates.

The capacity of the bureaucracy

The capital case review process depended on advice from PNG, and punishment selection depended on a belief in the capacity of the PNG administration to affect that punishment. Hasluck had serious doubts about the quality of the work undertaken in PNG, as revealed in his memoir. According to Hasluck, at the start of his tenure in 1951, the PNG public service commissioner had told him:

> If you assume that the Commonwealth Public Service is 100% efficient then you will be taking an optimistic view if you think of the PNG public service as being twenty-five per cent efficient.[105]

Hasluck explained that, while there were knowledgeable practitioners in areas like justice, health, agriculture and forestry, the fundamental bureaucratic process in PNG was ramshackle. He appreciated the courage and dedication of POs and civil servants in attempting service delivery, but not necessarily their administrative capacity in terms of forward planning and developing proposals for Cabinet and Treasury.[106]

---

103 Genty, *The Planter*; Martin D. Kerr, *New Guinea Patrol* (London: Robert Hale, 1973); Kenneth Read Papers Relating to Teaching Australian School of Pacific Administration (ASOPA) Courses.
104 Genty, *The Planter*, 28–9; Gloria Chalmers, *Kundus, Cannibals and Cargo Cults: Papua New Guinea in the 1950s* (Watsons Bay: Books and Writers Network, 2006), 17–25.
105 Hasluck, *A Time for Building*, 18.
106 Ibid., 83.

1. MEET OUR FRIEND, PAPUA NEW GUINEA

Rachel Cleland's memoir and Ian Downs's official history of the PNG administration present a contrasting picture of the bureaucracy's capacity to follow and to advise on policy.[107] According to them, Canberra-based Department of Territories bureaucrats and politicians did not understand the inappropriateness of mainland financial planning timetables and implementation schedules, which paid no heed to the vagaries of local contractors, infrastructure, climate and terrain.[108] Indeed, Downs described many of Canberra's policy demands as impossible or reckless given the unpredictability and diversity of the Papua New Guinean people.[109] For her part, Cleland regretted the impact of Hasluck's leadership style on the public service, especially his abrasive personality, which, she claimed, left the PNG public service more dispirited with every visit.[110] Thus, the question of competence cannot be easily settled using the accounts of those involved.

Recent studies, such as Waiko's, provide a more balanced view. Certainly, postwar public servants in PNG had complex duties; they were tasked with managing a poorly understood population and with trying to invent institutions to implement policy. Some opposed and/or ignored postwar advancement policies while others were quite new to their positions. According to Waiko, both groups had difficulties implementing, or were unwilling to implement, Hasluck's policies.[111] By contrast, and in direct contradiction of Downs's and Cleland's accounts, Nelson claims that most senior officials in PNG chose to work with Hasluck and found his style honest and direct.[112]

The capital case studies examined in this book provide further insight into the competency of the PNG bureaucracy and the challenges officials faced. Overall, they indicate that officials were inexperienced in formal procedure and were not familiar enough with Hasluck's liberal colonialism. The case studies also show that instances of administrative confusion became less common as time went on and the bureaucrats gained more experience. Even so, it can still be argued, based on the evidence presented in the capital case files and memoirs, that, over time, Hasluck relied less on the advice of bureaucrats and more on his own views, due both to his lack of confidence in the bureaucrats and his increased confidence in his own knowledge of PNG.

---

107 Cleland, *Pathways to Independence,* 147–8; Downs, *The Australian Trusteeship,* 126–7.
108 Ibid.
109 Downs, *The Australian Trusteeship,* 126–7.
110 Cleland, *Pathways to Independence,* 148.
111 Waiko, *A Short History of Papua New Guinea,* 94–7.
112 Nelson, 'Papua and New Guinea', 156–7.

Conclusion

The punishments meted out to murderers and rapists in PNG occurred within the context of a difficult and changing social, political and bureaucratic environment, as described in this chapter. Contested notions of the role of law, punishment, international obligations and advancement affected the arguments posed during capital case reviews. The enormous responsibility that officials felt, especially in the face of international scrutiny, made the arguments and discussions even more fraught, as will be seen in the historical case studies that follow.

2
'Why should the government want to fight us when we refuse to chip grass off the roads': The Telefomin killings of 1954

> Another patrol officer is missing—feared killed—in New Guinea as a result of a native attack last week in which a cadet patrol officer was killed. Native reports say that the missing man, Patrol Officer Gerald Leo Szarka, 30, of Leura, NSW, and three native policemen were killed before the attack on Cadet Patrol Officer Geoffrey Brodribb Harris, 22, of Cremorne NSW. Cadet Officer Harris was killed last Friday. An official statement from the Department of Territories tonight says fears are held for Szarka's safety, but the natives' report of the death of Szarka and his policeman have not yet been confirmed. The two officers were attacked by natives in the newly-opened Telefomin area.
>
> 'Second N.G. Patrol Officer Missing', *Advertiser* (Adelaide), 10 November 1953, 1.

The killings

In summary, a faction of Telefomin men conspired to kill Patrol Officer Gerald Szarka, Cadet Patrol Officer Geoffrey Harris, Constable Purari and Constable Buritori in three separate attacks while they were on patrol in the Telefomin subdistrict, located roughly in the geographic centre of the island of New Guinea. Patrol officers, also known as *kiaps*, exercised a wide variety of bureaucratic and policing powers to administer health, public works, taxation, economic development and censuses, and also served as magistrates for low-level offences.[1] The constables were Papua New Guineans in the Royal Papuan Constabulary, a police force, but they were not from the Telefomin area. Papua New Guineans sometimes resented official efforts as aggressive and shame-inducing interference.[2] The extent to which these killings reflected interpersonal or political motives was a subject of legal and public debate, which, ultimately, was unclear to Australian decision-makers; therefore, managing both possibilities was vital in the provision of clemency for the killers.

Located east of the centre of the island of New Guinea, the Telefomin subdistrict is a mountainous territory with narrow and steep river valleys and thick forests. Before the arrival of Europeans, there were established trade networks within the region and formal political groupings with alliances and rivalries. However, given its isolation from the coast and its position deep in the mountains, it was not an area readily accessible by Europeans until well into the twentieth century. Regular access was largely made possible by aeroplanes and the infrastructure of the war effort. Bill Gammage notes European accounts of the district prior to 1948 that describe a people amenable to trade and curious about outsiders, but also a people ready for war with rival groups.[3]

The primary point of outside contact for the Telefomin were patrol officers; therefore, the competence of such men was significant in being able to build relationships between local people and the colonial administration. Patrol officers trained at the Australian School of Pacific Administration in Sydney for a year and then served as assistant patrol officers, under more experienced officers, to refine their knowledge and abilities.[4] They were supposed to pre-empt trouble, provide services, enforce regulations, resolve conflicts and 'civilise the natives' using force of personality, a few rifles and

---

1   Clive Moore, *New Guinea: Crossing Boundaries and History* (Honolulu: University of Hawaii Press, 2003), 183; Hank Nelson, *Taim Bilong Masta: The Australian Involvement with Papua New Guinea* (Sydney: Australian Broadcasting Commission, 1982), 185.
2   John Dademo Waiko, *A Short History of Papua New Guinea*, 2nd ed. (Melbourne: Oxford University Press, 2007), 106–7.
3   Bill Gammage, *The Sky Travellers: Journeys in New Guinea 1938–1939* (Carlton: Melbourne University Press, 1998), ch. 10.
4   Nicholas Brown, *Governing Prosperity: Social Change and Social Analysis in Australia in the 1950s* (Melbourne: Cambridge University Press, 1995), ch. 2.

their belief in their own moral and cultural superiority. Yet not all patrol officers were skilled enough at their jobs to deal effectively with the cultural and political complexity of the role.

In the Telefomin subdistrict, according to anthropologist Barry Craig's research, during the Second World War, a serious epidemic of influenza affected the Telefomin people and was linked in their minds to the increase in contact with Australians. Prior to regular patrolling, there was also some resentment over a lack of compensation for the land on which the airfield had been built.[5] These issues began the slide away from friendly relationships commented on by early European visitors. Native Affairs officials established a permanent patrol base at Telefomin in 1948. From then onwards, officials were in residence in the district permanently as opposed to occasionally. As different cultures came into contact daily, the violation of marriage customs, conscription of labour and general dissatisfaction with foreign rule led to further tensions.

L. T. Nolen worked as a patrol officer from October 1951 to August 1953 and was assisted by Geoffrey Harris. Leo Szarka was appointed a patrol officer in mid-1953. The Australians were assisted in their work by up to ten constables from the Royal Papua New Guinea Constabulary, which was made up of men from other parts of PNG, particularly coastal areas where people were physically much larger.[6] William Lalor, the killers' lawyer, and Barry Craig recorded testimony about the problems that developed between these officials and the community they were supposed to manage and modernise.

First, local marriage customs were violated. Some of the constables married, or at least entered into liaisons with, local women without the provision of a bride price and, most importantly, without the reciprocal provision of a bride from the husband's family for a man in the woman's family. Further, Patrol Officer Nolen, in 1952–53, had a relationship with a local woman outside of customary procedures and, indeed, outside of Australian law.[7] This led to physical blows between police and members of the woman's family.[8]

---

5   Barry Craig, 'The Telefomin Murders: Whose Myth?', in *Oceania Monograph: Children of Afek: Tradition and Change among the Mountain-Ok of Central New Guinea*, ed. Barry Craig and David Hyndman (Sydney: Oceania Press, University of Sydney, 1990), 141–5.
6   Craig, 'The Telefomin Murders', 127–30.
7   W. A. Lalor, 'Investigation Made by Myself for the Purpose of the Defence of the Accused Natives in the Telefomin Trials', 26 August 1954, NAA: A4906, 4, item 209114.
8   Craig, 'The Telefomin Murders', 136, 146–7.

That Nolen was not punished for his actions added to local resentment. The fight followed other actions and enforcement measures by the police that were regarded as high-handed and disrespectful by locals. These had left the local men shamed but with no means of redress through traditional mediation systems.[9] Violent reprisal against the offending group was viewed as the only alternative means of redress.

Second, the conscription of labour for village cleaning, track building and bearing loads for the patrol took people away from their work and endangered their livelihood, which was hard-won from a less-than-generous landscape. The requirement to assemble for census taking had a similar effect. Tying people to the village on a weekly basis for these duties also caused social problems, as getting away to isolated garden plots in the forest was a traditional method for diffusing tensions in villages and a source of important food resources. To compound the resentment, work as a bearer was also feared, as bearers could be forced to enter enemy territory. Enforcement of these requirements could take the form of physical violence, including the burning of houses, and the rage felt by local people in the face of such tactics could be restrained for only so long.[10]

After the Second World War, administrative inefficiencies in Port Moresby caused additional problems on the ground in Telefomin. There was a long delay in bringing prisoners convicted of a range of offences to trial in the Telefomin area in 1952–53 because the Port Moresby bureaucracy neglected to appoint Patrol Officer Nolen a member of the Court of Native Affairs, as should have occurred. The absence of these prisoners from their duties and families was resented. This local resentment was focussed on the patrol station, despite Leo Szarka, appointed as a patrol officer in mid-1953, being able to clear the backlog, as the impression and effects of the long incarcerations were not ameliorated.[11] Further mistakes at the head office meant there had been a failure to compensate families for the death of local men who had drowned while conscripted into carrying equipment for a 1952 patrol. There were no good reasons for this other than understaffing and inefficiencies in the bureaucracy in Port Moresby. Once again, the patrol station bore the brunt of local displeasure.[12]

---

9   Ibid., 130. For a frank assessment of police use and abuse of the system, see August Ibrum Kituai, *My Gun, My Brother: The World of the Papua New Guinea Colonial Police, 1920–1960* (Honolulu: University of Hawaii Press, 1998), 268.
10 Craig, 'The Telefomin Murders', 147.
11 Lalor, 'Investigation Made by Myself'.
12 Ibid.

As well as head office inefficiencies, the practices of resident police also caused tension; there was resentment over the seizure of food, vegetables and pigs by police and patrol officers, including particularly large seizures in 1952–53, which threatened the livelihoods of people living in an ungenerous landscape.[13] After the killings, district commissioners Timperly and Elliott-Smith judged the seizures to be excessive. Their judgement highlights Nolen's poor record and the inexperience of Assistant Patrol Officer Harris.[14]

On top of these accumulating pressures, Patrol Officer Szarka and Assistant Patrol Officer Harris were dependent on local police officers for translation and to carry out orders. Not speaking the local language, and without a clear understanding of specific local customs, their perception of the mood and feeling in the community was not always clear. Szarka had inherited a good deal of anger against the administration as a consequence of Patrol Officer Nolen's lack of diplomacy and administrative deficiencies. Yet, Szarka's and Harris's own experience and skills were also limited. They were remembered as 'man bilong kros', that is, cranky and impatient and liable to deliver a boot to the backside if things did not go fast enough.[15] Their decisions and actions lacked tact and deftness.[16]

Underlying these specific complaints was a general dissatisfaction with rule by a foreign power whose unwelcome presence was enforced by the power of arms—by guns.[17] The Telefomins had established control of their territory by successful military strategy. They were skilled in the use of surprise tactics.[18] Political power in the mountains was traditionally established and defended by warfare and violence, and some Telefomin men were ready to engage with the administration on that basis. The Australians came to be seen as a rival political group against whom honour demanded redress.[19]

It would seem that Australian officials attempted to use (seemingly) arbitrary administrative actions, law and punishment to change the behaviours of the PNG people and modernise them. And that was resented. As with other

---

13 Craig, 'The Telefomin Murders', 130; Lalor, 'Investigation Made by Myself'.
14 Craig, 'The Telefomin Murders', 121.
15 Ibid., 129–30.
16 Ibid., 137.
17 R. Gore to administrator, 30 August 1954, NAA: A4906, 4, item 209114.
18 R. Gore, transcription of evidence, 'Case Book—Telefomin Cases Book "A"', Papers of Ralph Gore, 1930–1964, National Library of Australia (hereafter Gore Papers), box 9, 34.
19 Lalor, 'Investigation Made by Myself'. Lalor's account generally agrees with Craig, 'The Telefomin Murders'.

colonial administrations in Australia, there was a determination to use Western law to alter local culture.[20] Also similar was the extent of physical violence and conflicts over sexual and marriage practices between local people and Papua New Guinean constables, who nevertheless saw themselves as bringing civilisation to less advanced people.[21] Indeed, as Sepik District Commissioner Sydney Elliott-Smith wrote in his submission to the capital case reviews about the actions of the Australians and the constables, 'these incidents did much to set alight the already smouldering pile'.[22]

Summarising the feelings of the killers, Femsep, a community leader who had interacted closely with the first patrols, recalled this building anger fifteen years later:

> Why should the government want to hurt us when we haven't hurt the government? Why should the government want to fight us when we refuse to chip grass off the roads? Why should the government force us to make roads specially [sic] for the white men to walk along?[23]

Prior to colonisation, the Telefomin had been an independent and politically successful confederation of cultural groups. Australian colonialism chaffed. Anthropologist Barry Craig, reflecting on later oral accounts, and Justice Gore, in his submission to the capital case review, both argued that the Telefomin hoped to replicate their previously successful surprise tactics against the Australians.[24]

The conspiracy began in early November 1953 (a precise date was not clearly established in the trial) when some 'big men'—community leaders—met at Ankeivip in the Telefomin subdistrict.[25] They included Kabaramsep, the most influential figure, Novonengim, Kornsep, Okmansep, Foritengim and Dumarogim. In response to the multiple discontents described above, they agreed to kill the Australian officials and to spread the news of this decision to build support in the region's villages. In the end, Novonengim

---

20   Bruce Buchan, *Empire of Political Thought: Indigenous Australians and the Language of Colonial Government* (London: Pickering and Chatto, 2008).
21   Kituai, *My Gun*, 267.
22   S. Elliott-Smith, cited in D. M. Cleland, administrator, to Paul Hasluck, minister for territories, 30 August 1954, NAA: A4906, 4, item 209114.
23   Femsep of Telefomin, recorded by *Focus*, ABC, 1971, cited in Craig, 'The Telefomin Murders', 125. Femsep was also involved in the first regular contacts and was cited in Gammage, *The Sky Travellers*, 110–1.
24   Gore, transcription of evidence, 'Case Book—Telefomin Cases Book "A"'; Craig, 'The Telefomin Murders', 147–8.
25   In 1954, judges kept their own trial notes, and there was no official transcript other than those bench notes, which were sometimes subsequently typed up. In this case, there were handwritten bench notes as well as the typed judgements.

was among the men who carried out the killings; Kornsep, Dumarogim and Kabaramsep stayed at home. However, the Criminal Code of Papua and New Guinea—following Australian legal conventions—prescribed who could be a principal offender in a crime 'committed in prosecution of a common purpose', and that included conspirators who did not take direct physical action in the killings.[26] Employing this principle, the court found that Kabaramsep, Kornsep, Okmansep, Foritengim and Dumarogim together procured and counselled Novonengim and others to kill the Australian officials, and thus were also culpable of wilful murder.[27]

At midday on Friday 6 November 1953 at Uguntemtigin village, Constable Buritori was collecting firewood when Novonengim, Tobaronsep and Wavenasep set upon him with axes and stones. Buritori sought to escape, but an axe blow to the back brought him down. He rolled down the slope on which the village sat and, when he came to a stop, Asememnok, Sartengim, Kankosep and Arolengim finished him off with stone axes and arrows. Finally, with the blows of a stone axe, he was decapitated. His body was then dumped in the bush between the rest house and the village.[28] Pigs were eating his body when it was found by an investigating patrol.[29]

At the same time, Patrol Officer Gerald Szarka, who had only been in the posting for a few months, was ambushed. Village men engaged him in conversation and, once surrounded, Kaiobengal, Tigimnok, Irinsomnok, Warimsep and Olsikim attacked him. He was thrown to the ground in front of the rest house and he and his assailants rolled down the slope, struggling. Overwhelmed, he was bludgeoned to death. His killers then dismembered his corpse and threw it into a latrine.[30]

---

26   *Criminal Code (Queensland, Adopted) in Its Application to the Territory of Papua*, sections 7–8, Pacific Island Legal Information Institute, www.paclii.org/pg/legis/papua_annotated/cca254.pdf. This section was not subsequently amended, see NAA: A518, A846/6/45 PART 1, item 3272356; NAA: A518, A846/6/21, item 3272255; John Greenwell, *The Introduction of Western Law into Papua New Guinea*, unpublished manuscript given to author by John Greenwell, former first assistant secretary and director of Papua New Guinea Office Government and Legal Affairs Division, Department of External Territories, 1970–75, 20. On the relationship between Common Law and the Griffith Code, see Andrew Hemming, 'Impermissibly Importing the Common Law into Criminal Codes: Pollock v. The Queen', *James Cook University Law Review* 18, no. 6 (2011): 113–43; J. V. Barry, G. W. Paton and G. Sawer, *An Introduction to the Criminal Law in Australia* (London: McMillian and Co., 1948), 63; *Criminal Code (Queensland, Adopted) in Its Application to the Territory of Papua*, section 8.
27   *Criminal Code (Queensland, Adopted) in Its Application to the Territory of Papua*, sections 7–8; Justice Ralph Gore, 'Case Three, Reg. v. Kabaramsep of Telefolip and Others', NAA: A4906, 4, item 209114.
28   The house was used by the patrol officers when staying in a village and had to be maintained in a fit state by the village.
29   Gore, transcription of evidence, 'Case Book—Telefomin Cases Book "A"'.
30   Ibid.

Constable Mulai, a member of Szarka's party, was returning from gathering firewood when the sound of shouting alarmed him. He found his colleagues gone and the village largely deserted. Fearful and suspicious, he ran. Villagers pursued him until he came into the protection of an old couple who hid him physically and with taboos.[31] With the help of others, the couple escorted him safely to the patrol station at Telefomin, indicating the mixed feelings local people had about the Australian administration, and the fears and memories older people had of reprisals.[32]

Even though the people of Komdavip village had not been party to the initial plan, Novonengim's messengers, Awotingen, Telefakwansep and Bemsep, had informed the men's house, including Asogoning, Digimening, Arinening, Ivasimnok, Nasimnok and Aningapnok, of the plan. Hearing of the killings at Uguntemtigin, they were encouraged to kill the widely disliked Constable Purari (also called Buka) who was then in the village preparing for a census.[33] There was resentment of Purari in the village for his aggression and violence against villagers. Tinabirengim, the second headman, overheard the message and tried to dissuade the young men. The older man told them of a past attack on white men that had brought terrible consequences upon the attackers. Nasimnok dismissed that advice and insisted that: 'They have killed the kiap and now we will go and kill Buka.'[34] On the way to the rest house, the group of young men gathered Fobonening and Moriaksep, who were carrying axes for thatch gathering.[35] This large group of men—five armed with axes, Asogoning with a piece of wood and the rest unarmed—attacked Purari on the veranda of the rest house, overwhelming him and forcing him inside. Tinabirengim followed the young men but did not enter the house; he saw them exit carrying bloody axes. Argarming, the official translator, was left alone because he was of the village and had been conscripted into the role. The attackers testified to their assault within the house and to throwing Purari's body under a waterfall in a deep pool from where it was retrieved by Australian officials some days later.[36]

---

31 These taboos that forbade people from seeing them, were represented by an arrangement of sticks, cloth and vines.
32 'Native Bands Hunted Wounded Constable', *South Pacific Post*, 26 May 1954, 3; Gore, transcription of evidence, 'Case Book—Telefomin Cases Book "A"'.
33 Justice Ralph Gore, 'Reg. v Asogoning and Others', NAA: A4906, 4, item 209114.
34 'Kiap' was the Tok Pisin word for the various patrol officer/PNG native affairs department positions.
35 Gore, 'Reg. v Asogoning and Others'.
36 Ibid.

Cadet Patrol Officer Harris, accompanied by constables Paheki, Muyei and Kombo, a medical orderly, Bunat, an interpreter, Sinoksep, and Harris's servant Tegori, were patrolling the Iliptamin Valley from 28 October 1953. When they arrived in Terapdavip on 5 November, a pig was delivered to them as a sign of welcome.[37] However, that day messengers informed the headman, Yanmakalinin, of the planned murders, which he agreed to follow: 'All right, tomorrow we will go down and kill him [Harris].' Early on the morning of 6 November, while Harris lay in bed waiting for his shaving water to be heated, Kombo arose for his first cigarette and fortuitously covered his rifle with his blanket before leaving the barracks. He wandered over to stand under a tree near the warmth of a fire and was lighting his cigarette when he was seized and struck with a cudgel and an axe. Fighting off his attackers, he ran for his rifle. Although, during his retreat, he received an axe blow to the shoulder, he was still able to retrieve his weapon, the other police officers' firearms having been deliberately removed. Kombo returned to the doorway in time to see Damugim strike down Harris with an axe blow to the face. With a disabled shoulder, Kombo braced the rifle against his stomach and, due to his uncertain aim, shot Damugim in the shoulder; however, the shot still scattered the assailants. As Harris tumbled down the rise on which the rest house was sited, Kombo fired two more shots before handing the rifle to Paheki who, along with Bunat and Muyei, had just survived an attack themselves and whose assailants had also scattered at the sound of the rifle blast.

Paheki stood cover as Muyei and Bunat carried Harris to the safety of the barracks. The attack then developed into a siege, the limited ammunition and single gun of the government party facing fire arrows. With the barracks on fire, the patrol retreated to the rest house, from which Tegori was sent to the patrol station for assistance. By 2 pm, the men had retreated further to a nearby pigpen, a formidable structure designed to keep the village's most precious resource safe, but Bunat could do little to relieve the sufferings of the badly wounded Harris. The assailants attempted to get closer under cover of drainage ditches, while other locals warned the police party of impending attacks. Finally, at 5.20 pm, two armed constables reached the

---

37   Justice Ralph Gore, 'Case Four Reg. v. Sitkuningim of Afogovip and Others', NAA: A4906, 4, item 209114; Justice Ralph T. Gore, transcription of evidence, 'Case Book—Telefomin Cases Cook "C"', Gore Papers, box 9.

besieged officials and chased off the attackers, but Harris had succumbed to his wounds. The two armed constables were enough to cause the plotters to retreat into hiding in distant villages and seasonal encampments.[38]

The perpetrators were hunted down with cooperation from some local people over the course of December 1953 and January 1954.[39] A prosecution case was built as police located witnesses and as the perpetrators emerged from hiding. The search was made more difficult by the fact that innocent villagers had also scattered, fearing reprisal attacks by colonial authorities.[40] All the witnesses and accused were detained and taken to Wewak for trial, as allowed by the ordinances.[41] The accused were first arraigned in the Magistrate's Court in June 1954 and then subjected to four separate Supreme Court trials between 7 July and 17 August 1954, with Justice Gore presiding. There was no jury required under the law in a capital case when the accused was Papua New Guinean.[42] This meant that the judge determined the facts of the case, guilt or innocence, and the sentence.

Ralph Gore had been a judge in Papua since 1924. Prior to the unification of the two territories in 1949, he had been chief justice of Papua. Chief Justice Beaumont 'Monty' Phillips of New Guinea was senior in service to Gore by a month and so had been made chief justice of PNG.[43] Still, Gore was an established and respected person who had held various positions in the colonial administration in addition to his judicial duties, such as acting as lieutenant-governor of Papua prior to the Second World War.[44] His career reflected the close ties between the colony's executive, bureaucracy, police and judiciary. His sentencing record was consistent with his fellow judges.[45] As a long-term resident of PNG, he had a good understanding of the place; however, he also had a great deal of social contact with the expatriate community and shared many of their views, such as the view

---

38   Gore, 'Case Four, Reg, v. Sitkuningim of Afogovip and others'; Gore, transcription of evidence, 'Case Book—Telefomin Cases Cook "C"'.
39   'Wanted NG Natives Traced', *Courier-Mail*, 20 January 1954, 1.
40   Gore, transcription of evidence, 'Case Book—Telefomin Cases Book "A"', 18b, 22b.
41   Ian Downs, *The Australian Trusteeship Papua New Guinea 1945–75* (Canberra: AGPS, 1980), 154–5.
42   Donald Cleland, 'Report of the Administrator of Papua New Guinea and Appendices "A" to "E"', 30 August 1954', NAA: A4906, 4, item 209114.
43   Gore's attitudes in his memoir are similar to the views of Rachel Cleland and Ian Downs. Rachel Cleland, *Pathways to Independence: Story of Official and Family Life in Papua New Guinea 1951–1975* (Cottesloe: Singapore National Printer, 1985), 184; Downs, *The Australian Trusteeship*.
44   Paul Hasluck, *A Time for Building: Australian Administration in Papua and New Guinea 1951–1963* (Carlton: Melbourne University Press, 1976), 343.
45   See the tabulation of sentencing records for PNG judges in Table 6.1.

of old colonialists that the push, by the Liberal minister for territories, Hasluck, and the UN, for political institutions and a greater role for Papua New Guineans was too hasty.[46] He was popular with other expatriates and was known as 'Judgie' by the younger set, indicating a genial and good-humoured nature.[47]

The four trials, one for each of the victims, proceeded smoothly and were covered by Australian and international press. The spirited and principled defence was extremely critical of the conduct of Australian colonialism, highlighting the exploitation of local people, sexual misconduct of officials, seizures of goods and unnecessary use of violence to enforce regulations. This posed an actual and political problem for the administration and Hasluck in defending Australia from local, domestic and international criticism. Partially due to this defence, the accused—despite being found guilty—as well as the victims, received a good deal of sympathy from the Australian public.

The accused were found guilty of wilful murder and a sentence of death was mandatory under the legislation, except for Timengin, who was discharged on the basis of mental incapacity during the trial *Reg. v. Kabaramsep and Others*.[48] Justice Gore had two procedural options available to him. He could 'record a sentence of death', which meant he felt that the personal and cultural circumstances of the offenders mitigated the offence such that clemency should be enacted. Alternatively, he could 'pronounce a sentence of death', which meant that Gore judged the crimes to have had no significant mitigating circumstances and that he believed the convicted should hang.[49] The Executive Council could not, by custom and practice, hang an offender whose sentence had been 'recorded', giving Gore some control over their fate.[50]

Purari's killers had their sentences recorded, which meant, in effect, that the judge recommended clemency. Gore assessed these men as less culpable as they had been involved spontaneously in the killings: they 'were not party to the plan to wipe out the administration personnel'. However,

---

46 Ralph Gore, *Justice versus Sorcery* (Brisbane: Jacaranda Press, 1964), 217–8.
47 Ibid., 217–8; Cleland, *Pathways to Independence*, 183–4, 198–9.
48 Gore, 'Case 3, Reg v. Kabaramsep and Others, 1954', NAA: A4906, 4, item 209114.
49 On the meaning of a recorded sentence as opposed to a pronounced sentence, see Mark Finnane, *Punishment in Australian Society* (Melbourne: Oxford University Press, 1997), 126.
50 Murray Tyrell, interview by Mel Pratt for the Mel Pratt collection [sound recording], 1974, transcript, National Library of Australia.

the conspirators and killers of Buritori, Harris and Szarka were found to have plotted over time and thus received pronounced sentences, that is, a recommendation to execute.[51] This was an unusual sentence for Gore who, in his long career, had seldom delivered pronounced sentences and whose average sentence for murder was seven and a half years hard labour in prison.[52]

The minister for territories submitted the sentences to the federal Cabinet for review and consideration of clemency. Australian newspapers had covered the events, which meant that they were well known, and Hasluck's and the federal Cabinet's awareness of the incident ensured that the cases were referred to the governor-general.[53] The Cabinet, in its deliberation, had to consider numerous complex issues. Faced with the reality of local people trying to remove Australian authority from their ancestral lands and a trial defence that had blamed the actions of the administration for causing the violence, they had to decide whether capital punishment or clemency would better remediate these problems, while accounting for public interest in enacting mercy and the lobbying of various groups. Ultimately, the Cabinet and the governor-general made the decision on 22 September 1954 to direct the administrator to commute the recorded *and* pronounced death sentences to imprisonment for ten years with hard labour for all the men involved.[54]

Context

As described above, in November 1953, thirty-five men of the Telefomin subdistrict plotted and carried out a plan to rid themselves of Australian control by killing Australian officials. In the end, two Australian patrol officers and two Papua New Guinean constables were killed. In the public debate—in PNG, metropolitan Australia and internationally—that followed the murders, Australia's self-image as a benevolent friend in PNG was challenged by the rejection of the legitimacy of Australian colonialism suggested by the killings. From the beginning, discussions in Australia and overseas focussed on the reasons for, and consequences of, such a violent

---

51 Gore, 'Reg. v Asogoning and Others', 2.
52 PNG Crown Law Office, 'Tabulation of Sentencing by Judge', 10 July 1959, Gore Papers, box 1, folder 8; 'Few Executed for Murder', *South Pacific Post*, 26 November 1957, 3.
53 As this book will explore in the following chapter, such referrals did not always happen.
54 Notetaker A. S. Brown, 21 September 1954, submission 102, p. 124, NAA: A11099, 1/19, item 12105762; 'N.G. Natives to Serve Ten Years Imprisonment', *Canberra Times*, 23 September 1954, 6.

rejection of Australia's presence.⁵⁵ When the trials returned guilty verdicts for wilful murder, this questioning continued, growing to encompass the challenge of maintaining or repairing the legitimacy of Australian colonialism in the face of the killings, trials and punishment of the killers. These issues were also raised at a UNTC meeting during New Guinea's triennial review.⁵⁶ This was contemporary to colonial justice in British Kenya, where killers of government officials engaged in resisting authority were found guilty of treason and hanged.⁵⁷ It is theorised that clemency can bring legitimacy to the state through the extension of mercy, rather than execution, as people feel secure in a state in which justice is leavened with mercy.⁵⁸ Hence, Australian authorities gave serious consideration as to how to balance justice with the need to build Australian legitimacy for Australian colonialism in a decolonising world.

Authorities asked questions about the nature of the event to which Australian justice was responding. Was it a savage attack or a failure of colonial policy? In either case, how should the colonised—the killers—be treated? And how would the punishment be perceived by an international community that was increasingly aware of political violence in colonial rule? In terms of its role in PNG, Australia represented itself as an advocate for the UNTC's internationally sanctioned goals of 'advancement', peace, health and modernity.⁵⁹ Having presented its mission in PNG as civilising and just, Australia chose clemency for the killers as a means of demonstrating the benevolent character of its power to the United Nations, the Australian public and to Papua New Guineans in the subdistrict of Telefomin. The administration also had to manage the crisis of governance that had emerged in Telefomin. Mercy, it was hoped, would rehabilitate

---

55   The mother of one of the dead, Mrs Szarka, and the journalist cast doubt on the administration. 'Second N.G. Patrol Officer Missing', *Advertiser*, 10 November 1953, 1; 'White Prestige Must Be Restored', *Courier-Mail* (Brisbane), 18 January 1954, 2; United Nations, *Index to Proceedings of the Trusteeship Council*, Fourteenth Session 2 June to 16 July 1954 (New York: United Nations Headquarters Library, 1955), library.un.org/sites/library.un.org/files/itp/t14_0.pdf.
56   United Nations, *Index to Proceedings*.
57   David Anderson, *Histories of the Hanged. The Dirty War in Kenya and the End of Empire* (New York: W.W. Norton, 2005).
58   Tina Loo, 'Savage Mercy: Native Culture and Modification of Capital Punishment in Nineteenth Century British Columbia', in *Qualities of Mercy: Justice Punishment and Discretion*, ed. Carolyn Strange (Vancouver: University of British Columbia Press, 1996); Douglas Hay, 'Property, Authority and the Criminal Law', in *Albion's Fatal Tree*, ed. Douglas Hay (London: A. Lane, 1975).
59   Peter Fitzpatrick, *Law and State in Papua New Guinea* (London: Academic Press, 1980), 65–8; Allan M. Healy, 'Monocultural Administration in a Multicultural Environment: The Australians in Papua New Guinea', in *From Colony to Coloniser: Studies in Australian Administrative History*, ed. J. J. Eddy and J. R. Nethercote (Sydney: Hale and Iremonger, 1987), 220–1; Nelson, *Taim Bilong Masta*, 88.

the colonised's perception of the legitimacy of Australia. Ultimately, the outcome of the trials served to exonerate the administration of charges of wrongdoing, while also drawing attention to the need to maintain scrutiny of its colonial practice.

The Telefomin case file is the most voluminous clemency file in the archive of capital case files on which this book is based. This is because there were four trials, each with multiple defendants.[60] In addition, the public defence lawyer, William 'Peter' Lalor, submitted a lengthy report into the conditions in the district prior to the killings. Further, a long list of groups lobbied the Executive Council and administration and called for clemency in letters and petitions.[61] These were among the handful of PNG capital cases that received letters to the federal government on behalf of the condemned.[62] There was also considerable newspaper coverage of the killings, trials and sentencing, which indicated a level of public interest that politicians had to consider in their exercise of discretionary justice.

There is substantial evidence of grievances against Australian authority in the Telefomin subdistrict at the time of the murders. Oral accounts collated by the anthropologist Barry Craig some twenty years after the events correlate with the general evidence of maladministration presented by William Lalor. Both sources highlight unfairness in the conduct of Australian colonialism by constables and officials. Further intensifying the problem for the federal government, official submissions to the capital case reviews also noted administrative errors, while allowing that such errors might be attributed to cultural misunderstandings. More generally, accounts of the region suggest that the relationship between the people and the Australian authorities had become increasingly tense during the period of close contact, from 1948 to 1954, to the point that the condemned Telefomins had sought to remove Australian authority.[63] In this context, the authorities had to choose between the common use of capital punishment as a tool to assert control, or of clemency to build cooperation and legitimacy through mercy.[64]

---

60 'Reg. v. Asogoning and Others, 1954' (8 defendants), 'Reg. v. Tobaronsep and Others, 1954' (7 defendants) 'Reg. v. Kabaramsep and Others, 1954' (11 defendants), 'Reg. v. Sitkuningim and Others, 1954' (9 defendants), 9 September 1954, NAA: A4906, 4, item 209114.
61 'Representations Regarding the Sentences', NAA: A4906, 4, item 209114.
62 There were a few cases involving non-capital crimes that saw a good deal of lobbying, but that does not fall within this book. See, for example, NAA: A432, 1959/2208, item 7436109.
63 Gammage, *The Sky Travellers*, ch. 10; Craig, 'The Telefomin Murders'.
64 Michele Foucault, *Discipline and Punish: The Birth of the Prison* (London, Allen Lane, 1977), 11.

'Treat-them-gently-at-all-costs-and-please-the United Nations': When the news broke — Australian reactions to the killings

At first, as news of the killings broke, journalists and other observers scrutinised and critiqued the conduct of Australian colonialism. Such critique came from two fronts. Old colonialists pointed to the events in Telefomin and challenged Hasluck's assertion of a 'new relationship between peoples'.[65] However, there were also suspicions of colonialism in any form. A ready group of commentators who wrote regularly on PNG aired their views on the front pages of several major dailies in Australia immediately after the killings.

The first substantial discussion of the Telefomin killings in Australian newspapers built a narrative in which the killings were tragic, the result of various 'native' impulses and practices, but also that Australian policy and practice were to blame for creating the situation that allowed or even provoked the killings. Four days after the killings, on 10 November, both the Brisbane *Courier-Mail* and Adelaide *Advertiser*, the biggest newspapers in those cities, raised accusations of administrative malpractice. These papers regularly carried new about PNG.

The *Courier-Mail* raised the possibility that Australian mismanagement had provoked the killings. It reported on 12 November 1953 that:

> Szarka is believed to have been killed by natives in revenge for the drowning of five natives from a raft under the command of a patrol officer earlier this year.[66]

Also on 12 November 1953, the *Courier-Mail* argued that Hasluck's policies to expand the area under patrol and the pressures of international scrutiny had left the patrol officers exposed to dangers for which they were not sufficiently trained or equipped:

---

65   Nelson, *Taim Bilong Masta*, ch. 1; Fitzpatrick, *Law and State in Papua New Guinea*, 68; Healy, 'Monocultural Administration', 222; Hank Nelson, 'The View from the Sub-district', in *The Defining Years: Pacific Islands, 1945–65*, ed. Brij V. Lal (Canberra: Division of Pacific and Asian History, The Australian National University, 2005), 34–5; R. Gerard Ward, 'The 1950s and 1960s—An Information Age for the South Pacific Islands', in *The Defining Years: Pacific Islands, 1945–65*, ed. Brij Lal (Canberra: Pacific and Asian History, The Australian National University, 2005), 3–10; Anthony Yeates, 'The Patrol Officers and Tom Kabu: Power and Prestige in the Purari Delta', *Journal of Pacific History* 40, no. 1 (2005): 71–90.
66   'Search To-Day for Body of Missing Officer, Four New Investigators in the "Murder Area"', *Courier-Mail*, 12 November 1953, 1.

> The area in which the murders occurred has been described as one into which only patrols of maximum strength should be allowed to go. The murder of a cadet patrol officer in this area, while accompanied only by a small number of native police, seems to indicate that lives may be endangered to meet a Government deadline, which will, in turn, placate a committee of the United Nations.[67]

The *Advertiser* took a more personal approach, reporting comments from Mrs Szarka, the mother of the murdered patrol officer, that her son's predecessor had left 'a lot of cleaning up to do' and that Szarka and Harris 'had not received sufficient advice on this area before going there as they found a wild crowd of natives and apparently were caught without any or very little ammunition'.[68] Most major Australian newspapers paid close attention to the developing story of the parents' grief and their criticisms of the administration.[69] Mrs Szarka was able to quote from her son's letters about the situation in Telefomin, making her, in the newspapers' view, a credible source about events in PNG. According to Rachael Cleland, Mrs Szarka was 'very persistent' in questioning Donald Cleland and the administration as to their culpability.[70]

The *Courier-Mail*, over several months, continued to be critical of Hasluck's policies and the United Nations' intervention in Australian policy in relation to the Telefomin killings. Its editorial of 12 November 1953 suggested that:

> There is a connection between the murders, which have taken place in the New Guinea Mountains, and the talk, which goes on in the conference chambers of the United Nations.

Further, the editor developed the old colonial critique of Hasluck's policies by stating: 'Suggestions are being made that young men are now being pushed into responsible contact with remote tribes before they have had sufficient training.' On 18 January 1954, the *Courier-Mail* described Australian policy in PNG as a 'monumental bluff' and called on the administration

---

67 Editor, 'Danger Point in NG', *Courier-Mail*, 12 November 1953, 2.
68 'Second N.G. Patrol Officer Missing'.
69 'New Guinea Patrol Officer Killed by Natives', *Sun-Herald* (Sydney), 8 November 1953, 1; 'Geoffrey Harris', *Sun-Herald*, 8 November 1953, 2; 'Lost on Patrol; Fears of 2nd NG Murder', *Courier-Mail*, 10 November 1953, 1; 'Second N.G. Patrol Officer Missing'; 'New Guinea Patrol Locates Bodies of Murdered Men', *Mercury* (Hobart), 16 November 1953, 8; 'Hunt Murderers in NG Jungles', *Courier-Mail*, 17 November 1953, 1; 'Report on NG Massacre', *Sydney Morning Herald*, 2 December 1953, 5.
70 Cleland, *Pathways to Independence*, 273–5.

to rethink the rapid expansion of patrolled areas: 'But they were the first to be murdered since the post-war edict "treat-them-gently-at-all-costs-and-please-the-United Nations" came into force.'

The *Courier-Mail*'s advocacy of more vigorous action to control and police Papua New Guineans matched those who saw Australia retaining control over PNG long into the future.[71] This commentary was informed by prewar conceptions of colonialism that regretted the changing world and the new liberal colonialism begun under Labor and continued by the Liberal and Country parties.[72] The approach advocated by the old colonialists was a return to prewar forms of control and did not involve cooperating with the UNTC on advancement, development, devolution and eventual independence. The *Courier-Mail* and *Advertiser*'s criticisms sprang from old colonialists' critiques of the new direction of policy in PNG.

A different perspective was adopted by the *Canberra Times* (*CT*), the newspaper most accessible to foreign diplomats and that also spoke to an audience charged with policymaking in PNG. Rather than highlight accusations of malpractice, it attributed the killings to the vagaries of the Papua New Guineans. Perhaps not wanting to alienate its audience with trenchant critiques of federal bureaucrats, its customers, it chose to focus on Papua New Guinean culture as a causal factor. The representation of Papua New Guineans as 'primitive' and 'savage' and, therefore, in need of guidance was a common trope of Australian literature and media.[73] Exemplifying this approach, on 10 November, the *CT* reported that 'a patrol officer had been killed when natives attacked a party in New Guinea'; however, it noted that reports were unconfirmed. On 11 November, the *CT* led with a page one article dismissing rumours of a 'widespread native uprising in New Guinea'. Hasluck was reported as replying to a question in parliament, in which he emphasised that, while 'natives had said they had killed an officer … this statement might have been made only by way of boasting'. Such comments by Hasluck played to the trope of primitiveness. Subsequently, Hasluck confirmed the deaths but characterised the incidents as part of well-equipped, routine patrols into previously friendly areas; the patrols had been ambushed and the circumstances were being investigated.

---

71 Nelson, *Taim Bilong Masta*, 189–90; Gore, *Justice versus Sorcery*, 218.
72 Waiko, *A Short History of Papua New Guinea*, 95–6.
73 Regis Tove Stella, *Imagining the Other: Representation of the Papua New Guinean Subject* (Honolulu: University of Hawaii Press, 2007), 139.

The *CT* initially made no mention of Mrs Szarka or of her or others' criticisms of policy, only briefly recording on 17 November that Szarka's body was to be flown to his hometown of Leura, New South Wales, for burial, and that he had been 'the second patrol officer murdered during a tribal uprising within a matter of days'. By then, the *CT* was also reporting rumours circulating in PNG that the perpetrators had 'wiped out the government station at Telefomin so young men could hold ancient ceremonial rites during the next few weeks'. That commentary, which, in effect, highlighted the unsophisticated nature of the Papua New Guineans, seemed more focussed on justifying Australia's gradualist policy and the need for continued Australian guidance and trusteeship to an international audience.

As press coverage brought events into public discussion, Labor politicians joined the critique of the Menzies government. While Labor, unlike the *Courier-Mail*, was in support of policies to advance Papua New Guineans, it wondered if the colonialism of Blamey and Hasluck's 'New Deal' was being pursued genuinely. Between 10 November and 1 December, Labor asked pointed questions in both houses of parliament about whether there was an uprising in Telefomin and about the competence of the administration.[74] Mrs Szarka had passed her son's letters to her local member, Labor's Tony Luchetti, who used them to give specificity and authority to his questioning. By December it was clear that the administration had to defend its own record. In Port Moresby, Donald Cleland, the administrator of PNG, defended the quality of Australia's work in PNG and asserted to the *Courier-Mail* that the killings were not the government's fault.[75]

To some commentators, malpractice meant moving too fast in bringing Papua New Guineans under Australian control in pursuit of their eventual autonomy and independence. To others, it meant the continuation of an old dictatorial colonial determination to stay and control Papua New Guineans.[76] How was Paul Hasluck to address these contrary delegitimising criticisms of Australia's colonial project?

---

74 'Search To-Day for Body of Missing Officer, Four New Investigators in the "Murder Area"'; 'He Leads the NG Killers', *Courier-Mail*, 12 November 1953, 1; 'Report on NG Massacre: Specific Orders Disregarded', *Sydney Morning Herald*, 2 December 1953, 5.
75 'NG Killing "Not Fault of Govt."', *Courier-Mail*, 13 November 1953, 1.
76 'Consternation in New Guinea', *Advertiser*, 1 January 1954, 10.

Context of clemency

'To advance the welfare of native people': Administrative responses to the newspapers

Faced with such coverage, Hasluck reasserted the federal government's mission 'to advance the welfare of native people'.[77] On 9 November 1953, the minister argued that the expansion of patrolled areas 'was the essential preliminary to measures to advance the welfare of native people'. He also emphasised the bipartisan nature of Australia's efforts in PNG and that the welfare of the people had been Australia's priority for the previous five years. Scholars have noted that this rhetoric of nobility of purpose was a consistent theme in Australian policy statements on PNG.[78] This positive view of the goal of 'advancement' was in direct contrast to the criticisms expressed in press commentary to that point.

In trying to explain the killings, but also defuse criticism of his policy of expanding the scope of patrolled areas, Hasluck highlighted errors in procedure made by Szarka's patrol:

> Although the government accepted final responsibility for the territory, Canberra did not give detailed directions about how officers in the territory were to do their work, 'We rely on with confidence, the judgement of officers' he said.[79]

Going against the tide of sympathy being generated towards the officers, on 1 December Hasluck was reported in the *Sydney Morning Herald* (*SMH*) as stating that Szarka and Harris had 'disregarded specific instructions' to always patrol in pairs. Further exonerating the administration, while also providing some protection to Szarka and Harris, he explained that the attack could not have been, and was not, anticipated—the patrol officers, constables and translators had suspected nothing. In this way, Hasluck sought to protect both his policies and his officials, although the latter was only offered limited protection.

---

77 'Search To-Day for Body of Missing Officer, Four New Investigators in the "Murder Area"'.
78 Edward P. Wolfers, *Race Relations and Colonial Rule in Papua and New Guinea* (Brookvale: Australian and New Zealand Book Company, 1975), 125; Brown, *Governing Prosperity*, ch. 2; Tove Stella, *Imagining the Other*, 87; Cleland, *Pathways to Independence*, 195.
79 'Defence of N.G. Policy', *Advertiser*, 12 November 1953, 3.

Hasluck's other strategy to protect the administration was to cast doubt on the facts presented in early reports of the incident. In the *SMH* on 1 December he implied that such reporting had been sensational and offered himself as a source of calm statements of fact: 'until the true cause of the attack is known, as a result of careful investigation, speculation and surmise should be suspended'. He argued that the courts had not yet established the facts, and that the killings, rather than political, were criminal matters that required a judicial determination.[80] His statements suggested that all the information presented by most newspapers to that point was unreliable.

After several days of Mrs Szarka feeding trenchant criticism of Hasluck's management of the territory, the minister expressed his sympathy to her and her husband.[81] His words positioned them as grief stricken and, perhaps, irrational. He placed himself within a narrative of grief by expressing his own regrets and condolences. Continuing that strategy, when news of Harris's death became public, the Department of Territories ensured that the minister's condolence calls were reported: 'The Minister for Territories (Mr Hasluck) tonight expressed his deep sympathy with the relatives of the two officers.'[82] When Szarka's body was recovered and his death confirmed, Hasluck again represented himself as one of the mourners: 'Mr. Hasluck said he wished to extend the deepest sympathy to Szarka's parents, who were informed yesterday of the death of their son.'[83] He was also quoted as saying that: 'Patrol Officer Szarka, an ex-serviceman, went to the territory in 1950 … and by his personality and keenness had quickly gained recognition as a very competent officer'.[84] This formulation shows Hasluck's efforts to defuse criticisms that he had disregarded the safety and needs of his staff in implementing federal government policy by ensuring that the press was aware of his sympathy for the bereaved.

As Barry Craig has argued, Hasluck was keenly aware of the need to manage the international coverage as much as possible. As such, there was coordination between the PNG administration, the Department of Territories and the Department of External Affairs to ensure that consistent and accurate messages were being conveyed to both Australian and international audiences. The Department of Territories requested frequent updates from Port Moresby so that 'he [Hasluck] will be in the best possible

---

80   'Report on NG Massacre: Specific Orders Disregarded', *Sydney Morning Herald*, 2 December 1953, 5.
81   'New Guinea Patrol Locates Bodies of Murdered Men'.
82   'Second N.G. Patrol Officer Missing'.
83   'New Guinea Patrol Locates Bodies of Murdered Men'.
84   'Second N.G. Patrol Officer Missing'.

position to avoid pitfalls in shaping his replies'.[85] For the UNTC audience in particular, the Department of External Affairs requested briefings on the topic because: 'The Trusteeship Council's report has yet to come before the 4th Committee of the Assembly and questions might be asked and possibly exaggerated criticisms made by Soviet representatives.'[86] The Department of External Affairs began preparing responses, as Australian diplomats were certain that international critics in New York meetings would raise questions.

In the context of this heightened media and international attention, the trials became critical to determining which explanation of the events would be accepted as truthful. If the government's message of personal rather than institutional culpability was carried, could the killers be justly hanged according to the judicial norms? If there was an institutional failure, could the executions be justified politically? If the killings were the result of unprovoked 'savagery', could clemency be tolerated? What would satisfy a mother's grief, a minister's discomfort and a suspicious decolonising world?

'The illogical manner of the natives': The trial arguments and the problem of the defence of emergency

The accused were first arraigned in the Magistrate's Court in June 1954. Then, between 7 July and 17 August 1954, Justice Ralph Gore heard four separate Supreme Court trials in Wewak. Witnesses giving testimony included villagers, patrol officers, Papua New Guinean constables, administration officials and the accused. Importantly, there was consistency in the evidence as to the events of the killings. With the large-scale response of the administration to the killings, there were minimal doubts about issues such as witness reliability and translation, which sometimes made the authorities hesitate over punishment. Testimony was straightforward as the accused admitted to the killings; however, one man was exonerated as his intellectual capacity was considered to be too limited to be held culpable.[87] Indeed, in all the subsequent debate over appropriate penalties, the basic facts of the case and the fairness of the trial were not questioned; even Rachel Cleland, who went out of her way to discuss, and usually refute, accusations

---

85   Cited in Craig, 'The Telefomin Murders', 133–4.
86   The report went before the council during the trial the next year, cited in Craig, 'The Telefomin Murders', 133–4.
87   Gore, 'Summation, Cases 3 R. Kabaramsep and Others', NAA: A4906, 4, Item 209114.

of scandal in her memoir, made no reference to anyone criticising the fairness of the trial procedure. The eight killers of Purari had their sentences 'recorded', so it was impossible under PNG conventions for that group to hang. However, it was up to the Executive Council to decide on the fate of the remaining twenty-six men with 'pronounced' sentences.

The way William 'Peter' Lalor ran the defence was significant for the political calculations around determining whether the condemned would receive mercy. Lalor used the defence of emergency, a defence that has rarely been successful, and his argument focussed on the inadequacies of the Australian administration and colonial practice as the cause of the men's response to a crisis. The legal defence of emergency is central to understanding the implications of the trials for the capital case reviews. It was likely chosen to embarrass the administration and the federal government, even if unsuccessful. The Griffith Criminal Code defence of 'Emergency', section 25, draws on the common law defence of 'Necessity'.[88] It is a complete defence against murder and requires the defence to establish that the situation was so life threatening as to permit the suspension of normal moral rules for survival's sake.[89]

Lalor was new to the position of public defender in the PNG Crown Law Office but had been a patrol officer prior to retraining as a lawyer after a sustaining a serious injury. He was an active unionist in the Public Service Association and was known to be a reformist who was willing to challenge the administration and the federal government on behalf of Papua New Guineans. The nickname 'Peter' referenced the revolutionary leader of the 1854 Eureka Stockade uprising in Victoria, Peter Lalor. It was a nickname that reflected his iconoclastic personality. Yet, he also gained the respect of senior officials such as Cleland due to his sincerity and hard work.[90]

---

88   *Criminal Code (Queensland, Adopted) in Its Application to the Territory of Papua*, section 25, Pacific Island Legal Information Institute, www.paclii.org/pg/legis/papua_annotated/cca254.pdf. This section was not subsequently amended, see NAA: A518, A846/6/45 PART 1, Item 3272356; NAA: A518, A846/6/21, Item 3272255; David Lanham et. al, *Criminal Laws in Australia* (Annandale: The Federation Press, 2006), 50.
89   Lanham et al., *Criminal Laws in Australia*, 50.
90   Cleland, *Pathways to Independence*, 274, 304; Hasluck, *A Time for Building*, 162, 345; Barnes to McMahon, 10 December 1969, Department of Foreign Affairs, *Historical Documents: Volume 26: Australia and Papua New Guinea, 1966–1969*, www.dfat.gov.au/about-us/publications/historical-documents/volume-26/Pages/345-letter-barnes-to-mcmahon.

In constructing his defence, Lalor repeated some of Mrs Szarka's accusations of administrative malpractice, having been given Szarka's letters home as a part of discovery and due disclosure. There were also new accusations arising from Lalor's discussions with the accused and the villagers.[91] Witnesses spoke about seizures of food and supplies; sexual misconduct, such as concubinage or common law marriages without dowries; threats; beatings; uncompensated deaths; forced labour; and house burnings that outraged the pride of a previously independent people. Rather than being a desperate roll of the dice, the choice of the defence of emergency indicates that Lalor was disturbed by what he learned and wished to highlight the problems. He was known as a principled man with a deep concern for the welfare on Papua New Guineans and this attempt to both defend them as well as highlight injustice was in keeping with the character revealed in the source material.[92]

The court, however, found that there was no 'emergency' in the district as defined by the code: that is, an emergency sufficient to require the suspension of normal morality, and, most significantly, that the threat and crisis was imminent and immediate. Therefore, the culpability of the killers was not reduced and the men were found guilty of wilful murder.[93] If the defence of emergency had been accepted, Australian colonial policy would have been condemned, as the court would have found that the administration of the Telefomin region was so bad that people were driven to kill for their own survival. Nevertheless, just raising the possibility cast doubt on the quality of Australian colonialism and such doubts resonated with early reporting, creating a political problem for Hasluck.

Reinforcing the depths of Lalor's concerns, when he was called to provide a report on the matter for the capital case reviews as a bureaucrat rather than a defence lawyer, he doubled down on his criticisms and did not back away from the charges of malpractice he had levelled at the administration. Rather than temper his comments in the context of a confidential review process, he insisted on further highlighting the complaints of the region, which suggests that he had used the defence of emergency out of principle; it was not a desperate, or inexperienced, act. Lalor's defence and subsequent

---

91 Lalor, 'Investigation Made by Myself'.
92 Cleland, *Pathways to Independence*, 274, 304; Hasluck, *A Time for Building*, 162; Barnes to McMahon, 10 December 1969.
93 Gore, transcription of evidence, 'Case Book—Telefomin Cases Books "A", "B" and "C"', Gore Papers, box 9.

report ensured that Australia's potential maladministration in the conduct of colonialism remained in the minds of the members of the Executive Council during its clemency considerations.

Working against this, Gore's rejection of the defence of emergency obscured the realities of 'the incidents complained of'. Gore argued that the definition of the defence of emergency required a more immediate and specific threat than Lalor had adduced. The events Lalor referred to at trial were too diluted by time to be relevant to the case law of the common law defence of necessity upon which the code defence of emergency drew. As a result, the facts of maladministration were not disputed, but rather the meaning and significance of them. Indeed, according to the transcript of his judgement provided to the clemency deliberations, Gore found that:

> Whatever the incidents complained of were, and which had occurred so long before, they could afford no excuse for this murder, a relief from criminal responsibility for the crime. I am concerned in this charge with criminal responsibility and hardly at all with material advanced in mitigation. Perhaps the motive was revenge, and had in the illogical manner of the natives [*sic*], but my strong belief is that they wished to throw off administrative control, which they found irksome.[94]

As such, Gore's finding that there was not an emergency did not specify that there were not serious problems—although that is what it sounded like when reported by the administration and the Department of Territories.

Gore rejected Lalor's damning view of an Australian colonialism that drove people to kill and that was practised by the apparently bad-tempered misters Szarka and Harris and their predecessors, 'man bilong cross', as local people called them, according to Craig.[95] Gore found the cause of the killings in the irrationality and personal motivations of the killers. According to him, Papua New Guinean men killed because they were 'irked' personally—because they were shamed by assaults from constables and patrol officers and by those same men interfering with female relatives—and not because they were active political agents, warriors or rational actors. Gore's findings were consistent with the kind of images and stereotypes that Regis Tove Stella argued were used to justify colonialism. Such discourses painted a picture of

---

94 Gore, 'Case Four, R. v. Sitkuningim and Others', NAA: A4906, 4, Item 209114.
95 On being a bad-tempered or, in the lingua franca, 'man bilong cross', see Craig, 'The Telefomin Murders', 137.

people 'whose relegation [to a savage status] provided a justification for their domination'.[96] This is clear in Gore's finding that the accused were seized by emotional responses such as 'revenge' after finding things 'irksome'. In contrast to Lalor's depiction of a people engaged in a political struggle for survival, Gore presented an irritable and unthinking people who, rather than benefiting from Australian colonialism. reacted with violence in ways that ran counter to their own interests.

A senior judge who had sat in Papua and then PNG since 1924, Gore's doctrines held considerable influence in the PNG courts. In explaining his approach to law and sentencing in this case, we can turn to his writing on the practice of law in PNG more generally. For example, Gore believed that:

> Shame is a characteristic of most people no doubt, but among dark races the force of it seems to be more intense and its reaction takes queerer forms than in the instances amongst whites. Often the satisfaction for a sense of shame is quite illogical.[97]

Gore was predisposed to see the resort to violence by Papua New Guineans as an over-reaction to treatment that bruised their 'intense' sense of shame, such as the events cited by Lalor. Lalor's account of the events preceding the killings fed into Gore's narrative of an emotional people trapped in 'illogical' rituals of shame and redeeming honour. Gore believed that few defendants brought before him were 'what I call the true native criminal', that is motivated by premeditated, criminal intent and fully intending to break the law. Instead, most were operating under the demands of shame.[98] For this reason, he was in two minds about changing the names of prisons to 'corrective institutions', because, he argued, cultural impulses, such as shame, could not be corrected. In PNG, according to Gore, murder was almost never premeditated in the Western sense of criminal intent. Instead, men had social responsibilities to redeem the honour of their grouping that overrode any notion of Australian law. For him, this enabled their actions to be better understood, if not tolerated. Gore hoped that prisons might aid in Westernisation and thus militate against honour killing, even if they failed to be 'corrective' morally:

---

96 Tove Stella, *Imagining the Other*, 139.
97 Gore, *Justice versus Sorcery*, 103.
98 Ibid., 91.

> Though a delightful euphemism, there is, however, some merit in it in relation to the native offender because most of them are not criminals in the true sense of the word. In many cases the native custom, which supplies the motive, is such an ingrained part of the social system and the urge to commit crime in obedience to it so great that although the offender may have acquired sufficient conception of the law's demands, he is mentally incapable of resisting the impulse of his tribal creed.[99]

The Telefomin cases epitomised how Gore saw his career in colonial justice— as an attempt to correct unfortunate cultural habits with deterrence, rather than punishing criminal intent.

Following this pattern, Gore's judgement was that the Telefomin killers were rejecting Australian administration to return to a life more 'pleasurable' out of cultural impulses rather than necessarily murderous ones. Nevertheless, that was not acceptable to him:

> It [the conspiracy to kill] seems to have been engendered by the wish to be relieved of the white man's control, which was interfering to their way of thinking with their pleasurable existence.[100]

Therefore, despite some recognition that Australian control was unwelcome, Gore asserted that these were irascible people without awareness of the demands of the modern world: they were people in need of the instruction and correction that Australian colonialism provided. Gore intended punishment to instruct and provide boundaries for the community who observed the execution and imprisonment of the killers; he expected to correct their cultural impulses through deterrence.

On the surface, Gore's dismissal of the defence of emergency and guilty verdict appeared to be an official finding that the incidents of which Szarka and Lalor had complained had not happened. Ultimately, Gore's finding of an interpersonal murder, rather than the defence's implication of a legitimate rebellion, exonerated Australian colonial practice to its audiences.[101] Yet, this exoneration of the administration did not mean that the resentment and anger in the region went away. The events that Lalor described remained facts and his report to the administration on those matters would go on

---

99   Ibid., 88.
100 Gore, 'Summing Up', *R v. Tobaronsep and others*, 'Telefomin Cases Book', Gore Papers, box 9. This summing up is in a typed version and glued into the casebook.
101 This issue will be discussed in more detail below in considering Gore's reasoning.

to have an impact on considerations for clemency. The administration and the federal government had to find a punishment that would deter further violence, including murder, without inflaming an already angry community.

Choosing their fate: Cabinet decides

Once Gore's judgements were made, and so many condemned to death, the political authorities had to translate that matter of law and justice into a political solution to Telefomin's complaints in the context of heightened scrutiny within Australia and the UNTC. Advice from various officials on whether to hang the convicted men or grant them clemency makes up a significant part of the Telefomin killers' clemency file and reveals a great deal about the calculus of the different levels of the PNG administration, including what those with different ideologies of colonial law thought. Newspapers continued to cover the case, printing extended commentary on the matter of clemency, and such opinions also formed part of the context of the discretionary process, as did public lobbying, making for an unusually voluminous file. Cabinet more actively considered this case than any other clemency appeal during the 1950s.

During the capital case reviews, the Szarka and Harris families continued to be of interest to the press, to Hasluck and, therefore, to the Cabinet in its deliberations on clemency. Newspapers quoted both Mrs Szarka's and Mrs Harris's objections to the executions of the killers. For example, on 12 August 1954, the *Mercury*, reported:

> Mrs. Szarka said today that she wanted to find out why the natives murdered her son and who was responsible: 'I think these natives have been badly treated', she said. 'But my son got on very well with them … I know Gerald would not have wished the execution of the natives. He loved them and they highly respected him … When he arrived at Telefomin there appeared to be an unfriendly atmosphere.'[102]

The *Mercury* also transcribed the telegrams the grieving mothers had sent to the Cabinet: 'Mrs. Szarka's telegram to Mr. Menzies read: "Strongly object to death penalty passed on natives for the killing of my son".' The message from Mrs Harris in the *Mercury* similarly read: 'Natives must not die for Telefomin massacre. We request a full public inquiry.' The *Age* printed

---

102 'Parents Plead for Natives', *Mercury*, 12 August 1954, 5.

the same telegrams in their coverage of the trials.[103] Later, in August, the *West Australian* reported on the Harris family's visit to their son's grave in Wewak.[104] The administration had actively assisted Harris's parents to visit the gravesite and meet the Papua New Guineans who had worked with their son. Not only the grave visit but also the attitude of Mrs Harris, who was said to have 'no bitterness towards the natives', was reported. Mrs Harris was quoted as saying: 'They are just primitive creatures, and don't understand the white man's law.'[105] In this way, the grieving mothers' voices were able to influence the Cabinet's deliberations, albeit informally, through the press. Their comments reflected what Tove Stella, and also Buchan, have noted was an ongoing representation of PNG as undeveloped and dangerous and therefore needing colonial control.[106] The public attention they gained also then formed a part of the context of Cabinet deliberations, a point of view to be assuaged.

Discourse on the primitive state of Papua New Guineans built conceptual space for two Australian policies. First, it strengthened the argument for continued occupation to advance Papua New Guineans.[107] Second, it created conceptual space for policymakers to reaffirm the established sentencing precedent of commuting sentences for people thought to be too 'unsophisticated' to comprehend Australian justice.

The parents' views on maladministration were explicitly noted in the Cabinet submissions for the capital case reviews: 'It appears from the above information that there has been definite bad administration on behalf of the government.'[108] The Cabinet was also aware of the views expressed in the many letters to the newspapers critical of capital punishment for the Telefomin killers; no letters in favour of capital punishment for the Telefomin killers were printed. These effectively formed another pressure group in relation to the decision. For example, one correspondent to the *SMH*, a former New Guinea resident, wrote:

> Not so long ago the people of the British Isles were exhorted to defend their land from invaders 'to the last man and the last ditch'. The Telefomin natives of New Guinea, now under sentence of death for defending their place of living and way of life from invaders,

---

103 'Story of Heroism in Murder Case', *Age,* 18 August 1954, 8.
104 'Parents to See Wewak Grave', *West Australian,* 19 August 1954, 15.
105 'Not Bitter to Son's Killers', *Mercury,* 31 August 1954, 6.
106 Tove Stella, *Imagining the Other,* 139; Buchan, *Empire of Political Thought,* 5.
107 Nelson, *Taim Bilong Masta,* 201.
108 W. J. Hall, solicitor, to Watkins, 31 May 1954, NAA: A4906, 4, Item 209114.

should not be hanged. It is my belief that the patrol officers themselves would prefer that education take the place of the carrying out of the death sentence.[109]

Here, again, opposition to the death penalty was prefigured on the assumption that it was Australia's role to educate the Papua New Guineans and develop their country. While this justified Australia's continued occupation and colonial project, doubt was cast on the conduct of officials through arguments that implied a similarity between Australian colonial officials and Nazis.

Various concerned community groups made direct submissions to the Cabinet appealing for clemency. Hasluck informed the Cabinet that forty-two submissions had been made on behalf of the killers; he provided a list and a summary—not the actual letters.[110] The Howard League, a long-term opponent of capital punishment, wrote opposing its use in this case. Various unions, such as the Newcastle Branch of the Federated Engine Drivers and Firemen's Association, Brisbane Trades Hall and the Australian Council of Trade Unions, opposed the use of the death penalty in this case specifically and also more generally—the labour movement in Australia largely favoured the abolition of the death penalty.[111] Letters also came from other sections of the community, with the Australian Natives Association and the Churches of Christ in Australia making representations to the Cabinet on commuting the sentences of the men. Hasluck wrote that: 'some of these have an obvious political purpose; some are based solely on humanity'.[112] Indeed, groups such as the Howard League would have opposed any use of capital punishment. While there was little commentary on PNG in their opposition, it reflected increasing opposition to the use of capital punishment generally, which was itself of political significance. Neither Hasluck nor the newspapers drew attention to any support for carrying out the death sentences. The diversity of the representations clearly indicated to the Cabinet that they could exercise the mercy of the Crown with broad public and political support.

---

109 'Death Sentence in New Guinea', *Sydney Morning Herald*, 5 August 1954, 2.
110 'Representations Regarding the Sentences'. The text of all those submissions does not appear to be available.
111 R. N. Barber, 'The Labor Party and the Abolition of Capital Punishment in Queensland, 1899–1922', *Queensland Heritage* 1, no. 9 (1968): 3–12; Barry Jones, 'The Decline and Fall of the Death Penalty', in *The Penalty is Death: Capital Punishment in the Twentieth Century*, ed. Barry Jones (Melbourne: Sun Books, 1968).
112 Paul Hasluck, 'Summary of Cabinet Submission', NAA: A4906, 4, Item 209114.

To some extent, the critics of colonialism in Australia found similarities between PNG and other empires. The deficiencies of the traditional mode of colonialism and imperialism were obvious in the moral and practical collapse of regimes in the 1950s in Vietnam, Algeria and Kenya. Australian newspapers covered many stories about the decline of European empires in 1953 and 1954 and questions in federal parliament on PNG reflected this understanding of a changing world. For example, Labor member S. M. Keon compared PNG to Kenya, suggesting that it would become a hotbed of 'Maumauism' unless development and the movement to independence was better implemented.[113] Australians seemed to feel a duty to do better in PNG than other imperial powers had done in their colonies and they relayed that pressure to the Cabinet 'better' in this case meant clemency.

The priority of administration officials in PNG was to address the problem of the Telefomins' repudiation of Australian colonialism that PNG officials accepted had happened in response to 'incidents' and 'errors' in colonial practice. Therefore, submissions from within the administration focussed on the usefulness of both capital punishment *and* clemency in dealing with that. Gore believed that capital punishment would draw a firm line on violence and opposition to the administration; however, most favoured mercy to rebuild the relationship. Hasluck collated the views of the officials in PNG and raised two key problems for the Cabinet. First, there were clear indications that mistakes had been made and something had to be done about it. Second, there was the question of whether the condemned men were sufficiently civilised to make hanging them just.[114]

The first and most influential consideration for the Cabinet was how to deal with the reality of maladministration. William Lalor's albeit unsuccessful use of the defence of emergency and subsequent report to the Cabinet ensured that it and Hasluck were aware of the feelings and beliefs of the people who had experienced the administrative errors.[115] Had Lalor's critique been merely a contrivance—a defence tactic—he could have abandoned it in the clemency report. However, in maintaining it and continuing to shine a light on the issues, he showed that he was genuinely interested in assisting Telefomin to gain redress.

---

113 'Mau Mau Talk "Mischievous"', *Sydney Morning Herald*, 7 October 1953, 5.
114 Hasluck, 'Summary of Cabinet Submission', 1–4.
115 Lalor, 'Investigation Made by Myself'.

By convention, after handing down a mandatory sentence of death, the sitting judge was called upon to discuss what sentence a condemned person should *actually* receive. In making their recommendation, the judge could consider broad issues of justice and administration, rather than just the narrow context of a particular case and its burdens of proof and relevant case law. Justice Gore recommended hanging to Cleland and Hasluck, primarily for the deterrent value. His was a lone voice; no other Australian officials voiced support for the death penalty in this case. Considering Australian colonialism a net good, despite the 'errors', Gore wrote:

> The administration is at Telefomin to stay, and whatever the present generation might think, the administration must not be hampered in its undertaking for the future benefit of the people. There should be, I think, a punishment sufficient to make the people realise that there must be no interference in the future.[116]

Fundamentally, Gore believed that 'this was a war to exterminate the administration'.[117] Despite his characterisation of the men as 'irked' in his rejection of the defence of emergency, this meant that Gore was aware that there was serious dissatisfaction with the administration and that the Telefomin killers had had broader political goals and justifications for their actions. However, he evidently believed that the Australian project would bring benefits that outweighed those negatives. Gore was concerned that Papua New Guinean opposition to colonialism might limit the capacity of the Australian administration to carry out the mission to develop the land and people, and that whatever provoked the violence was not sufficient reason to stop the project to raise the people higher—that is, to stop 'advancement'.

Gore sought to follow the prewar colonial practice of being 'ruthless in dealing with any abuse of authority'.[118] His recommendation to use capital punishment to protect the work of the colonial administration is consistent with the observations of legal historians Bruce Ottley and Jean Zorn that a primary purpose of the practice of law in PNG was the preservation of the unitary state—that is, protection of the capacity of the central authority to rule.[119] Though Gore can, in no way, be considered a 'hanging judge',

---

116 Ralph T. Gore to administrator, 30 August 1954, NAA: A4906, 4, Item 209114.
117 Ibid.
118 I. P. Mair, *Australia in New Guinea* (Carlton: Melbourne University Press, 1970), 2.
119 Bruce L. Ottley, and Jean G. Zorn, 'Criminal Law in Papua New Guinea: Code, Custom and the Courts in Conflict', *American Journal of Comparative Law* 31, no. 2 (1983): 251–300.

he took a hard line in this case.[120] In his mind, this 'war' required Australia to act to preserve the power it had claimed for itself. If there was to be a deterrent, or expiation of some sort, it had to be in a language understood by Papua New Guineans: death. Having delivered 'pronounced' death sentences upon most of the Telefomin men, except the killers of Purari, Gore had, by legal custom, already recommended that most of them be hanged. As required, he had added an alternative sentence to execution; if the men were not to be hanged, ten years of hard labour for all would be appropriate, which was a relatively heavy penal sentence for murder.

Despite Gore having differentiated between the killers in 'pronouncing' sentence on some, but not all, Hasluck informed the Cabinet that: 'In this he [Gore] has indicated that he is not able to separate the thirty-two prisoners to suggest that some should receive greater or lesser punishment than others.'[121] In his clemency submission, Gore wrote: 'Neither could the rank and file appreciate a harsher treatment of their headmen.'[122] Here Gore was making the point that treating the men differently, which would have been more consistent with Australian law, would appear unjust to the Telefomin and provoke more trouble. To Gore, any sentence following from clemency was less about the merits of the men and justice, and more about how the colony should be managed on the ground. His proposal that all be punished equally, despite differences in culpability, was in keeping with his view that Papua New Guineans were a group that needed guidance and control, and that did not understand the nuances of law.

District Commissioner Sydney Elliott-Smith, a long-term official, former military officer and 'B4' whose jurisdiction included the Telefomin area, was asked by Cleland to make a submission to the capital case review board. His expertise in the Telefomin area and in colonial practice was of interest to the administrator and the minister. Like Gore, Elliott-Smith was less interested in the fine points of law and justice than in the question of how to manage the situation on the ground. Unlike Gore, he argued in favour of mercy. Due to the strong show of force used in the rapid capture of the accused, he maintained that 'the stick' had already been applied; therefore, mercy should be used as 'the carrot' to educate locals about the good intentions and superior morality of the Australians. Elliot-Smith also suggested that

---

120 Gore *Justice versus Sorcery*, 28, 218. On sentencing averages see Table 6.1.
121 Hasluck, 'Summary of Cabinet Submission'.
122 Gore to administrator, 30 August 1954; D. M. Cleland to Hasluck, 30 August 1954, NAA: A4906, 4, Item 209114.

the actions taken by the Telefomins might be understandable, as 'some of our past actions could be classed as unduly aggressive and in most instances thoughtless'.[123] He highlighted the problems that might arise from carrying out capital punishment on a people already dissatisfied with the violence of Australian colonialism. Drawing on the Murray system, he proposed using mercy to build confidence between Papua New Guineans and the authorities in this newly patrolled area.

Similarly, Administrator Cleland suggested to Hasluck that mercy would suit the mood of a people already smarting under maladministration. Relaying this advice, the minister informed the Cabinet that:

> although the Judge had held that there was not a complete breakdown of Administrative order, he [Cleland] could not exclude, in considering his own recommendations [as to sentencing] the fact that there had been, to say the least, bad administrative errors in the past, the memory of which may or may not have been in the native mind.[124]

Building on Elliot-Smith and Cleland's reservations, Hasluck was prepared to step carefully with a population that needed careful management—one whose sense of justice had been offended over several years.

The inability of a murder trial to deal with the question of maladministration and the legitimacy of authority in the minds of the Telefomin meant that the discretionary process was the last means by which a just, rather than a merely legal, outcome might be reached. Martin Wiener has shown that discretionary justice was sometimes able to serve this pacifying, backstop function in other colonial settings.[125] More specifically, the Telefomin capital case files support Sinclair Dinnen's suggestion that finding a balance between Western law and Papua New Guinean expectations of restitution was a question of long-term management by judges and Australian officials.[126] Dinnen shows that the legal system in PNG recognised the cultural pressures upon Papua New Guineans to act in ways not accommodated by Western jurisprudence, such as shame, and that judges and bureaucrats discussed, but did not always agree on, how to achieve that.

---

123 Cleland to Hasluck, 30 August 1954.
124 Hasluck, 'Summary of Cabinet Submission'.
125 See, for example, Martin J. Wiener, *Empire on Trial: Race, Murder, and Justice under British Rule, 1870–1935* (New York: Cambridge University Press, 2009), 158–9.
126 Sinclair Dinnen, 'Sentencing, Custom and the Rule of Law in Papua and New Guinea', *Journal of Legal Pluralism* 20, no. 27 (1988): 19–54, 8.

In addition to the question of how to manage the problem on the ground, all those consulted in the capital case reviews also addressed the question of how the local people understood the acts of execution and clemency. This supports Nicholas Brown's suggestion that the psychology of Papuans and New Guineans was a matter of great discussion among expatriate officials.[127] According to both Cleland and Elliott-Smith, the Telefomins did not understand the aims of the administration or the consequences of breaching the law. Cleland wrote to Hasluck that:

> I concur with the views of the District Commissioner particularly in that the accused were not fully informed about (a) the aims and desires of the administration and (b) of the penalties that follow breaches of our newly imposed laws.[128]

In light of such presumed ignorance, Elliott-Smith asked how hangings would 'help the cause of the administration?'[129] There was concern that hangings would be misunderstood, both by the Telefomin and by domestic and international observers. Conversely, clemency provided an opportunity for the colonial administration to be viewed as a merciful alternative system. Elliott-Smith argued that this had worked in other districts in PNG, the Murray system having brought peace to PNG by replacing reprisal and vendetta with policing and clemency. Indeed, it was common for PNG and federal government officials to celebrate the Australian repression of cycles of vendetta when justifying the Australian presence.[130] As such, Cleland's and Elliot-Smith's arguments were much more conventional and tested than Gore's and, therefore, more likely to be persuasive.

Hasluck and Cleland had to choose a punishment and they wanted the results to be useful to the administration as well as just. Their interest in potential Papua New Guinean responses was further revealed in their close attention to the views of Norm Draper, a Baptist missionary resident near the Telefomin patrol station who was invited by Cleland to make a submission on the specific situation in the Telefomin area after the killings. Hasluck was interested in the submissions of missionaries and missionary

---

127 Brown, *Governing Prosperity*, 67–72.
128 Cleland to Hasluck, 30 August 1954, 4.
129 S. Elliott-Smith, in Cleland to Hasluck, 30 August 1954, 3–4.
130 Hasluck, *A Time for Building*, 84; Nelson, 'The View from the Sub-district', 30; Buchan, *Empire of Political Thought*, 5.

groups working in Telefomin, as he valued specific knowledge over general moral argument.[131] His preference was such that he quoted Draper in his submission to the Cabinet. Hasluck also summarised Draper's thoughts as:

> the multiple death sentences would not further the cause of mutual confidence between the government and the natives, but would widen the breach to such an extent that for many years there would be no hope of achieving understanding.[132]

After understanding came stability, the rule of law and economic development—all of which amounted to 'advancement'. Hasluck wanted commentary on practical colonialism, which Draper and other colonialists provided along with the recommendation of mercy as a matter of managing that relationship. They seemingly believed that mercy would further the Australian project in PNG by bringing order to the Telefomin subdistrict.

There is no direct evidence of UN concerns over Telefomin in 1954 in the Australian archives; however, as Wolfers has suggested, fears of international criticism were often a matter of perception—officials anticipated critiques and acted accordingly to avoid them. Indeed, the Department of External Affairs warned the Department of Territories that there would be international and, particularly, UN interest in the Telefomin matter from the very first days of the crisis, and that the message Australia sent to those international audiences had to be carefully managed.[133] The Department of External Affairs was prompted to write because UNTC deliberations on the state of Australia's governance in PNG were scheduled to occur at the same time as the trials.[134]

That UN scrutiny affected PNG policy and practice seemed to be commonplace knowledge, as the Adelaide *Advertiser* opined:

> The recent sentencing of New Guinea natives for the murder of a patrol officer in the Telefomin district will inevitably be publicized far beyond. The natives' primitive state will be discussed. References

---

131 Hasluck, 'Summary of Cabinet Submission', 4.
132 Ibid., 4.
133 Cited in Craig, 'The Telefomin Murders', 133–4.
134 '8 New Guinea Natives to Die', *New York Times*, 16 July 1954, 3; 'The Proceedings in the U.N.', *New York Times*, 16 July 1954, 5; 'Clemency Advocated for Natives', *Leader-Post* (Regina, Saskatchewan), 3 September 1954, 20; 'News in Brief', *Times* (London), 9 November 1953, 6; '54 Police Search New Guinea Valley', *Times*, 11 November 1953, 7; 'News in Brief', *Times*, 17 March 1954, 7; 'New Guinea Murders', *Times*, 23 September 1954, 5.

to the subject in the UN Trusteeship Council must be expected ...
But such questioning may be salutary, if it prompts a review of the
Commonwealth's programme for New Guinea.[135]

The *Advertiser*'s dislike of international pressure and its suspicion of maladministration at Telefomin were repeated in articles printed after the conclusion of the trials. Given the expectation of foreign criticism, such reporting placed pressure on the Cabinet despite there being no evidence of any actual international criticism.

Links between the Telefomin situation and suspected international scrutiny and criticism were repeatedly made in newspapers. For example, the decision to keep Lalor's investigation into the administration in the Telefomin area from the public fuelled suspicions about the impact of international scrutiny on domestic decisions. The *SPP* linked the secrecy over Lalor's report to Australia's announcement of its commitment to SEATO and its desire not to offend its postcolonial allies with stories of its own colonialism.[136] In August 1954, the state secretary of the Australian Labor Party in Queensland, Jack Schmella, wrote to the *Courier-Mail* of his concerns about the impression the UN might form of Australia's actions in Telefomin and PNG more generally.[137] The risk to Australia's international reputation must have been apparent to Cabinet and Hasluck during their consideration of clemency for the Telefomin killers. The problem for Cabinet was the strong perception in Australia that the world cared about its conduct in PNG. The politics of discretionary justice enabled such perceptions and fears, whether real or imagined, to be carefully managed.

Mercy keeps things quiet

The federal Cabinet instructed the administrator to commute all the death sentences for the Telefomin killers to ten years imprisonment with hard labour.[138] Hasluck told Cabinet that, in his view, there was little difference between the four crimes so similar punishments were suitable. The Cabinet notebooks recorded that as 'all the people with knowledge agree on ten years' the recommendation was approved. The description of advisers from

---

135 'Progress in New Guinea', *Advertiser*, 23 August 1954, 2.
136 'Telefomin Report to be Kept Secret', *South Pacific Post*, 11 August 1954.
137 Jack Schmella, 'Party's Concern on New Guinea Affairs', *Courier-Mail*, 11 August 1954, 8.
138 Notetaker A. S. Brown, 21 September 1954, submission 102, p. 124, NAA: A11099, 1/19, item 12105762.

PNG as 'people with knowledge' suggests that extra credence was placed on submissions from PNG that recommended ten years, such as Gore's. At this stage in the evolving process of clemency decisions across the period covered in this book, Canberra paid close attention to the judgement of PNG officials in clemency cases. Further, despite some sentences being 'pronounced' and some being 'recorded', indicating that some were considered more serious than others, the Cabinet made no such distinction in deciding on punishment. Evidently, regaining the confidence of the community by presenting an identical punishment to aid in the understanding of the local people was prioritised over finer points of justice or differentiating between levels of culpability, which was the approach recommended by PNG officials. This indicated a poor view of the capacity of the PNG people.

Despite the Cabinet representing officials in PNG as 'the people with knowledge', it wanted to direct the administrator in the final decision over clemency via the Executive Council, which would then advise the governor-general. As such, the Cabinet determined to continue with plans to legislate to remove the royal prerogative of mercy in PNG from the hands of the administrator to the governor-general: 'It looks from the act as though it is the administrator's business to commute. Decisions by the Cabinet and not the Executive Council. Form of amendment to be discussed.'[139]

This indicates that, although a decision had been made in late 1952 to amend the *Papua and New Guinea Act, 1949* to move the royal prerogative of mercy to the governor-general, it had not been enacted. However, it was eventually presented to the Parliament of Australia in 1954 and was enacted.[140] It also indicates that these cases reminded the Cabinet of the decision to transfer that power to Canberra and that it needed to refine its legislation. The determination to take control suggests that there was some discomfort with leaving the power of life and death in the hands of the chief colonialist. Hasluck's suspicions in 1951 of the Raj-like B4s and old colonialists seemed to manifest itself in this measure. In addition, it regularised the process in PNG to be more like other Australian jurisdictions, which had the prerogative invested in the formal head of state. This regularisation reflected Hasluck's liberal, legal ideological leanings, as it made the Australian territories consistent with the states and more equal in applying the rule of law.

---

139 Ibid.
140 Hasluck, 'Summary of Cabinet Submission', 3–4.

Having determined to commute the sentences, Cabinet also discussed how best to represent the use of mercy to the public. Cabinet determined to make it clear that the trial and sentence review process was what an Australian would have been entitled to. It was noted that: 'Whole process available to the condemned person available to native.' Cabinet wanted Australians and other audiences to know that Papua New Guineans experienced the due process of law. In regard to the wording of the press release announcing its decision, Cabinet noted: 'Commutation should be accompanied by the sort of statements in judges and others reports … Judge's report not to be quoted from.'[141] Cabinet decided not to mention Justice Gore's warning of possible warfare if the killers were not executed, but it accepted his conclusion that there was no emergency in the district, an approach consistent with producing an outcome acceptable to international audiences. Indeed, clemency was useful to colonialists in presenting colonialism as merciful and just in contrast to Papua New Guinean violence.[142] A court case run on liberal principles of equality of justice ending in clemency was something that could be sold to the world. Moreover, it was something in which Hasluck firmly believed, as shown in his attempt to bring liberal colonialism to PNG to replace the old colonial variety.

Once the decision to commute the sentences was made, Hasluck made the public announcement, which was reported in depth by the *SPP* and the *SMH*.[143] The *SPP* focussed on those aspects of Hasluck's speech that exonerated the work of PNG officials, reporting that the minister dismissed allegations of mismanagement as 'incidents [that were] alleged to have happened'.[144] Seemingly, Hasluck sought to build on the findings of the court that there had been no emergency. He was also reported as emphasising the minimal level of influence the patrol had achieved in the area. In this way, he tried to position the colonial government as less liable—that is, as not really having been in a position to affect people for good or ill. This seems to have been Hasluck's own contribution, as it was not included in the reports. The *SPP* also drew attention to Hasluck's claims that the Cabinet had considered the lobbying efforts by expatriates, families and officials.

---

141 Notetaker A. S. Brown, 21 September 1954.
142 Loo, 'Savage Mercy'; Hay, 'Property, Authority and the Criminal Law', 135.
143 Hasluck's statement to the press was not included in the file.
144 'Cabinet Commuted Telefomin Murder Sentences', *South Pacific Post*, 29 September 1954, 9.

In his public announcement, Hasluck was reported as arguing that Papua New Guineans demonstrated their lack of 'awareness of the administration' in their actions. However, reflecting Gore's arguments, he asserted that the most irrational act would be to remove colonial control:

> They acted to exterminate the administration as they knew it so that they could lead their old life … Any sense of grievance on any particular matter would appear to have been used as an excuse and was not the actual motive. The attack apparently occurred when it did because a long-awaited opportunity was seen and not because of any recent events or, any event with which the victims were personally associated.[145]

Hasluck configured the Telefomin as ignorant people who acted violently out of an irrational desire to return their own lives, thereby justifying Australia's continued colonial occupation.[146] Indeed, at a time when progress and modernity were so prized in the Western world, the image of the Telefomin clinging to their old life marked them as needing Australia's assistance. Murder, according to Hasluck, revealed the nature of the colonised and highlighted the challenges Australians faced. His careful wording drew attention to the principal justification for Australia's presence in PNG—its UNTC-endorsed project to advance Papua New Guineans. These propositions also played to the precedent of clemency for offenders deemed too 'unsophisticated' to comprehend Western justice. Thus, Hasluck placed this mercy within a context of similar decisions and made it conventionally just.

In the same article, the *SPP* quoted Hasluck's statement that the Cabinet had been influenced by the advice from the territory on how to bring order and peace to the Telefomin:

> Cabinet was influenced by a belief that the execution of the death sentences would not help the cause of the Administration in bringing law, order and improved conditions to the people of Telefomin.[147]

The *SPP* highlighted Hasluck's reference to the dynamics of colonialism to position those closest to the events as the greatest advocates for clemency, further presenting the administration as enlightened and benevolent.

---

145 Ibid.
146 Loo, 'Savage Mercy'; Nelson, 'The View from the Sub-district', 30; Buchan, *Empire of Political Thought*, 5.
147 'Cabinet Commuted Telefomin Murder Sentences'.

The statement suggested that mercy was chosen because of local advice that it would not exacerbate the dissatisfaction of the Telefomin, even if Hasluck had previously characterised them as 'irrational'. Having publicly criticised the conduct of officials in PNG in the initial phase of the crisis, giving credence to views from PNG might have been the *SPP*'s way of trying to remediate the relationship with administration staff; alternatively, praising PNG officials, the *SPP*'s main readers, may simply have been the *SPP* continuing its editorial practice of supporting and defending the colonial project in PNG.

In configuring the Telefomin as 'irrational', Hasluck was able to present the announcement to grant clemency without having to acknowledge the 'bad administrative errors' that Cabinet intended clemency to ameliorate. He agreed with PNG officials that clemency would better serve the needs of the administration in bringing peace to the area.

The *SMH* endorsed the act of clemency by suggesting it was a politically successful choice for Cabinet. Apparently satisfied with the rightness of Australia's project and Hasluck's policies, the *SMH* editor wrote: 'The decision, announced yesterday, to commute the death sentences passed on 32 Telefomin natives will be generally acknowledged as wise and humane.'[148] The editor cited two reasons for this view: first, the Telefomin could not understand 'white' justice; second, their motives 'were not even entirely discreditable in the context of tribal resentment of white interference'. Yet, curiously, the editor also wondered if it might not have been better to grab a few of the accused killers and hang them on the spot. Just as curiously, even as the *SMH* advocated for coercive Australian control, it was suspicious of Australian colonialism and mercy. To the *SMH*, there were good reasons for holding PNG and acting humanely, but Australia also needed to make sure it was the boss. Rife with the tensions and contradictions inherent in the modern colonial project, the *SMH*'s commentary highlights the difficulties Hasluck faced in navigating this policy area. Overall, the decision to grant clemency was one that pleased most parties. The focus of much of the commentary in the press indicates that Hasluck, despite his best efforts, was not able to shift public attention away from the administration's errors at Telefomin—notwithstanding the fact that the decision to grant clemency represented a generally approved policy measure to address those errors.

---

148 Editorial, 'The Telefomin Murders', *Sydney Morning Herald*, 23 September 1954.

Administrator Cleland was also attempting to shape the media's representation of the case. However, while Hasluck's focus was on a broad audience, his was on PNG expatriates. After the clemency decision, Cleland was reported in the *SPP* as saying that 'we are there and there we must remain particularly after recent events … The people of the Telefomin area still need close watching with care and patience.'[149] Cleland was not satisfied with relying on the capital case reviews to bring peace to the district. Bringing peace and restitution, he pointed out, would be the continuing work of the administration, which needed to make investments in agriculture, health, education and policing. This formulation fits with the style of paternalism and authoritarianism that characterised Australian colonialism according to Wolfers and Healy.[150]

There are few accounts of the reaction of the Telefomin to the sentencing. Craig's collection of oral history shows that the events were well remembered, including the misconduct of the patrol officers and constables; however, the testimony of witnesses in court indicates that the killings had limited support at the time, with much aid being given to the police and officials even in the midst of the attacks. If not for the history of violent reprisals against such attacks on officials before the war, and testimony that the conspirators were warned about such reprisals by the old people, such evidence could be read as minimising the notion of widespread dissatisfaction with the colonial administration in Telefomin. Some people could have been both dissatisfied *and* fearful of attacking colonial officials.

It seems that clemency and prison went some way to reconciling the parties. A report written by the administration for the UNTC in 1961, when the killers' sentences were almost complete, showed that most of the offenders had cooperated with the administration during their incarceration, learning farming and/or brick-related trades and also acquiring proficiency in Tok Pisin.[151] While a few of the imprisoned men took up jobs with the administration upon completion of their ten-year sentences, most returned home, perhaps indicating their common desire to minimise further contact with the colonial project.[152]

---

149 'Telefomins Still Need Close Watching, Mr Cleland Says', *South Pacific Post*, 20 October 1954, 2.
150 Wolfers, *Race Relations*, 126–7.
151 Crown Law Officer W. Watkins to secretary, Department of Territories, 28 February 1962, NAA: A452, 1961/4256, 3500477.
152 Ibid.

Conclusion

It is significant that Hasluck's memoir of his work in Papua and New Guinea, which is in many ways a justification of his work there, is silent on Telefomin. This unexpected silence suggests that he was aware that the events that occurred there detracted from his narrative of just governance. Hasluck's omission points to an unresolved question of legitimacy. The Telefomin incident and trials raised questions about whether Australia's place in PNG was just and legitimate and, as Hay and Loo suggest, whether executive clemency—mercy—was a way of reclaiming political legitimacy.[153] The use of mercy in the face of Papua New Guinean violence also drew attention to the purpose of, and justification for, the colonial project in PNG, namely advancement. The justification was that the Telefomin needed help and guidance to become clement and law-abiding Westerners. Therefore, clemency served the purpose of colonial administration.

The decision to grant clemency to the killers accommodated the many concerns of the federal government, including its awareness of the Telefomins' dissatisfaction with Australia. Hasluck determined that the best way to achieve justice in that context was to depend on the experience and judgements of the B4s and their approach to handling justice on the ground. At the same time, he was able to point to the defensible liberality of the conduct of the trial and clemency. At the beginning of this period, the administration was in control of justice, but not to the extent that it was allowed to carry out punishments that appeared autocratic and unjust.

This case reminded the Cabinet to legislate the process that became standard post-Telefomin: the referral of all death sentences for a capital case review by the governor-general-in-council, instead of it being the administrator's decision. Cabinet commentary indicates that it was just this kind of case—well-known and with international implications—that prompted the decision to alter the legislation so as to have the royal prerogative exercised in Canberra. There was too much danger that the wrong decision might be made by the administrator in PNG.

This notorious case offered the Australian government the chance to legitimise its colonial rule. The commutations cast the administration in a favourable light. This counteracted the possibility of a controversial

---

153 Hay, 'Property, Authority and the Criminal Law'.

legal case delegitimising Australian colonialism. Calavita has argued that a controversial legal case that highlights a dying discourse in the public eye can act to extinguish support for that discourse entirely.[154] Calavita's insight into causation suggests that, with colonialism viewed as a dying discourse by the world and by Australians, there was a danger that hanging the Telefomin killers would have emphasised Australia's disagreeable colonial past and undermined the ennobling discourse with which Australia justified its presence in PNG. Hasluck's handling of the killings avoided that. Clemency gave sanction to the idea that the administration had a legitimate role to play in bringing McAuley's 'seal of peace' to the rugged mountains of New Guinea.[155] Yet the question of Australia's goals and colonial legitimacy in PNG was again raised in 1954, far from the rugged mountains, when a Papua New Guinean man raped a white woman in Port Moresby. That case is discussed in the next chapter.

---

154 Kitty Calavita, 'Blue Jeans and the "De-constitutive" Power of Law', *Law and Society Review* 35, no. 1 (2001): 89–116.
155 James McAuley, 'In Memory of Arch-Bishop Alain de Boismenu, MSC', in James McAuley, *A Vision of Ceremony*, cited in Brown, *Governing Prosperity*, 46.

3
'Mentally upset and a nymphomaniac': *R. v. Kita Tunguan, 1954*

On 2 June 1954, the *South Pacific Post* reported that 'a native houseboy had raped a European woman who had once saved his life'.[1] The story was reported on page one. A week later, on 9 June, the weekly Port Moresby paper reported that Justice Gore, the presiding judge, had concluded: 'I don't see any indication in this case which calls upon me to record the sentence.'[2] This chapter tells the story of how Gore came to this conclusion and what happened next.

According to a report prepared by Police Sub-Inspector John Fisher of Port Moresby, the accused, Joseph Kita Tunguan, was born in 1928 or 1929 in Sutmili in the Sepik district. His widowed mother died when he was fourteen or fifteen, after which a foster mother in Sutmili cared for him.[3] Between 1948 and 1950, like many village boys, he was a part-time student at the village school. As a result of his perceived potential, he was then sent to a Catholic mission school on Kairo Island near Wewak, but he was sent home after seven months for fighting.[4]

---

1 'Native on Trial', *South Pacific Post*, 2 June 1954, 1.
2 'Native Sentenced to Death', *South Pacific Post*, 9 June 1954, 1.
3 His age was uncertain as census processes were still rudimentary in the 1920s and the Second World War destroyed many NG records.
4 John Fisher to superintendent of police, 12 June 1954, NAA: A518, CQ840/1/3_PART1, Item 3252669.

Subsequently, Tunguan found work in Wewak as a labourer for a month, returned home, found more work in Madang, and was then hired as a contractor in Bulolo. In 1951, he changed jobs and worked as a house servant in Lae, a well-paid position for a largely unskilled person, and one that indicates he had good Tok Pisin and English language skills—the key skills required for the job. He then moved with his employer to Port Moresby. In December 1951, he changed jobs to work for the Australian Petroleum Company until he fell ill and was hospitalised for two months. Dr Nesbit treated him at the Ela Beach Native Hospital. He was sick long enough that he had to find a new job, which he lost for brawling with Australians from his previous workplace, but the report does not explain why they fought.

Tunguan could read and write in Tok Pisin, Motu and, at the time of his arrest, his English was reportedly 'reasonably good'.[5] In 1953, his language skills enabled him to move between several employers, using variations of his names before being hired by the Port Moresby European Hospital. However, he was dismissed for threatening one of his previous short-term employers, Captain Barr. Then came two more jobs, and again he was dismissed for fighting with his employer's colleagues at the Department of Civil Aviation. He promptly found work at the Steamship Company Mess, but then, in early 1954, was employed by Lloyd Nesbit of the Civil Aviation Office to work in his home. Tunguan's employment history creates an interesting picture of labour mobility for a Papua New Guinean with language skills in the 1950s.

Even though his work life was disrupted, the defence adduced that Kita Tunguan attended his Port Moresby Catholic Church regularly and did odd jobs for a priest at Taurama. It was also mentioned that he pursued classes in English and in reading and writing. His former employer Sub-Inspector Collins described Kita Tunguan as a large and strong man with a quick temper. He was also described as 'difficult to manage'. Indeed, he appears to have been a man who would not tolerate being treated poorly and was willing to use violence in search of respect. Yet, he kept getting jobs, so Kita Tunguan's demeanour was perhaps persuasive, or his skills were considered worthy of employment. Kita Tunguan was both an example of advancement and of the social change that old colonialists found discomforting: he was skilled and adapted to an expanding labour market yet was also volatile and independent and commonly used violence to redeem offended honour.

---

5   Fisher to superintendent of police, 12 June 1954.

Born in Yugoslavia in 1922, Blanka Parcen qualified as a medical doctor, achieving high scores in her studies at Graz, Austria, during the Second World War. She subsequently worked in a research facility in Croatia, Yugoslavia, before migrating to Australia in 1949.[6] Like other migrants to Australia, she experienced difficulties in having her qualifications and experience recognised. Parcen was working as a cleaner when she applied to the PNG Department of Health, which was then actively recruiting 'New Australians' due to skill shortages in the territory. She went where she could practise medicine, and was joined by her married lover, Dr Otruba, also a European-trained doctor. She worked at Ela Beach Native Hospital (see Figure 3.1). A report was prepared on Parcen's background by the police for the clemency process. It noted that Parcen and Otruba's relationship had ended when Dr Gunther, head of the PNG Department of Health, had posted them far apart after learning of their relationship.[7]

Figure 3.1: Ela Beach Native Hospital, Port Moresby, Papua New Guinea, 1953.
Source: Terence E. T. Spencer and Margaret Spencer, National Library of Australia, nla.gov.au/nla.obj-145544518.

---

6   D. J. Bock to Australian Military Mission, 16 January 1951, NAA: A518, 280/3/2544, Item 3309370; Blanka Parcen, Passenger Arrival Index, 1921–50, NAA: K269, 8 MAY 1949 MOHAMMEDI, Item 9245201.
7   C. Normoyle to administrator, 15 June 1954, NAA: 518, CQ840/1/3 PART 1, Item 3252669.

In the small, gossipy community of expatriate PNG, Parcen and Otruba's relationship had been common knowledge. Shortly after their separation, Otruba attempted suicide and was subsequently deported. In 1951, Dr Parcen met and married Mr William Nesbit, who worked for the Department of Civil Aviation. However, her life seemed to remain emotionally troubled. In 1953 she took leave from the native hospital in Port Moresby, suffering depression after a fellow doctor, also a European immigrant, had attempted to engage her in a suicide pact. It is easy to imagine her distress amid such dramatic transformations in her life. Compounding matters, she was dismissed from her position later in 1953, in part because of her protracted sick leave and in part because she was reported to have demonstrated hostility towards Papua New Guineans.[8] Her circumstances, again, were the subject of much gossip and appear in several sources.[9]

On 25 May 1954, Dr Nesbit was home alone. Her husband had been working away from Port Moresby for several weeks. That afternoon she was engaged in sewing a skirt. At the trial, it was stated that her husband's servant, Kita Tunguan, who had been hired seven weeks earlier, knocked at the back door. As he had before, he asked permission to iron his own clothes for his day off. He was the gardener and did the heavy laundry. However, true to established etiquette, he did not wash Blanka Nesbit's clothes.[10] He began to iron and she sat down to sew in an adjoining room, with no door separating them, until she joined him, seeking to press a part of the skirt she was making. The evidence presented at Kita Tunguan's trial did not clearly establish whether Nesbit had demanded that he iron the skirt panel, and, if so, whether he had refused.[11] Neither did the court rule clearly on what happened next. Either Nesbit kneed Kita Tunguan sharply and painfully in the buttocks while passing him, and he then grabbed her from behind; or, while peacefully returning to the dining room, Nesbit was grabbed from behind and thrown to the floor. It is clear that Nesbit was thrown to the floor as her head damaged the woven palm wall near the dining room door. What is unclear is whether she first assaulted Kita Tunguan. He claimed that she did, and he was enraged:

---

8   Normoyle to administrator; D. M. Cleland to secretary, 5 October 1954, NAA: A518, CQ840/1/3 PART 1, item 3252669.
9   Cleland to secretary, 5 October 1954; Gloria Chalmers, *Kundus, Cannibals and Cargo Cults: Papua New Guinea in the 1950s* (Watsons Bay: Books and Writers Network, 2006), 67; Normoyle to administrator.
10   J. Wyatt, *Guide to Newcomers to Papua-New Guinea by a Port Moresby Housewife* ([Port Moresby]: Country Women's Association, 1957), 12.
11   Cleland to secretary, 5 October 1954; Gore, 'R. v. Tunguan—Transcription of Trial', Papers of Ralph Gore, 1930–1964, National Library of Australia (hereafter Gore Papers), box 1, folder 6. Gore compiled a full transcript only a handful of times in the 1950s.

she claimed she did not.[12] Despite the prosecutor's interest in pursuing this matter, Justice Gore determined not to rule on the matter as he found it irrelevant to what followed. Yet, Kita Tunguan's claims were not dismissed out of hand, indicating Nesbit's precariously balanced reputation.

In 1957, J. Wyatt's *Guide to Newcomers to Papua-New Guinea* provided a guide to what most long-term expatriates accepted as precepts for relationships between white women and their Papua New Guinean male servants in the years preceding its publication. Wyatt suggested that servants could interpret familiar behaviour, such as physical contact, as an invitation to sex.[13] As Amirah Inglis argued, the pamphlet is revealing about attitudes and expectations around women's behaviours in PNG in the 1950s.[14] The notions revealed in the pamphlet help to explain the prosecutor's interest in trying to establish that physical contact had occurred prior to the rape. The ambiguity surrounding Nesbit's actions, especially her proximity to her husband's servant, shadowed understandings of the case.

Other servants testified that they heard Nesbit call Tunguan's name. Justice Gore accepted testimony that Nesbit had struggled against Kita's grasp and shouted his name asking him to stop. Nesbit testified that she then tried to shame him into letting her go by reminding him that she had cared for him when he was sick and that he was a mission boy and a Christian. She explained to the court that she then tried to trick Tunguan by asking to be placed on her bed. She hoped for a chance to run away. However, the defence construed this as further evidence of her consent. Tunguan placed her on the bed, but without releasing his hold on her. He tore at her clothes and he raped her. He kept his hold on her and threatened that if she told anyone, he would tell Mr Nesbit that she had been sleeping with many men while he was away. In his own evidence, Tunguan claimed that he had watched her with her lovers through the window while sitting in a mango tree.[15]

Nesbit testified that, fearing for her life, she had agreed to his terms. When he left, she ran to the nearby single women's quarters. Finding no one home, she ran to the house of her neighbour, Mrs Woodmansey. Taking note of Nesbit's torn clothes and distressed state, Woodmansey called the police. Nesbit then telephoned a friend to come and help her. However,

---

12 Cleland to secretary, 5 October 1954; Gore, 'R v. Tunguan—Transcription of Trial'.
13 Wyatt, *Guide to Newcomers*, 12.
14 Amirah Inglis, *The White Women's Protection Ordinance: Sexual Anxiety and Politics in Papua* (Sussex University Press, 1975).
15 Cleland to secretary, 5 October 1954; Gore, 'R v. Tunguan—Transcription of Trial'.

as the telephone call was not conducted in English, Woodmansey could not confirm what was said. Shortly afterwards, a doctor examined Nesbit and found physical injuries consistent with rape. The police set out to arrest Tunguan, who was found at the Nesbit house wearing his freshly ironed shirt. He was arrested on the charge of rape.[16]

Kita Tunguan's trial began on 3 June 1954 and ended five days later. In his judgement, Gore stated that he found Dr Nesbit to be honest, while he found Tunguan 'cleverly evasive'. He believed Nesbit's testimony and took into account her physical injuries and the accounts of neighbours and other servants. Gore found Tunguan guilty of rape and pronounced a sentence of death.[17] Kita Tunguan, given his experience of trouble with the police, was apparently unwilling to incriminate himself by confessing as usually happened in capital cases. He had some understanding of the processes of the Australian law.

A 'pronounced' sentence was an explicit recommendation that Tunguan should hang and also indicated that Gore had determined him to be a more dangerous criminal than the many murderers and violent men he had convicted in his career and for whom he had 'recorded' a sentence instead.[18] In thinking about Papua New Guineans and the law, Gore's view was that violent crime was usually a result of what he saw as the irresistible demands of custom and pride rather than individual criminal intentions, as assumed by Australian law.[19] By pronouncing the sentence on Kita Tunguan, Gore indicated that, in this case, he saw a vicious crime, not some compulsion of custom: in other words, he believed that Tunguan's actions were those of a criminal who knew what he was doing—an observation compounded by his perception of Tunguan's 'evasive' testimony. However, Gore also noted that the executive would make the ultimate decision and he knew from experience that very few convicted criminals were ever hanged.

The case was referred to Administrator Donald Cleland who commuted Tunguan's pronounced sentence of death to a sentence of life with hard labour—a severe sentence compared to the five to eight years most murderers received.[20] But, whatever past practice might have been, Cleland's decision violated a federal Cabinet decision of 1952. Once the *Papua and New*

---

16 Cleland to secretary, 5 October 1954; Gore, 'R v. Tunguan—Transcription of Trial'.
17 Ibid.
18 See Table 6.1 for sentencing statistics.
19 Ralph Gore, *Justice versus Sorcery* (Brisbane: Jacaranda Press, 1964), 91.
20 'Women Sign Petition', *South Pacific Post,* 11 August 1954, 7.

Guinea Act 1949 (Cth) was amended, the power of mercy would be given to the Executive Council and governor-general; however, in the meantime, the prerogative of mercy in such cases was to be left in the hands of the federal Cabinet, which would then advise the administrator.[21]

The Tunguan case came to Minister for Territories Paul Hasluck's attention when he noticed a newspaper article in the *South Pacific Post* (*SPP*) about some members of the Port Moresby Country Women's Association's (CWA's) opposition to the commutation of Tunguan's sentence. The minister wrote to Cleland and demanded to know why he and the Cabinet had not reviewed this case. Unaware of his mistake, Cleland sent the full capital case file, a precis of the reports on which his decision had been based and a letter explaining his decision, which included his suspicions regarding Nesbit's character that drew on gossip about Nesbit's sex life to which he had been privy. Hasluck was shocked at his administrator's candour and requested that Secretary of the Department of Territories Cecil Lambert inform Cleland that what he wanted was an explanation as to why the new procedure had not been followed, not the details of Nesbit's affairs. Cleland was apologetic and wrote that he had not intended to 'thwart' the minister. Cleland wrote back that he had not remembered that verbal direction and had received no paperwork to support the 1952 decision. Cleland went on to explain that he had commuted this case along with numerous other 'recorded' sentences that had come across his desk. Evidently, the process for clemency Hasluck had ordered in 1952 had not been clear to Cleland in 1954.

Cleland was subsequently instructed to continue giving his attention to the recorded cases until the legislation was amended transferring that duty to the governor-general. The amendment was passed in October 1954. However, Cleland kept commuting recorded sentences beyond that date and had to be reminded by Lambert in May 1955 to forward all such cases to the department. All the recorded cases were sent from November 1955 onwards, including a backlog of cases from between October 1954 and May 1955.

The Tunguan case, and the chain of mistakes that followed it, reinforced Hasluck's mistrust of territory officials that first arose after touring PNG in 1951 at the start of his ministry. He wrote of that trip in *A Time for Building*

---

21 'Case of Gebu-Ari', notes of meetings, 30 October 1952, NAA: A11099, 1/30, item 11584983; 'Minute to the Minister—Papua and New Guinea Act—Proposed Amendments, Draft', 4 August 1954, NAA: A518, CQ840/1/3 PART 1, item 3252669.

and noted that: 'The incompetence of the senior men was frightening.'[22] As well as highlighting their incompetence, Hasluck satirised expatriates in his memoir as having been intent on reliving the Raj, describing:

> the oddities of an officers' mess full of temporary gentlemen in white ducks giving a repertory club performance of a pukka sahib who had just come in from a dammed awful day of taking up white man's burden.[23]

He recalled being mistrustful of the PNG administration, and, in that vein, insisted that, in an age of modern communications, the Department of Territories in Canberra could and would take a more interventionist approach to the administration of PNG and to meeting Australia's obligations to advance Papua New Guineans.

Context of the clemency decision

Joseph Kita Tunguan raped Dr Blanka Nesbit and was tried at the same time as the highly publicised Telefomin murders were being investigated. Tunguan was convicted under the *White Women's Protection Ordinance, 1926–1934* (*WWPO*), which, under sections 2 and 3, made the rape, or attempted rape, of a European female by a Papua New Guinean man a capital offence, whereas the rape of a Papua New Guinean woman was punishable by imprisonment under the Criminal Code.[24] As mentioned above, a sentence of death was pronounced upon Tunguan; however, it was commuted to life with hard labour, a determination that reflected the intersection of gender and interracial relations with the themes discussed in the previous chapter. The administrator, being conscious that if PNG was to advance and be seen to advance in the eyes of the world, it could not do so under racist ordinances, commuted the sentence.

Anxiety about contact, especially sexual contact, between white women and colonised males was evident in most colonial societies.[25] Australian expatriates were concerned about domestic situations that placed white

---

22   Paul Hasluck, *A Time for Building: Australian Administration in Papua and New Guinea 1951–1963* (Carlton: Melbourne University Press, 1976), 18.
23   Ibid., 13.
24   Text of legislation cited in Amirah Inglis, *The White Women's Protection Ordinance: Sexual Anxiety and Politics in Papua* (Sussex University Press, 1975), 71; 'The Criminal Code (Queensland, Adopted) 1903', sections 347–9, NAA: A432, 1958/3143, item 7801743.
25   Ann Laura Stoler, *Carnal Knowledge and Imperial Power: Race and the Intimate in Colonial Rule* (Berkeley: University of California Press, 2002), 2.

3. 'MENTALLY UPSET AND A NYMPHOMANIAC'

women in contact with colonised men in open spaces, bathrooms, bedrooms, kitchens and gardens, and so legislated to control the movements of Papua New Guinean men.[26] The *WWPO* was one such piece of legislation. Amirah Inglis has argued that executive clemency and oversight limited the impact of this racist ordinance upon Papua New Guineans, with only one execution carried out under it after 1934, and that for the rape of a child.[27] Tunguan's case allows for the examination of the application of this ordinance after the Second World War, a period affected by the pressures of decolonisation, and extends Inglis's argument to the postwar period. I will build on Inglis's injunction to consider the ways in which the administration worked around the *WWPO*, with its most serious penalties rarely being considered relevant or invoked, rather than viewing its presence as indicative of the pervasive use of executions. Indeed, indicating the self-consciousness of the administration in relation to the ordinance, it was not reported separately in the justice statistics sent to the UN and the Australian Parliament after 1953/54, a change in reporting that was contemporary to the prominence of this case.[28]

Despite the anxieties of long-term PNG residents, 1954 was not a year of high crime against women in the territory (see Figures 3.2 and 3.3). Nevertheless, concern about the possibility of Papua New Guinean men committing crimes was translated into calls for sterner punishments for such men who endangered the security of white women. Yet, by 1954, recent expatriate arrivals were developing a stronger sense of confidence and security in working and living with Papua New Guineans, particularly in urban areas. Long-term expatriates, seemingly incapable of escaping their prewar racial prejudice, rejected the newcomers' outlook and were anxious that any relaxation of boundaries between white and black would undermine colonial power and authority.[29] The cultural change afoot made for a complex picture of gendered racial anxiety.[30]

---

26 Edward P. Wolfers, *Race Relations and Colonial Rule in Papua and New Guinea* (Brookvale: Australian and New Zealand Book Company, 1975), 127–9; Chilla Bulbeck, *Australian Women in Papua and New Guinea: Colonial Passages 1920–1960* (Melbourne: Cambridge University Press 1992), 37.
27 Inglis, *The White Women's Protection Ordinance*, 89–90, 123. On not hanging offenders, see, for example, *R. v. Hahaea-Koaeia, 1948*, an attempted rape prosecuted under the ordinance, Papers of Ralph Gore, 1930–1964, National Library of Australia (hereafter Gore Papers), box 1, folder 2.
28 Statistics taken from Australia, Department of Territories, *Territory of Papua: Annual Report for the Period [1949–1965]* (Canberra: Government Printer, [1949–66]); Australia, Department of Territories, *Report to the General Assembly of the United Nations on the Administration of the Territory of New Guinea [1946–1966]* (Canberra: Commonwealth Government Printer [1947–1967]).
29 Wolfers, *Race Relations*, 127–8.
30 See, for example, Margaret Spencer, *Doctor's Wife in New Guinea* (Sydney: Angus and Robertson, 1959), 52; Chalmers, *Kundus, Cannibals and Cargo Cults*, 17–25.

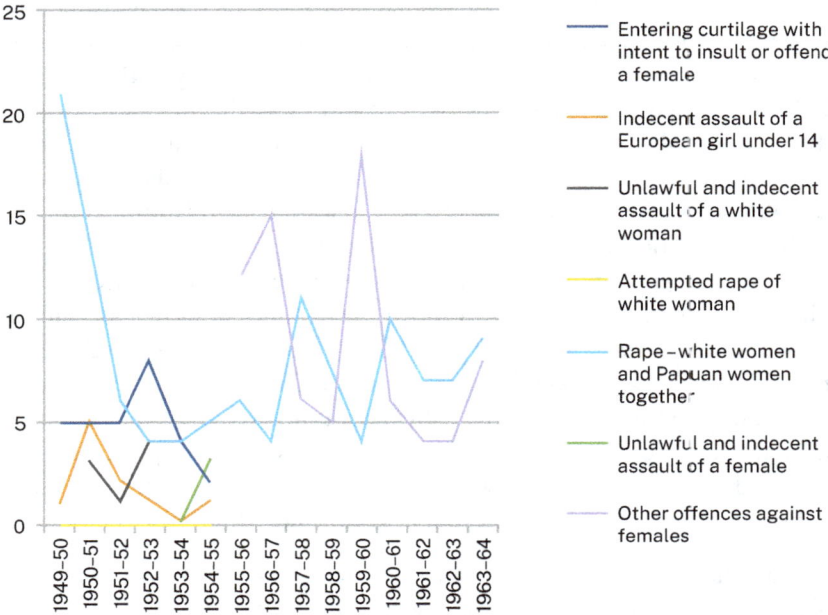

Figure 3.2: Offences against women in Papua.
Source: Australia, Department of Territories, *Territory of Papua: Annual Report for the Period [1949–1965]* (Canberra: Government Printer, [1949–66]).

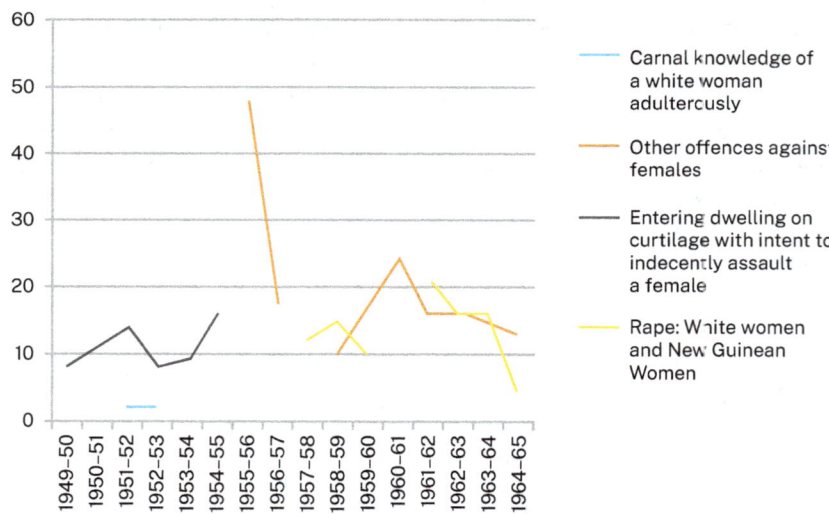

Figure 3.3: Offences against women in New Guinea.
Source: Australia, Department of Territories, *Report to the General Assembly of the United Nations on the Administration of the Territory of New Guinea [1946–1966]* (Canberra: Commonwealth Government Printer [1947–1967]).

As with the Telefomin trials, the punishment of Kita Tunguan was determined amid tensions within the white community as much as between colonisers and colonised. Central to these tensions was contestation over the place of white women's bodies in the policy hierarchy of the PNG system. Indeed, the decision to grant clemency to Kita Tunguan shows that white women's bodies had shifted from being a valorised repository of colonial power and authority to the degree described by Ann Stoler and Inglis in their studies of pre–Second World War colonies. Instead, and stemming from the approval of the international community, the treatment of Papua New Guinean bodies had become much more important as a source of colonial power and authority. Australia had to be a careful provender of advancement for Papua New Guineans under the UN Trusteeship Council's requirements, which had begun to moderate racist thinking, or at least policy, about the perceived strength and honour of the colonial white racial regime. Indeed, Cleland's decision to grant clemency reflected the policy goal of producing a positive perception of the regime.[31]

Race and gender in the PNG expatriate community

Cleland had made the decision to commute Tunguan's sentence and Hasluck could not override it, even had he wanted to, because that power was technically still invested with the administrator. Hasluck could only instruct Cleland to exercise such power under the minister's instructions in the future.

The question remains as to why Cleland commuted the sentence in the first place. Why did he decide not to hang a Papua New Guinean man who had raped a white woman? In considering the degree of influence brought to bear on Cleland, it is important to take into account that the administrator, a bureaucrat, probably felt less pressure to respond to the community than politicians in Canberra who needed to be mindful of electoral politics and popular opinion if they hoped to retain office. As a result of this greater discretion, Cleland's decision to commute Tunguan's sentence can be seen

---

31 See, for example, Tina Loo, 'Savage Mercy: Native Culture and Modification of Capital Punishment in Nineteenth Century British Columbia', in *Qualities of Mercy: Justice Punishment and Discretion*, ed. Carolyn Strange (Vancouver: University of British Columbia Press, 1996); Stacey Hynd, '"The Extreme Penalty of the Law": Mercy and the Death Penalty as Aspects of State Power on Colonial Nyasaland, c. 1903–47', *Journal of East African Studies* 4, no. 3 (2010): 542–59, 552.

as a reflection of his own notions of gender, race and justice; the general direction of Australian norms for the punishment of rape; and the desire to protect PNG's international reputation. Cleland made his decision in spite of the judge's preference for hanging and lobbying in favour of the judge's ruling by a significant section of the expatriate community.

Politicians' and officials' ideas about gender influenced PNG's advancement policies and were also a significant factor in the clemency cases examined in this book, particularly Kita Tunguan's. Officials' understandings of masculinity and femininity affected their judgement of the seriousness of capital cases and the characters of the people involved.[32] Scholars of colonialism prior to the Second World War have similarly proposed that interracial relationships and ideas of appropriate masculine and feminine roles were the loci of social tension in other colonial settings.[33] Further, scholars have argued that discourses of savagery and civilisation surrounding Papua New Guinean men led people to view them as dangerous company for white women.[34] Moving into the postwar period, the case studies examined in this book show that officials in PNG and Canberra held similar ideas about gender, which reflected metropolitan Australian views, and that the attitude of federal government officials influenced outcomes in PNG, as technology, such as reliable telephone connections, allowed them to intervene more readily.

Despite the distance, the way politicians and lawyers thought about the punishment of gendered crimes, such as rape and attempted rape, were similar in PNG and mainland Australia. For example, the punishment handed down in PNG in the case of *R. v. Gebu-Ari, 1952*, was very similar to a number of notorious sexual assault cases in Queensland at the same time.[35] In both places, flogging as a punishment was contemplated to protect

---

32   See, for example, Gore, *Justice Versus Sorcery*, ch. 26.
33   See, for example, Durba Gosh, 'Gender and Colonialism: Expansion or Marginalisation?' *Historical Journal* 47, no. 3 (2004): 739-41; Stoler, *Carnal Knowledge and Imperial Power*, 2.
34   Regis Tove Stella, *Imagining the Other: Representation of the Papua New Guinean Subject* (Honolulu: University of Hawaii Press, 2007), 144–5.
35   Notes of meetings, 2 December 1952 (Cabinet), NAA: A11099, 1/30, item 11584983. See *Criminal Code (Queensland, Adopted) in Its Application to the Territory of New Guinea*, sections 18–9, 208–16, 315, 350, 420, 425–66, 319, 655, 666, Pacific Islands Legal Information Institute, www.paclii.org/pg/legis/newguinea_annotated/cca254/; Lisa Durnian, 'Research Brief 21: Whipping as a Criminal Punishment', *Prosecution Project*, 14 March 2016, prosecutionproject.griffith.edu.au/whipping-as-a-criminal-punishment; 'The Charleville Rape Case. Three Youths Found Guilty', *Charleville Times* (Queensland), 7 August 1952, 8; 'Would the Cat Reduce Sex Crimes?' *Courier-Mail*, 18 January 1951, 2.

women and children; however, in the end, similar terms of imprisonment were imposed, despite the option of hanging or flogging Gebu-Ari under the *WWPO*.

More generally, the sexual lives of men and women were also significant to judgements about appropriate punishments for offenders in both PNG and Australia. Historians of gender and sex in postwar Australia and PNG have noted that the attempt to return to traditional gender roles in the 1950s was in conflict with gender relations that had been recalibrated by the Second World War towards freedom from social restrictions.[36] The PNG administration, like the Australian government, was concerned about the independence and sexual autonomy it observed in young women. Old colonialists in the Port Moresby community were afraid that such independent women would incite Papua New Guineans into acting on their presumed desire for white women. The punishment of death for the rape of a white woman indicated the seriousness of the assault on colonial authority that was perceived to be encapsulated in the assault of a white woman; it was an offence comparable to treason and piracy, both of which also rejected the primacy of white authority. Accordingly, the expatriate community, as well as the authorities, sought to police the sexual behaviour of white women. Mrs J. Wyatt and the CWA in PNG wrote a pamphlet in 1957 advising women, particularly new arrivals, on how to treat Papua New Guineans. Called *Guide to Newcomers to Papua-New Guinea by a Port Moresby Housewife*, the pamphlet recommended behaviours that would ensure physical and social distance thereby maintaining power over the Papua New Guineans in the household.[37] Wyatt was concerned about the welfare of 'newcomers', particularly the new category of 'business girl'.[38] 'Newcomers' was, in part, a code for 'New Australians'—that is, non-Anglo-Saxon migrants like Blanka Nesbit née Parcen. Consistent with my analysis of Wyatt's pamphlet, Lisa Featherstone and Amanda Kaladelfos have also

---

36 Anne Summers, *Damned Whores and God's Police* (Ringwood: Penguin Books, 1994), 471; Frank Bongiorno, *The Sex Lives of Australians: A History* (Collingwood: Black Inc., 2012), ch. 7; Jill Julius Matthews, *Good and Mad Women: The Historical Construction of Femininity in Twentieth Century Australia* (Sydney: Allen and Unwin, 1984); Christine Stewart, 'Men Behaving Badly: Sodomy Cases in the Colonial Courts of Papua New Guinea', *Journal of Pacific History* 43, no. 1 (2008): 77–93; Robert Aldrich, *Colonialism and Homosexuality* (London: Routledge, 2003), 247–8; Human Rights Watch, *This Alien Legacy: The Origins of Sodomy Laws in British Colonialism* (New York: Human Rights Watch, 2008); Garry Wotherspoon, 'The Greatest Menace Facing Australia: Homosexuality and the State in NSW during the Cold War', *Labour History*, no. 56 (1989): 15–28.
37 Inglis, *The White Women's Protection Ordinance*, 146.
38 Wyatt, *Guide to Newcomers*, 5–9. See, for example, 'Public Aid Sought to Check Port Moresby Crime Wave', *South Pacific Post*, 16 May 1954, 3.

noted the anxieties that Australians expressed about the sexual behaviour of non-Anglo-Saxon migrants.[39] These newcomers were of particular concern to Wyatt, who feared such women would place themselves in vulnerable positions through excessive familiarity and thus break the taboo around interracial sexual encounters that lay at the heart of white solidarity and power.

The provision of live-in servants created complex relationships between white women and Papua New Guinean men, which Wyatt was most anxious about, especially as most Australian colonial officials were unused to servants. Consequently, expatriate men and women thought that women living in villages, outstations and suburbs, often isolated from the immediate protection of men, were vulnerable. Stoler found a connection between the increased numbers of white women in pre–Second World War Java and Sumatra and increased anxiety among colonists over the sexual and social practices of white women in the community.[40] This suggests that, in PNG, anxiety was heightened by the increasing number of white women arriving there in the 1950s.

Demonstrating PNG's practice of policing colonial relations in the home, in 1952, Mrs Fawkner was investigated and prosecuted for her consensual, but still illegal, relationship with a Papua New Guinean man under section 9 of the Papua and New Guinea Criminal Code in which: 'Any European woman who voluntarily permits any native (other than a native to whom she is married) to have carnal knowledge of her shall be guilty of an indictable offence.'[41] Clearly, Mrs Fawkner did not share the racial and sexual anxieties of other expatriates, as she chose a relationship with a Papua New Guinean man. The determination to protect colonial authority by deeming inviolate the white home and the white female body was an important policy objective for many expatriates. However, the nature and extent of that concern changed in the postwar period as the focus shifted from white women's bodies to male Papua New Guinean bodies.

The level of official scrutiny of the sexual lives of Papua New Guinean men and expatriates is shown in the amount of knowledge an administrator might come to possess about members of the small expatriate community. Nesbit's superiors knew about her relationships and rumours about Mrs Fawkner's

---

39　Lisa Featherstone and Amanda Kaladelfos, *Sex Crimes in the Fifties* (Carlton: Melbourne University Press, 2016), ch. 6.
40　Stoler, *Carnal Knowledge and Imperial Power*, 2.
41　R. T. Gore, 'R. v. Fawkner (1952), Judgement', handwritten notes, Gore Papers, box 1, folder 6.

relationship led to a police investigation. In addition to formal channels of information, such informally acquired knowledge was important to Cleland in making his decision to grant clemency in the Tunguan case.

Cleland's decision was consistent with similar contemporary cases in New South Wales (NSW), where rape could likewise be punished by death. Indeed, comparisons to NSW rape cases and punishments were explicitly made in newspaper coverage of the Tunguan case in PNG. NSW legal decisions were on the minds of *SPP* readers such as Cleland, even as he chose to oppose the direction advocated by the paper.[42] The *SPP* was the mouthpiece of the expatriate society: as Nelson has suggested, the English language paper was written for expatriates, by expatriates.[43] In reviewing Tunguan's sentence, Cleland's role was to ensure that the punishment was in line with community expectations and standards. The expatriate writers and readers of the *SPP* may have favoured execution, but, given the high level of international scrutiny of Australian colonialism in PNG, those community standards encompassed Australian and international observers, not just those in Port Moresby.

After considerable debate, capital punishment for rape was repealed in NSW in 1954.[44] This brought NSW in line with the rest of Australia, leaving PNG the only Australian jurisdiction able to hang rapists—or, more precisely, able to hang the Papua New Guinean rapists of white females. The rapists of Papua New Guinean females could not be executed. Officials in PNG were clearly aware of this change, as the debate in NSW was discussed in relation to Tunguan's case in the *SPP*. The *SPP* used the abolition of the death penalty for rape in NSW to warn PNG against taking similar action, claiming that it would result in an upsurge in sexual crimes in PNG and NSW.[45]

The most significant rape case in NSW that allows insight into normative understandings about justice for rape victims, and which was discussed in relation to penalties in PNG in the *SPP*, was the Lawson case. Lawson,

---

42 Editor, 'The Death Sentence', *South Pacific Post*, 7 July 1954, 12; Jo Lennan and George Williams, 'The Death Penalty in Australian Law', *Sydney Law Review* 34 (2012): 659–94, 668, 680; *Crimes Act 1900* (NSW), ss63.
43 Hank Nelson, *Papua New Guinea: Black Unity or Black Chaos?* (Pelican Penguin, 1972), 126.
44 'Widespread Search in Rape Case', *Singleton Argus*, 8 March 1954, 2; 'Appeal of Rape Case, Solicitor', *Sydney Morning Herald*, 22 June 1954, 11; 'Savage Penalties for Rape', *Sydney Morning Herald*, 18 June 1954, 2; 'Q'land Men Gaoled Ten Years', *Sydney Morning Herald*, 18 June, 1954, 7; 'Changed Law Urged on Rape Penalty', *Sydney Morning Herald*, 18 June, 1954, 3; 'Youth 14 Gaoled for Life', *Barrier Miner* (Broken Hill, NSW), 22 June 1954, 2; 'Letters', *Sydney Morning Herald*, 19 June 1954, 2; 'Letters', *Sydney Morning Herald*, 21 June 1954, 2.
45 Editor, 'The Death Sentence'.

a Sydney photographer, was condemned to death for raping his models, but then had his sentence commuted.[46] The Lawson case was discussed in conjunction with the Kita Tunguan case in an editorial in the *SPP* and was used as a touchstone by the editor for the failure of NSW's legal standards around rape:

> In his pronouncement of sentence, Mr. Justice Gore made specific mention to the fact that the case had nothing in it which merited clemency. In Sydney last month Mr. Justice Clancy in the NSW Supreme Court when sentencing a man to death for a similar offence said that he could see no reason why the death sentence should not be carried out. There is apparently a hardening of the mind to this form of offence no doubt brought about by the increasing numbers of people who have been tried and convicted for it and the consequent increase in the numbers of life prison sentences which have been imposed on those found guilty.[47]

This comparison led the editor to conclude that a judge's verdict, such as Gore pronouncing death upon Kita Tunguan, should be upheld for the purpose of deterrence, rather than law and order being undermined by executive mercy. The *SPP* did not regard imprisonment as sufficient deterrence for rape: it argued that only death would deter rapists. Cleland apparently disagreed and aligned himself more with the NSW executive, though he still gave Tunguan a life sentence—a severe punishment. Cleland, involved as he was in the social life of his community, was well aware of the position of the newspaper and the preference for deterrent penalties among its expatriate readers. However, he also knew that the *WWPO* was an unusual law and that it isolated PNG morally. PNG was outside the mainstream of metropolitan thought on punishment for rape and the administrator knew this when he chose clemency, even as PNG expatriates and the *SPP* pushed for harsher punishments for rape.

The perpetrator was not the only person judged during a rape trial in the 1950s in metropolitan Australia. The victim experienced their own inquisition and judgement, as the men making the decisions also made moral judgements about the victim in deciding on a just punishment. Yet, surprisingly given the dreadful history of interracial sex and violence in the Western and colonial world in the 1950s, this case study indicates that

---

46 'Sentence of Death for Rape', *Sydney Morning Herald*, 25 June 1954, 1; Onlooker, 'Candid Comment', *Sun-Herald* (Sydney), 27 June 1954, 18.
47 Editor, 'The Death Sentence'.

it was little different in the colonial setting of PNG, even in the context of interracial rape.[48] Historians have shown that ideas and ideals about gender in Australia helped determine the nature of questioning and arguments in rape cases.[49] They have also revealed the flip side of traditional gender ideas in the 1950s, as chivalry dictated an increased condemnation of sexual violence across this period.[50] Nevertheless, the input of social ideologies was what the discretionary process was for, to ensure justice was done in the eyes of the community, rather than the law being carried out without reference to contemporary standards. Building faith in the state through just punishment seems to have manifested itself in NSW and PNG by enforcing traditional gender modes upon men and women as rapists and victims, and these attitudes towards victims were explicitly discussed in the mainstream media and in private conversations in 1954. Despite the expectations that might arise of punishments in PNG as a colonial legal regime, this case suggests that PNG generally followed mainland standards, as outlined below, both in determining the justness of penalties for rape and in the ways that it questioned the conduct of victims of rape.

This can be seen in the case of Blanka Nesbit and the clemency granted to Joseph Kita Tunguan, despite what the *SPP* called a 'hideous crime'.[51] The *SPP*'s ideas about gender were similar to ideas in the mainstream Australian media. For example, Kay Melaun, a regular advice and social affairs columnist, wrote a feature article for the hugely popular *Australian Women's Weekly* (*WW*) on 14 July 1954. She asked as the title of her essay 'Is Virtue Old Fashioned? No!' Written in response to the NSW debate on penalties for rape, the article argued that many of the rapes highlighted in the recent cases could have been avoided if 'old-fashioned' virtue and rectitude were practised by more young women. According to Melaun, young women needed to behave more modestly and remain in the protection of their families longer. She equated rapists and single mothers morally: 'Sympathy and pity? For the girl who is to become an unmarried mother? For the man who raped a young girl?' To Melaun, such people were victims of a permissive society and women who slept with men before marriage foolishly destroyed their reputations. Therefore, women who put themselves in a situation that

---

48   See, for example, Joanna Bourke, *Rape: Sex, Violence, History* (Berkley: Counterpoint Press, 2007).
49   Matthews, *Good and Mad Women*, ch. 7.
50   Featherstone and Kaladelfos, *Sex Crimes in the Fifties*, 8.
51   The editor, 'Death Sentence'.

endangered their physical security foolishly increased the chances of being raped. 'Men of today', she warned, were less trustworthy and less chivalrous than in the past and girls most certainly did need protection.

Melaun's *WW* article, and the correspondence it subsequently engendered, reveal a normative understanding of rape in Australian society in the 1950s. Rape was regarded as a wicked crime, but it was also largely avoidable. A victim, such as Dr Nesbit, was both blameworthy and to be avenged; the perpetrator, Tunguan, was to be pitied and also punished.

This harsh standard for rape victims in NSW in the 1950s is consistent with literature on the history and legal theory of rape in other jurisdictions. Looking at the history of rape trials in the UK, Zsuzsanna Adler noted that:

> We have seen that the victim's chastity and sexual reputation remain crucial issues in rape trials. Her general character, however, also seems to be a salient factor and attempts are frequently made to discredit her in this respect. Anything other than totally 'proper' and 'respectable' behavior may be used for this purpose.[52]

This includes psychiatric history, such as Nesbit's depression and institutionalisation. In an Australian context, J. E. Newton argued that:

> Within the ambit of this broad approach courts give recognition to factors such as the use of violence, the circumstances and behaviour of the victim and the degree of mental ill-health of the defendant in terms of sexual deviance.[53]

As in other Western jurisdictions, in Australia, a lack of injuries, familiar behaviour and the victim's sexual history affected the calculus of determining a just sentence. Such considerations usually reduced the sentence given to the offender—if they were found guilty at all. These considerations likely played a role in Cleland's decision to commute Tunguan's sentence for rape.

Further, as Adler noted, 'one of the main rape myths … is that women have a marked tendency to make hysterical, unfounded allegations of rape for a variety of somewhat obscure psychological reasons'.[54] An allegation of rape was not taken at face value. Susan Estrich echoed this in reflecting on the legal history of rape trials:

---

52   Zsuzsanna Adler, *Rape on Trial* (New York: Routledge and Kegan Paul, 1987), 102.
53   J. E. Newton, *Factors Affecting Sentencing Decision in Rape Cases* (Canberra: Australian Institute of Criminology, 1976), 23.
54   Adler, *Rape on Trial*, 105.

Evidentiary rules have been defined to require corroboration of the victim's account, to penalize women who do not complain promptly, and to ensure the relevance of a woman's prior history of unchastity.[55]

Estrich analysed rape cases in which the victim was not believed.[56] 'Real rape', a perception that Estrich incisively critiqued, was thought to have a definite moral and physical character by judges and officials. Such men imagined a hierarchy of rape within which some women might be blamed for some types of rape. As these were the criteria judges and politicians used to resolve equations of victimhood and blame, pity and punishment in 1954, these criteria will be used to judge the treatment of the perpetrator and victim in the Kita Tunguan case.

How a Papua New Guinean was defended like a white man

The prosecutor worked to establish a vision of Blanka Nesbit as matronly and respectable. They emphasised her virtues to prove that she was worthy of the law's full protection. For example, Blanka Nesbit was not called 'Dr Nesbit' during the trial, though her career was briefly cited.[57] The prosecutor's insistence on the more traditional and matronly title 'Mrs' represented her as a respectable woman entitled to the protection of the law.[58] Using Mrs and her married name also obscured her 'foreign' origins. Such implied respectability was vital in a rape trial. Nesbit's domesticity and respectability were further emphasised through detailed and repeated descriptions of her sewing. Even the particular panel of the skirt she was making at the time of the rape was precisely identified, as was the process she was using to construct the garment: what was more respectable than sewing?

The prosecution used witness testimony to confirm Nesbit's injuries, bruises and torn clothing. The hole in the wall made by her head, her distress and her dishevelled state after the assault were also highlighted.[59] This evidence of resistance, as Estrich has noted, was a key evidentiary matter for the prosecution to adduce, as it was perceived to demonstrate what Estrich

---

55   Susan Estrich, *Real Rape* (Cambridge: Harvard University Press, 1987), 5.
56   Ibid., ch. 2.
57   Her medical qualifications were recognised in PNG.
58   Cleland to secretary, 5 October 1954; Gore, 'R v. Tunguan—Transcription of Trial'.
59   Gore, 'R v. Tunguan—Transcription of Trial'.

satirically called 'real rape'.⁶⁰ As there were no witnesses to the crime, such evidence bolstered Nesbit's credibility as a witness. Alongside her prompt reporting of the crime, such testimony was strongly suggestive of rape. Further, Gore found her testimony to be more reliable than Tunguan's.⁶¹ Her word as a white woman carried more weight with him, however much the expatriate community found otherwise. In this way, Nesbit's lack of witnesses was overcome by her whiteness, trappings of respectability and some physical evidence.

The defence raised Nesbit's past and her character. The scholarship suggests that if the defence could paint the victim as a 'loose woman', the accused would likely be exonerated.⁶² Thus, references were made to the attempted suicide and suicide of the men construed to have been her previous lovers. Her affair, prior to her marriage, with a married man, Dr Kocenas, who later committed suicide in an attempted suicide pact with her, was highlighted.⁶³ Seeking to further discredit Nesbit, the defence asked several times if she had kicked or kneed Tunguan while he was ironing, thus provoking the attack; or, as outlined by Wyatt in her guide to behaviour, whether she had invited sexual advances by physical contact.⁶⁴ Nesbit denied all prior physical contact.⁶⁵ To prove she was a loose woman, she was asked if she had had men in the house while her husband was away, as Tunguan had charged.⁶⁶ She replied that she had had many friends to visit. When pressed in cross-examination with the proposition that men had been sleeping in her house while her husband was away, she refused to answer the question. The defence went on to suggest, repeatedly, that she had consented to sex with Tunguan and had only decided to call rape when she thought Tunguan might tell stories about the encounter, or that perhaps people had heard her calling his name. She denied this absolutely.⁶⁷ Further, the defence suggested that, immediately after the rape when she fled to her neighbour's house, she made phone calls of a suspicious nature, perhaps to her lovers. They found it suspicious because the calls were not conducted in English.⁶⁸ Additionally, the defence subjected the medical evidence of bruising to questioning to

---

60 Estrich, *Real Rape*, 7.
61 Gore, 'R v. Tunguan—Transcription of Trial'.
62 Estrich, *Real Rape*, 7; Adler, *Rape on Trial*; Newton, *Factors Affecting Sentencing*; Matthews, *Good and Mad Women*, ch. 7; Featherstone and Kaladelfos, *Sex Crimes in the Fifties*, 47–8.
63 Gore, 'R v. Tunguan—Transcription of Trial', 32.
64 Wyatt, *Guide to Newcomers*.
65 Gore, 'R v. Tunguan—Transcription of Trial', 26.
66 Ibid.
67 Ibid., 30–1.
68 Ibid., 31–2.

try to indicate that it was the result of consensual sex rather than rape. An attempt was made to cast doubt upon the extremity of Nesbit's injuries, describing them as evidence of depravity rather than rape, in the hope of having them excluded as evidence to corroborate Nesbit's story.[69]

Thus, the defence did his best to cast Nesbit's character into disrepute, suggesting that in her depravity she was the type to have had sex with her '*haus boi*' and then cry rape when she thought it might get out. She was this type because she had had lovers in the past and one of them had killed himself.[70] Nesbit was painted as the kind of woman the *WW* felt might have invited an attack by her own behaviour. Certainly, according to the prosecution, she had broken Wyatt's test of distance and respect with Papua New Guinean men by allowing Kita into the house to perform personal tasks and she may even have touched him.

The defence's attack on Nesbit's character is significant to a study of colonial justice, as the perpetrator was defended in the same manner as a white rapist in Sydney. This was not a 'kangaroo court' determined to hang him, as literature on gender and colonialism might suggest; the defence and the prosecution were both members of the administration. Further, to protect a Papua New Guinean man, the defence built much of its case around the notion of consensual, interracial sex initiated by a white woman. Rather than being railroaded, Tunguan was accorded an all-too-common defence against a rape charge. Featherstone and Kaladelfos's survey of rape cases suggests that it is highly unlikely that an Aboriginal man would have received such a defence on the mainland in the 1950s.[71] While the final penalty Tunguan received was severe, it was not as severe as death, indicating that this case marks a shift in the way gender, crime and colonial authority interacted. The scope of the arguments was consistent with rape cases cited by Adler, Newton and Estrich. Thus, even in the PNG context, Western ideas about gender were significant; rather than only colonial ideologies that might have demanded hanging to expiate the assault on white authority, Western ideas about gender influenced the way the case was defended and prosecuted.

---

69 Ibid. 35b, 37.
70 Chalmers, *Kundus, Cannibals and Cargo Cults*, 67.
71 Featherstone and Kaladelfos, *Sex Crimes in the Fifties*, 43.

Community pressure on Cleland

In Port Moresby, news of the rape of Blanka Nesbit made the front page. It came in the midst of the widely reported Telefomin trials, which created a local context for Cleland's deliberations—a context that expected harsh punishment for Tunguan. As seen in Chapter 2, the Telefomin trials created anxiety in PNG over the territory's image overseas and how best to punish offenders. Formal and informal representations of Nesbit also influenced Cleland's deliberations on clemency. Regarding these, it is plain from the defence's line of questioning and the tone of a petition proposed by the CWA, analysed below, that private discussions of Nesbit were less sympathetic than most arguments seen in the *SPP*.

The *SPP* presented Nesbit as a largely blameless victim of Kita Tunguan's perfidy and emphasised the likelihood of his hanging. Designed to place pressure on the administration, it is suggestive of the type of informal commentary Cleland likely encountered in his social life in PNG. 'Native on Trial' was the relatively mild header for the story that launched the news of the rape into the public domain. However, as the *SPP* was a weekly newspaper at that time, it was likely that the rape was already known about by most townspeople.[72] The front-page article opened with a narrative of ingratitude: 'A native houseboy had raped a European woman who had once saved his life, the woman told the Port Moresby District Court last week.'[73] The characterisation of Kita Tunguan as ungrateful resonated with the storytelling of the Telefomins' irrational ingratitude for Australian colonialism that was in the courts and newspaper at the same time. The Telefomin, too, were blamed for not appreciating the opportunities they had been given.

The *SPP* story emphasised Nesbit's matronly and respectable nature by reporting that she was quietly 'sewing in her living room in Konodobu' prior to the attack.[74] This was followed by a paragraph of explanation about why Tunguan was in the house. The length of the explanation seems to suggest that it was an unusual privilege for a servant to be allowed to iron his clothes in the main house. This was followed by a description of Nesbit's injuries, especially the bruising on her wrists and arms, as this was a key element in proving a rape charge. To emphasise the idea that he

---

72 'Native on Trial'. As the *Post* was a bi-weekly paper, this was first opportunity to report on the events.
73 Ibid.
74 Ibid.

3. 'MENTALLY UPSET AND A NYMPHOMANIAC'

was dangerous, Tunguan was described as 'a powerfully built Sepik River native'.[75] The Sepik River was an area known to *SPP* readers for the warlike propensities of its people: the Telefomin subregion is also near the Sepik. This description played to the fears readers had about the servants in their midst: Stoler's 'troubled intimacies'.[76] The *SPP* characterised Kita Tunguan as dishonest by reporting that the police said he told conflicting stories. This again resonated with the dishonesty of the Telefomin ambushes. The *SPP* was campaigning for a severe penalty.

Finally, the plaintive words of Tunguan upon his arrest were reported: 'No matter you kill me. No matter. I go along calaboose. I make this trouble.' This could be read as a confession or recognition of his weak position in a colonial context, as he did not plead guilty. Inglis noted the extreme caution of Papua New Guinean men in their dealings with white women even into the 1970s due to the *WWPO*.[77] Inglis's analysis further suggests that Kita Tunguan believed that he could not win once the accusation was made 'no matter' what he said. From his experience of accusations of violence against whites, he knew that he would be punished as an example 'no matter' what the facts of the case might be. He believed that the penalty was likely to be death, reflecting a Papua New Guinean understanding of the way gender and colonialism interacted in PNG. It would seem that Papua New Guineans believed that whites in Port Moresby would react in a prewar colonial manner to a rape charge and that death was likely.

Indeed, as mentioned, the *SPP* lobbied for hanging. They endorsed Gore's judgement and carried the story of the sentencing on the front page in its next edition the following Wednesday.[78] The article led with Gore's pointed refusal to merely record the mandatory sentence of death and his determination to pronounce the sentence: 'I don't see any indication in this case which calls upon me to record the death sentence.'[79] This indicated that Gore thought Kita Tunguan was too Westernised, due to his work experience and trouble in Port Moresby, to receive merciful treatment on the basis of incomprehension of Australian society and justice, as often happened to non-Westernised offenders. Further, offenders under the

---

75 Ibid.
76 Stoler, *Carnal Knowledge and Imperial Power*, 2.
77 Inglis, *The White Women's Protection Ordinance*, 146.
78 'Native Sentenced to Death'.
79 Ibid.

115

WWPO were usually given pronounced sentences.[80] The newspaper quoted at length Gore's recitation of evidence that pointed to rape and included his characterisation of Tunguan: 'This is a powerfully built native and she had little chance against him. The accused is a highly intelligent native who was cleverly evasive in answering questions.'[81]

Pointing to Gore's doubt that a hanging would actually occur, the article concluded with him washing his hands of the ultimate sentencing process: 'What the Executive chooses to do after I have done my part is their business.'[82] This choice of words suggests that the judge and newspaper thought a commutation was likely, even if Kita Tunguan did not. The newspaper gave prominence and authority to Gore's finding that Kita Tunguan could hang in conjunction with a warning that the process would be political, in the sense of being influenced by diplomatic expectations and Australian policy. The *SPP* and Gore, in their comments about the executive and punishment, obviously sought to influence the capital case review and Cleland; they recognised that Cleland and Hasluck held liberal ideas that might well lead to commutation.

The lobbying by expatriates in the newspaper after the commutation indicates that they believed there had been pressure to commute from Canberra and internationally. Such lobbying continued after Cleland's decision was announced, seemingly in the hope of influencing future cases by countering or mitigating the influences they believed had led to it. Cleland's mercy prompted the *SPP* editor to write:

> The Administrator's decision to commute the death penalty recently imposed on a native found guilty of a hideous crime against a European woman was to be expected, but nonetheless will be received with misgivings among a wide section of the community.[83]

According to the *SPP*, while people had expected clemency, they still railed against it and feared that crime, particularly sexual crime, would escalate as a result. That they expected clemency shows their awareness, if not acceptance, of the punishments and racial ideologies beyond the islands. PNG exceptionalism, as noted by historians such as Allan Healy and Peter

---

80 For example, notes of meetings, 2 December 1952, NAA: A11099, 1/30, item 11584983; *R. v. Hahaea-Koaeia, 1948*, an attempted rape prosecuted under the ordinance, Gore Papers, box 1, folder 2; Inglis, *The White Women's Protection Ordinance*.
81 'Native Sentenced to Death'.
82 Ibid.
83 Editor, 'The Death Sentence'.

Fitzpatrick, was clearly at work in this case. Despite not seeing themselves as colonialists, the B4s and old colonialists continued to hold prewar gendered notions of colonial power.[84] Hence, they thought it was suitable to punish crimes against white women more severely than crimes against Papua New Guinean women.

There was also pressure on the capital case review from Australian norms. The *SPP* editor cited Australian rape cases and punishments in building his argument for execution, regardless of the fact that these had been commuted too. His conclusion was that a rise in rape cases in Australian jurisdictions had led to a 'hardening of the legal mind to this form of offense'.[85] In echoing arguments printed in NSW newspapers, the editor of the *SPP* sought to show continuities between Australian and PNG legal norms. However, there is little evidence to support a rise in the number of rape cases in PNG.[86] Nevertheless, the *SPP* wanted to place pressure on future decisions by asserting a nexus between commutations and rising crime.

The discussion indicates that expatriates in PNG believed that Cleland was influenced by international scrutiny and anti-colonial sentiment in Australia. The *SPP* documented the general mood of PNG expatriates who sympathised 'with the political difficulties which could face the Administrator had he confirmed the court's verdict'.[87] 'Political difficulties' could refer to the policies of Hasluck and other liberals who were focussed on advancement and a more colourblind approach to the law; the *WWPO*, of course, was the most unequal of all PNG laws. Alternatively, or also, it could refer to the UNTC and its scrutiny of the Department of Territories. The *SPP* editor pointed out that expatriates in PNG were aware that the administrator faced international political pressures to appear benevolent to satisfy UN concerns. They were also aware that Australia would be engaged in a triennial review of its trusteeship in New York in June and

---

84 Allan M. Healy, 'Monocultural Administration in a Multicultural Environment: The Australians in Papua New Guinea', in *From Colony to Coloniser: Studies in Australian Administrative History*, ed. J. J. Eddy and J. R. Nethercote (Sydney: Hale and Iremonger, 1987); Peter Fitzpatrick, *Law and State in Papua New Guinea* (London: Academic Press, 1980), 68.
85 Editor, 'The Death Sentence'.
86 Australia, Department of Territories, *Territory of Papua: Annual Report for the Period [1949–1965]* (Canberra: Government Printer, [1949–66]). Note the shifting of reporting categories. Australia, Department of Territories, *Report to the General Assembly of the United Nations on the Administration of the Territory of New Guinea [1946–1966]* (Canberra: Commonwealth Government Printer [1947–1967]).
87 Editor, 'The Death Sentence'.

July 1954, and that embarrassing legal cases were best avoided.[88] The *SPP* often reported on criticisms of PNG colonialism, so it was aware of how outside opinion of Australian colonialism might be affected if a Papua New Guinean was executed for raping a white woman and how this might be seen as an extraordinary penalty.

Cleland's justification of his sentence to the expatriate community in statements to the *SPP* revealed some of the considerations that were significant to him in reaching his decision. He justified the life sentence as a harsh deterrent, and indeed it was, as most murderers were sentenced to around seven years or less hard labour. Cleland emphasised to the *SPP* that his sentence meant Kita's release 'would remain at the Administrator's discretion'.[89] Gore's declaration that there was no reason to recommend mercy stood in stark contrast with Cleland's clemency. Vastly different approaches to colonialism were evident in these contrasting decisions made by Gore, an old colonialist, and Cleland, who usually acted as Hasluck's leading agent of the liberal project for advancement.

Informal sources of knowledge and their influence on the discretionary process

Politics, both international and Australian, had to be considered by the administrator in exercising the royal prerogative of mercy. Expatriates in PNG were in favour of capital punishment for their own security; however, signalling awareness of the racist overtones of that view, the editor of the *SPP* acknowledged that there were 'political difficulties'.

Yet, for advocates of B4 colonial justice, the matter could not rest there. Mrs M. H. Jewell, a B4 from a family long resident in Papua, attempted to mobilise the local branch of the CWA in Port Moresby to support both capital punishment for interracial rape and migration control through a petition, but failed.[90] Her attempt was reported in the *SPP*:

---

88   United Nations, *Index to Proceedings of the Trusteeship Council,* Eleventh Special Session, 10 April 1961, Twenty-Seventh Session, 1 June to 19 July 1961 (New York: United Nations Headquarters Library, 1961), library.un.org/sites/library.un.org/files/itp/t27_0.pdf.
89   'Death Sentence Commuted', *South Pacific Post,* 7 July 1954, 9.
90   The CWA is a large and influential national organisation. While focusing on providing social and community connection for women in rural areas, it has also engaged in commentary and campaigning on issues.

The petition points out that a similar petition was successful several years ago and the government of the day allowed the death sentence to be carried out. It says that there were no more cases of rape against women for fifteen years. The petition also asks that people who apply for Territory entry permits should be more thoroughly screened before they are allowed into the country.[91]

The historical basis for the claims made in the petition is unclear. The last person hanged for rape was most likely Stephen Gorumbaru in 1934. His case, which involved the rape of a white female child, had resulted in much community activism in which Mrs Jewell's father-in-law, Arthur Jewell, had played a leading role.[92] Jewell's comments reflected two beliefs apparent among some B4s: deterrence by hanging was the best response to serious crime by Papua New Guineans and the rape of a white woman was more serious than the rape of a black woman.

Jewell's failure to convince the CWA branch to pursue this course of action suggests two things: first, that women did not feel as vulnerable in 1954 as they apparently had in 1926 when the ordinance was passed; second, that not all expatriates agreed with Jewell's views and that most members of the local CWA did not feel comfortable calling for the Papua New Guinean rapists of white woman to be hanged in 1954. Of course, it should also be noted that the wife of the administrator, Rachel Cleland, was active in the CWA and may have had a hand in the defeat of a measure that implicitly critiqued her husband.

The criticisms of Nesbit's character that Cleland made in his comments to Hasluck, mentioned above, were apparently general knowledge. It is likely that Cleland gained his information about Nesbit, which influenced his decision to commute the sentence, from gossip and talk, which also resulted in the petition. The public reputation of a woman was apparently significant to reasoning around the justness of penalties for rape, as the petition's call for 'screening' immigrants was also a veiled reference to Blanka Nesbit, a migrant; the gossip surrounding her supposed affairs with Dr Kocenas and Dr Otruba; and the state of her mental health.[93] Seemingly, the careful screening process proposed by Jewell was intended to catch people such as Nesbit. Implicitly, Nesbit was being blamed for her mismanagement of Kita Tunguan. Her general conduct was being explicitly conflated with

---

91 'Women Sign Petition'.
92 Inglis, *The White Women's Protection Ordinance*, 130–5.
93 'Women Sign Petition'.

discussion over the appropriate punishment for Tunguan, indicating that some sections of the community saw these as being connected. Nesbit's sexual conduct was obviously widely known and thought to be germane to clemency deliberations.

Indeed, drawing on such widespread gossip, Cleland told Hasluck that the screening proposition in the petition was motivated by Nesbit: 'It is no doubt inspired by the knowledge of the woman's history whilst in the territory.'[94] The petition attacked both Nesbit and Tunguan. The screening issue also highlights the anxieties that Anglo-Saxon Australians held about new migrants to Australia and their different sexual habits, as noted by Featherstone and Kaladelfos.[95] Local gossip was not kind towards Nesbit, but such unkindness was not directly expressed in the paper. Publicly, there was racial solidarity in maintaining the direct attack on Kita Tunguan. The disjunction between public and private discussions suggests that officials and expatriates believed that Kita Tunguan had to be punished despite Nesbit's failure to manage her sexual behaviour properly, but not as severely. The question for Cleland then became about how much Nesbit was to blame for Tunguan's actions and how this should be accommodated. Estrich's theories about, and criticism of, the concept of 'real rape' seem to be highly relevant here, for while Cleland thought there had been a rape, it seems, as Estrich theorised, that Nesbit's past meant that the assault on her was not considered 'real rape'. Judgements were being made about the victim.

Clemency: Cleland decides

When Hasluck enquired as to why clemency had been granted to Kita Tunguan without reference to the federal Cabinet, he was asking a procedural question. However, the reply from Cleland mistakenly went to the substance of his decision to grant clemency. Hasluck's handwritten note suggests that he was shocked enough not to wait for his response to be typed, as would have been usual. His note to Secretary Lambert of the Department of Territories points out Cleland's misapprehension. Nevertheless, Cleland's letter, which outlines his and his community's low opinion of Dr Nesbit, provides a good picture of both how the decision to grant clemency was made and the cruel view that the rape of such a woman was a lesser sort of crime.[96]

---

94 Cleland to secretary, 3 September 1954, NAA: A518, CQ840/1/3 PART 1, item 3252669.
95 Featherstone and Kaladelfos, *Sex Crimes in the Fifties*, 144–8.
96 Cleland to secretary, 3 September 1954.

3. 'MENTALLY UPSET AND A NYMPHOMANIAC'

Cleland drew on both formal documents and the recollections and opinions of officials in forming a picture of Dr Nesbit and Joseph Kita Tunguan for the commutation process. This included a report on Nesbit prepared by C. Normoyle, the assistant commissioner of police, which Cleland forwarded to Lambert and Hasluck. Normoyle's report contained an unflattering account of Nesbit's life and rumoured affairs in PNG.[97] Reports were also prepared on Tunguan; however, unlike the further information garnered on Nesbit, they mainly covered material that was adduced in court.

The head of the PNG Department of Health, Dr John Gunther, reported that Nesbit had spent several months from June 1953 in 'a halfway house in lunacy' due to her depression and anxiety after her alleged lover Dr Kocenas's suicide. Cleland wrote:

> In a recent conversation with Dr. Gunther he informed me that he considered Mrs. Nesbit to be mentally upset and a nymphomaniac. According to local gossip she is a woman of loose morals. However, in examining the evidence in the case of Kita Tunguan, there is no doubt in my mind that she was raped.[98]

Cleland developed a picture of Nesbit based on imprecise and informal knowledge that drew on traditional ideas of gender, such as those promoted by Melaun: namely, that women should not place themselves in situations in which men might attack them, and that women could invite attacks through their conduct and reputation. Gunther characterised Nesbit as 'mentally upset and a nymphomaniac' and Cleland did not challenge that view. These perceptions and rumours go to questions of character of the type raised by theorists of gender and rape who argue that some people believed that 'mad and loose' women were not raped in the same way as 'good' women.[99] In relaying this gossip and innuendo about the victim to the very formal Paul Hasluck, Cleland showed that he found such ideas to be perfectly reasonable—further underscoring their acceptability.[100] Indeed, Cleland was engaging in a conventional discussion for mainland Australia and the Western world: Nesbit made a very poor example of someone whom the ordinance had been designed to protect.

---

97   Normoyle to administrator.
98   Ibid.
99   Estrich, *Real Rape*, 7; Featherstone and Kaladelfos, *Sex Crimes in the Fifties*.
100 For commentary on Hasluck's frosty reactions to violations of procedure and hierarchy, see, generally, Tom Stannage, Kay Saunders and Richard Nile, eds, *Paul Hasluck in Australian History: Civic Personality and Public Life* (St Lucia: University of Queensland Press, 1999).

Joseph Kita Tunguan's background and reputation were also germane to the decision to grant mercy. This was because being 'unsophisticated' was usually a significant reason for a sentence to be commuted; therefore, Tunguan's level of 'sophistication' had to be established. There was also the question of character and just deserts. Police Sub-Inspector John Fisher prepared a report for Cleland that indicated that Tunguan was known to the police and that he was prone to being provoked by insults into violent crime, such as fighting and assault. He was proud, stiff-necked and volatile. Further, he was also an educated Papua New Guinean who had language skills and had received a basic school and vocational education.[101] The testimony of Tunguan's priest, Fisher reported, was that he was honest and ambitious. Therefore, Cleland could not use ignorance or lack of 'sophistication' as grounds for commutation. He had to search for other grounds.

Tunguan was part of a growing cohort of urban, educated and advanced Papua New Guineans who were—in a future still very indefinitely sketched—the aim of the colony, yet PNG had difficulty treating them with respect and providing them with meaningful work. Further, as mentioned, Tunguan seems to have challenged traditional colonial demarcations of power and authority with violence. In short, he was the kind of man who could expect the full force of the law to go against him. However, while Gore condemned him, and despite the convention that a Westernised person should probably hang, Cleland commuted his sentence. Why?

In postwar PNG, the ideologies of liberal paternalism and liberal justice seemed to trump racism and colonialism. The wide reporting in mainland newspapers and the *SPP* of contemporaneous rape cases and NSW's abolition of capital punishment for rape and murder meant that Cleland had clear information about how to make a decision that would be both consistent with NSW and Australian law and acceptable to the wider world. Consequently, his use of discretionary justice ensured that a Papua New Guinean rapist was punished similarly to a white man in Sydney. In this way, Cleland's decision kept PNG more in step with Australia and Australian norms for punishment than Gore's.

In his letter to Hasluck and Lambert, Cleland outlined the steps he had taken to reach his decision to commute the sentence. After précising the information from the reports of the judge, the police and the investigators, Cleland highlighted several points that were germane to his decision.

---

101 Fisher to superintendent of police, 12 June 1954.

First, Tunguan claimed that Nesbit had kicked him, although Gore had been unsure about this. Second, Tunguan had not attempted to escape; in Cleland's view, this showed that his actions were from a flare of temper and just as soon regretted, so he was not irretrievably bad. Third, despite his history of brawling, Tunguan's priest told Sub-Inspector Fisher that 'the native was a good lad and regular communicant'. Fourth, Cleland claimed that:

> it is also known that she [Nesbit] had a strange vindictiveness against natives in general. This was in evidence when she was employed at the Native Hospital and because of it she was removed from employment therein.[102]

This story had not been mentioned anywhere else. Cleland's letter made it clear that, even if he accepted that the rape had occurred, it was not a 'real rape', or at least a much less serious one, due to Nesbit's seemingly provocative actions.[103]

In repeating gossip about Nesbit's alleged affairs and mental health, Cleland engaged in a discourse common to rape trials and discussions of rape—namely, that promiscuous women brought rape upon themselves and did not deserve the same protection as virtuous women. Nesbit, having broken the rules of female behaviour laid out by B4s such as Wyatt, had 'brought it upon herself'. If she had been provocative, then, in Cleland's mind, Tunguan's execution was not just. To be clear, Cleland's thinking did not extend to disbelieving that the rape had occurred; rather, he regarded it as a lesser sort of rape better punished by imprisonment. When Tunguan's character and other factors such as international scrutiny were considered, Cleland felt that Tunguan did not deserve to die and that a lesser punishment was more just.

Despite Cleland not mentioning it directly to Hasluck, the *SPP* argued that Cleland was being pressured by Australian liberals and international observers to grant clemency. Since such pressures were noted in other cases examined in this book, it seems plausible. International and domestic Australian suspicions of colonialism were the main drivers of such pressure. Rather than write about them explicitly, Cleland noted that, given the 'circumstances', life in prison would be punishment enough.[104] The 'circumstances' encoded

---

102 Cleland to secretary, 3 September 1954.
103 Estrich, *Real Rape*, 7.
104 Cleland to secretary, 3 September 1954.

Cleland and Hasluck's shared understanding of the colonial context and its vulnerability to critique in a decolonising world. It is a clear signal of the shift in thinking on race and colonialism that, in 1954, the 'circumstances' of the rape of a white woman in a colonial setting did not require expiation in blood, as had the last use of this penalty against Stephen Gorumbaru in 1934. Neither was the idea of corporal punishment raised, as in the Gebu-Ari attempted rape case in 1952.[105] In 1954, hanging a colonial subject using a racist law would not have encouraged critical powers to see Australian colonialism as legitimate, temporary and benevolent, as required by liberal colonialism. This is because the punishment was so extreme compared to general standards for the punishment of rape and other sexual offences in Australia, including metropolitan NSW, the only other place that might have executed an offender for rape.[106] Cleland, in noting the 'circumstances', indicated his desire not to delegitimise the colonial project with a fundamentally racist use of capital punishment; rather, he wished to use mercy as a bulwark to colonial legitimacy.

The times had changed. Sexual violence against white women was answered with imprisonment, and the contrast between brutal rape and gentle mercy emphasised the legitimate role Australia had in colonising and advancing PNG. The Kita Tunguan case demonstrates that colonialism in PNG, under Cleland and Hasluck, had begun to adopt a more colourblind, liberal ideology of justice, and that, for Cleland, advancing Papua New Guineans was incompatible with inequitable laws such as the *WWPO*. Moreover, as Inglis has argued of the prewar period, the case demonstrates that, in some circumstances, discretionary justice could fix the disjunction between a desire for benevolence and harsh laws. The B4s, the *SPP* and Gore acknowledged the changing times when they accepted that it was unlikely that Tunguan would hang, even though they thought he should.

Conclusion

This historical case study addresses several questions raised in the introduction: How did the international climate of decolonisation affect clemency decisions? How did contested legal ideologies affect clemency

---

105 Notes of meetings, 2 December 1952, NAA: A11099, 1/30, item 11584983.
106 On liberal paternalism and colonialism see Peter Gibbon, Benoit Daviron and Stephanie Barral, 'Lineages of Paternalism: An Introduction', *Journal of Agrarian Change* 14, no. 2 (2014): 165–89.

decisions? How did concerns of the day affect clemency decisions? How did clemency happen? Was it discretionary justice? And what was the significance of formal and informal sources of information?

The discussion around the punishment of Kita Tunguan in the clemency file and newspapers shows that both expatriates in PNG and Cleland were aware of international scrutiny regarding Australian colonialism: Gore and the *SPP* cited 'political' pressure and Cleland cited 'the circumstances' that affected his decision to commute the sentence. As established in Chapter 1, concern about the reaction of the international community was recurring and therefore axiomatic to most policy decisions. The B4s and the liberals were aware of Australian norms of punishment that militated against the hanging of a rapist being acceptable to domestic or international observers' sense of justice and morality. As Hay, Loo and Hynd have theorised, Cleland had to consider the wider reaction to an execution in the context of maintaining the legitimacy of the colonial government. As with Telefomin case, the discretion of a capital case review allowed the administration to play both sides of the fence—to foster and protect colonial governance by punishing the crime with a life sentence, while also allowing for doubts as to the moral worth of its victim by commuting a death sentence.

Nevertheless, there was a contest of ideologies of law: old colonial ideas of justice based on deterrence and the sanctity of white bodies were put forward by Justice Gore and the editor of the *SPP*, despite considering themselves likely to lose. They were aware that a shift away from old colonial notions of law enforcement was occurring, and they regretted the change. Representing the change, Cleland opted for a more colourblind version of justice: he refused to respond reflexively with colonial vengeance to protect white female bodies, which, from the reaction of some expatriates, suggests it might have been expected, and certainly was expected by Kita Tunguan.

This change was affected by the gendered beliefs about women and sex, more specifically about Nesbit's sexual conduct, held by Cleland and the expatriate community. The perception of Nesbit as a bad, mad woman entered the calculus of discretionary justice when Cleland determined not to hang Kita Tunguan. The documents show that Nesbit's reputation was at the forefront of Cleland's mind when he explained his commutation decision to Hasluck. The petition developed by Mrs Jewell of the CWA also shows that this case was connected, in the minds of B4 expatriates, to concerns about changing gender roles and the influx of new Australians into the Anglophone community.

Significantly for this book, this case was also a turning point in the process of determining clemency in PNG. Newspaper reports drew Hasluck's attention to the fact that Cleland had commuted a pronounced sentence against directions from Canberra, focusing Hasluck's attention on changing the process. The time it took to clarify the status of recorded sentences and finalise a coherent process for referring all sentences to Canberra, even after the amendments passed in October 1954, contributed to Hasluck's suspicions about the reliability of the PNG public service.[107] Cleland's references to both formal submissions and general gossip indicate that both sources of information were significant in his decision to commute Kita Tunguan's sentence.

As Martin Wiener has suggested, and has been done here, looking at the uniqueness of colonial settings is vital in examining and evaluating their legal processes.[108] This case highlights the relative significance of ideologies of gender and race in PNG and Australia in 1954 and the ways that the legal system both cooperated with and resisted those ideologies in an attempt to build a positive image of PNG in Australia and across the world. In another case in 1954, analysed in the next chapter, the calculus fell the other way, and execution was used to reach the same goal of legitimacy.

---

107 Cleland to secretary, 5 October 1954; R. March to minister, 26 October 1954, NAA: A518, CQ840/1/3 PART 1, item 3252669; 'Commutation of Death Sentences', NAA: A518, CQ840/1/3 PART 1, item 3252669.
108 Martin J. Wiener, *Empire on Trial: Race, Murder, and Justice under British Rule, 1870–1935* (New York: Cambridge University Press, 2009).

4

The limits of mercy in Australian PNG: *R. v. Usamando, 1954*

It is for the court to say what will happen to me. I have been in gaol nine years altogether. If I don't go back to my place and remain in prison, these thoughts will come into my mind—the thoughts of killing. Before the war, I was never like this. I worked for seventeen years in Wau without any trouble. It is now for the court to decide. If you feel sorry for me, you can send me back to my village. If not, it rests with you. I have said everything I want to say and you are the judge: but I have spoken the truth. This is all. If you want to send me to another gaol, or if you want to kill me, I would like to get tobacco, sugar and betel-nut. That is all.[1]

Members of the Australian federal Cabinet were informed in a submission about the particulars of Usamando's criminal career. A New Guinean man from the Madang area, in 1928, Usamando had murdered a man, Iwar, who had been sleeping with his wife and had served five years in gaol.[2] On 12 January 1946, he had murdered his wife and her sister; much to the villagers' disgust, the sister had become Usamando's lover without her family receiving the bride price. Usamando attributed the murders to their neglect of their gardening responsibilities and failure to cook for him. Presumably, it would have been concluded at sentencing that, in killing them, he was seeking to redress the shame he felt at their disrespect of him according to

---

1 'Usamando's Allocutus', in F. B. Phillips to administrator, 29 September 1954, 5–6, NAA: A4906, 205, item 4678943.
2 NAA: A4906, 205, item 4678943.

the mores of the village. The Australian New Guinea Administrative Unit (ANGAU) court, the military legal apparatus in place during the war and its immediate aftermath, recorded a sentence of death for those murders, which was subsequently commuted to life in prison with hard labour.

Usamando was serving this sentence at Madang Gaol, when, in September 1951, he killed Lula, a fellow prisoner, because the other prisoners were gossiping about the two of them of having a homosexual affair. The prisoners' gossip had not caused an immediate reaction, but then Lula had moved his bed in the open barracks away from Usamando's. Usamando felt that this confirmed the accusation in the eyes of the other men. Feelings of shame, perhaps, at being seen as a sodomite and possibly as predatory were compounded by this public rejection. Usamando plotted to acquire a knife and then stabbed Lula to death. Indicating his shame, he immediately attempted suicide but was unsuccessful. He was charged and convicted of the wilful murder of Lula.

Chief Justice Monty Phillips, the presiding judge, only learned of the first murder conviction from Usamando's statement, or allocutus, prior to sentencing during the trial. No documentation for the 1928 conviction was put to the court by the prosecution, possibly because of the destruction of records, and all of Rabaul, by a volcano. Phillips was able to note a short entry in the defunct *Rabaul Times* that cited a conviction for the murder of a man with a similar name in 1928. Usamando's unguarded confession was accepted as indicative evidence and evaluated in Phillips's determination of sentencing. The judge found Usamando guilty of murdering Lula and recorded a sentence of death.

Following sentencing, Phillips received a delegation from Usamando's community who confirmed the first undocumented murder. The villagers insisted that he be hanged or, they warned, he would kill again. They also thought that executions helped prevent violence. However, all Phillips could do at that stage was warn the prison authorities that Usamando might kill again. Accepted as the killer of four people, not three, Usamando, Phillips cautioned, was very dangerous and should be watched carefully. Given the nature of his crimes, his perceived demeaned status, his personality and the flaws within the administrative system, Usamando was already a complex figure for the exercise of colonial law.

4. THE LIMITS OF MERCY IN AUSTRALIAN PNG

Figure 4.1: Native prisoners weaving house walls, Minj Station, Wahgi Valley, Papua New Guinea, 1954.
Source: Terence E. T. Spencer and Margaret Spencer, National Library of Australia, nla.gov.au/nla.obj-145553519.

Over time, Usamando's behaviour and demeanour in prison led to him being trusted, suggesting that he had some capacity to behave in ways that a colonialist expected of a servant. By 1952, he was no longer perceived as dangerous by experienced prison officials who ceased watching him carefully. He was given additional responsibilities, including the job of gardening at an employee's family quarters (similar to the work pictured in Figure 4.1). This trusted position gave him access to axes and machetes, called bush knives in PNG, as well as to other prisoners and other weapons. Around 15 June 1954, the chain of events that culminated in Usamando's fifth and final murder began. Usamando either raped, or had consensual sex with, another prisoner called Kago: Usamando did not give precise dates or details of the sexual encounter in his testimony. Kago then refused to speak to Usamando. On 22 June, Usamando walked away from gardening at the gaoler's house to where Kago's work party was engaged in tending cattle. According to Phillips's summary of the trial, Usamando either requested, or demanded, that Kago 'submit to sodomy' again, but Kago refused. Usamando was carrying his machete from his gardening duties and Kago felt threatened enough to call for help from his workmate, Monkap. When Monkap came running, Usamando threatened to kill him if he came closer. Kago again refused a demand to go into the bush for sex. Monkap then witnessed Usamando hit Kago on the head with the machete. Monkap ran for the warders. The coroner found that, on 22 June, Usamando struck Kago six times fatally and then ran off into the bush. A protracted search failed to find him.

In the early hours of the following morning, 23 June, cold and hungry, Usamando gave himself up to the senior gaoler, Kelleher, whose garden he had been tending. He insisted that he had wanted to give himself up to Kelleher rather than a native policeman, as he mistrusted native policemen, further indicating his marginal status. When questioned, Usamando told Kelleher: 'I asked him to commit sodomy with me; he refused; I got wild and cut him with a knife. I then became frightened and ran away.'[3] Kelleher reported that Usamando seemed dazed and spoke brokenly but was coherent. Some of his confusion was put down to the cold. Yet his confusion and inadvisable frankness was not necessarily a sign of a sophisticated man with a clear understanding of his situation.

---

3   Phillips to administrator, 29 September 1954.

Usamando's trial occurred, again before Phillips, on 23, 24, 27 and 30 August. The defence called no evidence and did not dispute the presentation of facts by the prosecution. The accused made no statement. During his closing address, the defence lawyer presented one factor in mitigation, arguing that Usamando's past record should have precluded his access to weapons and that the gaol had been negligent in its duty to Usamando and Kago. The defence played to existing concerns about the disorganised and unstructured nature of PNG prisons and highlighted the need for alternative means of enforcing order, as the prison reform process had been unsuccessful.

Given Usamando's four previous murders, with the fifth being so blatant, Phillips ordered an investigation into his psychological health before final sentencing. This suggests that, even though the matter of criminal capacity had not been raised in the trial, the judge, a man with extensive experience of Papua New Guinean criminality, felt that Usamando's conduct was unusual and that he was possibly mad. Phillips was also concerned that Usamando could become more violent as he aged and possibly grew senile. In evaluating the question of mental illness, Phillips may also have been responding to the tendency in the 1950s to see sodomy itself as evidence of mental illness.[4] The psychological expertise available to the judge was limited, the only doctor being a general practitioner who found Usamando to be in good mental health. Dr Bruce remarked: 'had I not known about this business I would have thought him a normal native'.[5] Without an insanity plea or evidence of mental illness, the sentence could not be mitigated by mental illness, yet Phillips seemed to consider Usamando's sexual behaviour anomalous within the conventions of both 'native' custom and Western pathology.

After Usamando was found guilty of murdering Kago on 27 August 1954, he made a statement, or allocutus, to the court in which he pleaded his general good behaviour. His rambling and fatalistic remarks gave no compelling reason for commutation; however, they did highlight his ambiguous place between two cultures. This was also suggested by his apparently limited understanding of codified law. His approach, with its appeal to personal relationships and feeling, was more suitable to the Papua New Guinean manner of settling disputes by interpersonal negotiation and consensus building. He concluded by saying, through the translator:

---

4 Lisa Featherstone and Amanda Kaladelfos, *Sex Crimes in the Fifties* (Carlton: Melbourne University Press, 2016), 175–82.
5 Phillips to administrator, 29 September 1954, 3.

> It is for the court to say what will happen to me. I have been in gaol nine years altogether. If I don't go back to my place and remain in prison, these thoughts will come into my mind—the thoughts of killing. Before the war, I was never like this. I worked for seventeen years in Wau without any trouble. It is now for the court to decide. If you feel sorry for me, you can send me back to my village. If not, it rests with you. I have said everything I want to say and you are the judge: but I have spoken the truth. This is all. If you want to send me to another gaol, or if you want to kill me, I would like to get tobacco, sugar and betel-nut. That is all.[6]

The statement is remarkable for its naivety and lack of comprehension of the circumstances in which Usamando was placed, even though the court considered him to be relatively sophisticated and Westernised. His request for a 'last meal' shows that he was resigned to his fate.

Phillips had been sympathetic enough to Usamando's situation to investigate his mental health but also concerned enough about the extremity of his behaviour to gather what documentation could be found about his previous murders so that these facts could be considered during sentencing and clemency. These papers were added to what became an extensive file to be forwarded to Canberra. Then, on 30 August 1954, Phillips took the unusual step of pronouncing a sentence of death on Usamando, making no recommendations as to alternate sentencing as per standard practice. It seems that Phillips was either resigned to the likelihood or determined that Usamando would hang.

The case then went to Cleland to be forwarded to Hasluck and the Cabinet. Cleland also took advice from the Crown Law Office, commissioning a report from its head, Wally Watkins, who also recommended execution. Cleland's covering letter endorsed Phillips's and Watkins's reasoning. Hasluck, however, made no written commentary or recommendations to the Cabinet in the submission as he had done in other cases. After the Cabinet made its decision on 21 November, Hasluck informed Cleland that:

> When Cabinet was considering your recommendations regarding the sentence of death passed on the native Usamando, today, some concern was expressed at the fact that a prisoner, who was in the custody of the Administration and was known to have a record as a killer, was able to find further opportunity for murdering a fellow

---

6   Ibid., 5–6.

prisoner. It was felt that close administrative attention should be given to the conditions under which such prisoners are held in the territory and the nature of the supervision over them.[7]

On 23 November, the decision to execute was transmitted to PNG.[8] This was officially confirmed by the paperwork from the governor-general-in-council on 8 December.[9] The announcement of execution was made on 16 December; Usamando was executed promptly on 17 December 1954.[10]

The father of Kago, Usamando's last victim, and the *luluai* of Usamando's village, an elder who liaised with the administration, were witnesses to the hanging. Usamando received the last rites from Reverend Father Bernarding and was given a 'heavy sedative dose of morphia'; the latter was recorded in the file but not mentioned in the press. Despite his sedation, Cleland noted in a letter to Canberra that those who witnessed the execution considered Usamando's conduct brave. This was the point at which extensive media attention began. Usamando's execution received newspaper coverage in Port Moresby, Australia and London. He was represented both as a multiple killer and stoic in his death. Seemingly unaware of the hangings conducted by military authorities in the 1940s, the coverage also highlighted that it was the first hanging in PNG since 1938.[11]

The preceding narrative of the case and capital case review process is based on the reports that Chief Justice Phillips of the PNG Supreme Court and Walter Watkins, secretary of the PNG Crown Law Office, wrote on the matter for the administrator, Donald Cleland, and in turn for a Cabinet Submission on the question of clemency. For Cleland and Watkins, the issues at stake included wider concerns for the administration. Usamando also presented distinct questions of principle and procedure for the presiding judge.

Frederick 'Monty' Phillips had been resident in Melanesia since 1920, first as a lands commissioner in the Solomon Islands then as a magistrate and judge in New Guinea. Having a few months seniority on Ralph Gore, chief justice

---

7   Paul Hasluck to D. M. Cleland, 23 November 1954, NAA: A4906, 205, item 4678943; NAA: A518, CQ840/1/3 PART 1, item 3252669.
8   Cabinet minute, 'Decision No. 207', 23 November 1954, NAA: A4906, 205, item 4678943; Paul Hasluck, 'Confidential Submission No. 25', NAA: A4906, 205, item 4678943.
9   'Native Murderer Died Silently on Lae Scaffold', *South Pacific Post*, 22 December 1954, 5.
10 'First N.G. Hanging For 16 Years', *Advertiser* (Adelaide), 17 December 1954, 28.
11 'Native Murderer Dies Silently on the Scaffold', *South Pacific Post*, 16 December 1954, 5; Hank Nelson, 'The Swinging Index: Capital Punishment and British and Australian Administration in Papua and New Guinea 1888–1945', *Journal of Pacific History* 13, no. 3 (1978): 130–52.

of Papua, he was made chief justice of New Guinea in 1938. The first chief justice of a unified PNG, he was lauded by his biographer and colleague, Paul Quinlivan, as both an experienced judge and a sympathetic and kind man. He had travelled widely in the territories and was known to many Papua New Guineans and expatriates.

Quinlivan presented Phillips as a defender of Papua New Guineans, as his decisions through the 1920s and 30s did much to repress the flogging of Papua New Guinean workers. Phillips had an extensive knowledge of the administration of the colony from acting as the administrator of New Guinea during emergencies, including the volcanic eruption that destroyed Rabaul in 1937. He had also taken on an administrative role during the reconstruction effort immediately following the Second World War, before returning to the bench.[12]

To Rachel Cleland, his contemporary, Phillips, like Gore, was a 'mighty' man of the law. She described him as a leader among the expatriate society, jovial and approachable.[13] Hasluck paid him the compliment, but also the criticism, of being 'the best of the old school'—a group that Hasluck thought sometimes made decisions on the merits of the law or due to a 'kindly interest' in Papua New Guineans, but, at other times, made the interests of the colony, as they understood them, the deciding factor.[14] Such men were, the minister considered, less concerned with the fine details of the separation of powers and the rules of evidence and more in favour of managing outcomes for Papua New Guineans and keeping order as they saw fit. These standards, with their implicit suggestions of paternalism, inconsistency and unaccountability, concerned Hasluck, as he sought a more ordered system of government and law—one that would be more acceptable to a critical world audience in the Trusteeship Council.

Little about the individual killings in Usamando's case would have surprised Phillips; it was the number that surprised him. Killings by machete and axe were common. Men murdering wives and murdering due to shame and pride were also not unusual. Phillips's long residence in Melanesia had given him broad experience of these and other cultural differences and, as Aldrich

---

12   Paul Quinlivan, 'Phillips, Sir Frederick Beaumont (1890–1957)', *Australian Dictionary of Biography*, adb.anu.edu.au/biography/phillips-sir-frederick-beaumont-8034.
13   Rachel Cleland, *Pathways to Independence: Story of Official and Family Life in Papua New Guinea from 1951–1975* (Cottesloe: Singapore National Printer, 1985), 183–6.
14   Paul Hasluck, *A Time for Building: Australian Administration in Papua and New Guinea 1951–1963* (Carlton: Melbourne University Press, 1976), 177.

suggests, expatriates were broadly aware of the diverse sexual practices among some Melanesian groups.[15] As acting administrator, Phillips had been involved in earlier attempts at prison reform, and so was well aware of the deficiencies, disorder and violence in PNG's penal system.[16] Indeed, Phillips was familiar with Usamando himself, who had been brought before him for the murder of Lula.[17] The judge would not have been surprised by Usamando's reactions to shame, his sexual conduct or the means of the murders. Murdering five people across twenty-six years, however, was surprising.

Context

Usamando's fifth murder was not a crime that drew the attention of newspapers in PNG or Australia. That a Papua New Guinean man had killed another Papua New Guinean man in prison was of little interest to Europeans in PNG who were the primary readership of the *SPP*. Indeed, the *SPP* rarely reported crimes that only affected Papua New Guineans, despite such crimes being regularly investigated and prosecuted by the authorities. The press in PNG, Australia and abroad did, however, report the execution of Usamando, as it was unusual and also judged to be significant to wider perceptions of colonialism in PNG.

In Chapters 2 and 3, Papua New Guineans were found guilty of serious crimes against colonial authority but their sentences were commuted. Yet, Usamando was hanged. In accounting for that outcome, an analysis of the trial and the discretionary process exposes many questions and problems. As Martin Wiener reminds us, 'neither the narrative of celebration, nor that of indictment prepares us for the complex struggles that these [colonial] trials stimulated and focused'.[18] Wiener's observation encourages us to ask why Usamando's crime was so much more serious than the many other murders that crossed the desks of the minister and the Federal Executive Council. How can his hanging be reconciled with the liberal approach

---

15   Robert Aldrich, *Colonialism and Homosexuality* (London: Routledge, 2003), 262.
16   F. B. Phillips to secretary, External Territories, 18 January 1951, NAA: A452/1959/4611, item 231528.
17   Phillips to administrator, 29 September 1954, 4.
18   Martin J. Wiener, *Empire on Trial: Race, Murder, and Justice under British Rule, 1870–1935* (New York: Cambridge University Press, 2009), 231.

to the law that Minister for Territories Paul Hasluck championed? These questions speak to the threshold for capital punishment and the limits of mercy in PNG.

The decision about whether to hang Usamando became entangled in four important issues for Papua and New Guinea's relationship with Australia. First, the case highlighted debates over the safety of prisons and their effectiveness at reforming and 'advancing' Papua New Guineans to Australian ways. The decision to hang Usamando should be understood in the context of processes of prison reform that spanned from 1949 to 1958 and an intention to deter violence and sodomy in prisons.

Second, *R. v. Usamando, 1954* revealed how officials engaged with gender ideologies and social anxiety during clemency matters in ways comparable to the issues raised in *R. v. Kita Tunguan, 1954*. Usamando hovered between two worlds and violated the mores of both. He was a test of the proposition that only those sophisticated enough to understand the law and punishment would hang. Indeed, his execution reflects the difficulties of making such judgements when retributive justice and deterrence were at stake.

Third, the punishment of this serial murderer occurred with conscious reference to anxieties about violence and crime in the PNG community, as well as to international and national norms. Australian officials and other observers were conscious of the possibly critical reception of the execution; however, they also sought to address the perception in PNG among Papua New Guinean and expatriate communities that a hanging was needed, both to deter further crime and to maintain the precedent for hanging in the face of what seemed to be a de facto abolition of the penalty. Advisers to the Cabinet—more explicitly than usual—took international scrutiny of the PNG criminal justice system into careful account in their recommendations. They considered ways to maintain the sanction of the death penalty while still seeking to present a positive image of Australian colonialism to a range of audiences. Usamando's case illuminates the limits of international pressure in a UN trust territory and the ways in which old colonialists and liberals found common causes despite such pressure.

Further, Usamando's case highlights gaps in bureaucratic capacity in PNG. Justice Phillips struggled to construct Usamando's criminal history because so many records were destroyed in the war and by the eruption of Mount Tavurvur and Mount Vulcan in 1937. The information that initially classified Usamando as a serial killer in 1951 came to the judge accidentally through a delegation of local people, and through the inadvisably frank testimony of the accused, rather than through official processes. It reflects the peculiarities of a system re-establishing itself over territories that had been subject to war and disaster and that had only partially been under control prior to the war.

Finally, Papua New Guineans made their views clear on capital punishment and on Usamando. They wanted hangings for punishment and to deter further crime. In this case, the judge and officials knew that people from Usamando's area found him dangerous and had favoured his execution since his fourth murder. There was much less ambiguity than usual about the possible impacts of the execution on the community. As such, in the execution of Usamando, the administration could find a common cause with its subjects.

Having introduced the chapter with a narrative of events, this chapter will examine the particular policy context of those engaged in determining the ultimate punishment for Usamando. Subsequently, the clemency discussions will be analysed and the arguments that were presented for and against execution will be discussed in relation to the particular confluence of interests.

Discretion: Enforcing security and public safety

The administration was aware of lingering concerns raised by the commutations of the perpetrators of previous well-publicised and disturbing capital crimes, including the Telefomin killings and the rape of Blanka Nesbit. Hasluck and his administration were also aware that Papua New Guineans generally preferred capital punishment for violent offenders. The executive had the option of using the discretionary justice process to address those concerns. Equally, at that time, officials were concerned that the consistent commutation of capital crimes was setting a precedent against hanging. The option of executing Usamando addressed those concerns, yet it also seemed to be in a category of its own, given that Usamando's crimes were so numerous. There were also qualms about hanging a prisoner in PNG, an Australian territory. However, the execution of a multiple murderer was in line with the punishment of white Australian offenders on the mainland. Therefore, such an execution could be represented as a just punishment for a Papua New Guinean. As well as for purposes of deterrence and security in the wider community, discretionary justice from the executive in the form of an execution could address prison disorder. Further cementing Usamando's fate, the administration was also concerned about sodomy and homosexuality, particularly in prisons but also in the wider community. The punishment's presumed deterrent effect, it was hoped, would impact the prevalence of such behaviour in prisons and beyond.

Sodomy was of concern to the PNG legal system as a behaviour representing the worst of both cultures, which Usamando seemed to embody. These concerns about sexuality in PNG were paralleled by heightened concerns in Australia and the West in general. Gary Wotherspoon traced an increase in investigations, prosecutions and penalties for sodomy across the early 1950s in NSW, the UK and the US.[19] Lisa Featherstone and Amanda Kaladelfos's research on sexual violence and crime in Australia in the 1950s places Wotherspoon's findings in the context of an increase in prosecutions for all sexual offences.[20] Similarly, the case studies in this book show that Australian legal practitioners in PNG were enmeshed, both culturally and legally, in this stringency that was occurring across the West, but with aspects of concern that reflected the particular mediating role of law in colonies.

Reflecting this general trend in the West, authorities also policed gender behaviour more actively in PNG in the 1950s than before the war. There was an awareness among expatriates that homosexual practices were common in some Papua New Guinean cultural groups, both ritually and as a matter of sexual pleasure, but that did not lessen the administration's anxieties at the interface of law, custom and morality. As Robert Aldrich shows, authorities in PNG policed sexual crime and gender boundaries more actively in the 1950s than before the war when homosexual practices among Papua New Guineans had been of little concern.[21] For expatriates, too, there were lines that could not be crossed. In her memoir, for example, Gloria Chalmers recalled an Australian being deported from PNG in 1953 for propositioning another white man.[22]

---

19 Garry Wotherspoon, 'The Greatest Menace Facing Australia: Homosexuality and the State in NSW during the Cold War', *Labour History*, no. 56 (1989): 15–28.
20 Featherstone and Kaladelfos, *Sex Crimes in the Fifties*, ch. 7.
21 Aldrich, *Colonialism and Homosexuality*, 250–2, 253–6.
22 Gloria Chalmers, *Kundus, Cannibals and Cargo Cults: Papua New Guinea in the 1950s* (Watsons Bay: Books and Writers Network, 2006), 25.

Indicative of this changed stance, prosecutions for sodomy and permitting sodomy were actively pursued at the PNG Supreme Court level in the 1950s. The offence of permitting sodomy under the Criminal Code made it a crime to be penetrated. According to Christine Stewart's analysis, anxieties around gender were such that it is probable that male rape victims were prosecuted on that basis.[23] The reports of the colonial administration show that there were three successful and three unsuccessful prosecutions for the crime of sodomy between 1952 and 1955. The extent of concern was such that authorities began pursuing such cases despite the apparent difficulty in mounting a prosecution, as the three incidents of nolle prosequi (in which the prosecutor withdraws their own charges) in Table 4.1 show. From 1955 onwards, prosecutions for sodomy/permitting sodomy in New Guinea's reports to the UN were collected under the category 'Unnatural Offences', with crimes such as bestiality and necrophilia making the statistics difficult to read.[24] The nomenclature alone indicates the role that homosexual practices played in the imagination of the territories' administrators. The penalties were serious, with terms of imprisonment comparable to those for assault.[25] With the sex lives of Papua New Guineans and expatriates being captured by policing and the courts, the administration was making plain what was and what was not appropriate behaviour on the path to advancement, reflecting the typical use of law as a didactic institution in colonies.[26] The determination to prosecute and the serious penalties imposed demonstrated the administration's willingness to use punishment and the courts to police the boundaries of sexual behaviour in PNG.

Capital case reviews required judgements regarding the character of an offender, including their moral fitness to continue to live, and judgements about whether the punishment would deter similar criminal behaviour in the wider community. Ideas about gender played a significant role in such

---

23 Christine Stewart, 'Men Behaving Badly: Sodomy Cases in the Colonial Courts of Papua New Guinea', *Journal of Pacific History* 43, no. 1 (2008): 77–93; *Criminal Code (Queensland, Adopted) in Its Application to the Territory of Papua*, chapter XXII, section 208 (1–3), Pacific Island Legal Information Institute, www.paclii.org/pg/legis/papua_annotated/cca254.pdf.
24 See Aldrich, *Colonialism and Homosexuality*, 251, on lower court prosecutions.
25 Australia, Department of Territories, *Report to the General Assembly of the United Nations on the Administration of the Territory of New Guinea [1946–1966]* (Canberra: Commonwealth Government Printer [1947–1967]).
26 Rick Sarre, 'Sentencing in Customary or Tribal Settings: An Australian Perspective', *Federal Sentencing Reporter* 13, no. 2 (2000): 74–8; Heather Douglas and Mark Finnane, *Indigenous Crime and Settler Law: White Sovereignty and Empire* (Basingstoke: Palgrave Macmillan, 2012), 5–8; Bruce L. Ottley, and Jean G. Zorn, 'Criminal Law in Papua New Guinea: Code, Custom and the Courts in Conflict', *American Journal of Comparative Law* 31, no. 2 (1983): 251–300.

decisions. The authorities were concerned to find and prosecute people who they regarded as possessing serious moral flaws or characters that were difficult to redeem to send a message of deterrence to the community. Conversely, they also wanted to model good behaviour. It was widely understood that being a person of good character—a manly character—could save you from the rope when authorities deliberated on clemency.

Table 4.1: Supreme Court prosecutions for sodomy.

New Guinea, reporting year: July–June	Charged	Convicted	Discharged	Nolle prosequi	Sentence
1952–53: Sodomy	2	2			9–12 months with hard labour (IHL)
1953–54: Sodomy and permitting sodomy	4	1		3	5 months IHL
1954–55: Sodomy and similar not reported as a category					
1955–56: Unnatural offences; a new category including bestiality, necrophilia and sodomy	6	4		2	18 months to 3 years

Source: Australia, Department of Territories, *Report to the General Assembly of the United Nations on the Administration of the Territory of New Guinea [1952–1956]* (Canberra: Commonwealth Government Printer [1953–1957]).

In addition to anxieties about sodomy in prisons and in the community, there was also anxiety about crime and a belief that a lack of hangings was encouraging criminality in PNG among expatriates and Papua New Guineans. The high-profile capital cases discussed so far—the Telefomin cases and *R. v. Kita Tunguan, 1954*—had resulted in clemency. However, the old colonials felt that imprisonment was ineffective at deterring serious crime and that public confidence in the law was faltering.[27] The role of sentencing and punishment was evident in the general law text used in

---

27 'Women Sign Petition', *South Pacific Post*, 11 August 1954, 7; Editor, 'The Death Sentence', *South Pacific Post*, 7 July 1954, 12. Experts in punishment, such as the Howard League, had long argued—and shown—that deterrence did not, in fact, work. See, for example, *Howard Association Annual Report, October 1899*, Queensland State Library: G 365189—1901, Prison System Reports.

training *kiaps* at the Australian School of Pacific Administration (ASOPA). The eminent Australian jurist of the 1940s and 1950s J. V. Barry counselled that capital punishment was reserved for 'cases which present some features which shock the public conscience'.[28] Sentencing was to restore public confidence in the law and provide security through retribution, deterrence, rehabilitation or exclusion from the community.

So, while the community had been shocked by Kita Tunguan's offences, as seen in Chapter 3, the expatriate community's outrage had not been substantially assuaged by the punishment. There followed a rise in public campaigning in favour of the death penalty.[29] In 1954, newspaper editorials both enhanced and reflected wider calls for the use of the death penalty, such as those surrounding Kita Tunguan's commutation. Adding to this disquiet, the sparing of the Telefomin men begged the question of why, previously, Papua New Guineans who had killed officials had been hanged and their villages burned.[30] Both expatriates and Papua New Guineans were asking questions about the efficacy of the current system of penalties in deterring sexual violence and crime, particularly the practice of almost automatic commutation across Australian jurisdictions. After a string of serious crimes, the capital case reviews provided an opportunity for the executive to attend to the outrage of the community. In Usamando's case, Phillips was able to gauge community sentiment relatively easily due to the village deputation that waited on him after the trial.

Yet, the expatriate and Papua New Guinean communities, with their feelings of insecurity and desire for retribution, were not the only constituencies that the executive considered. Australian policy was to make justice and punishment uniform in PNG and comparable to mainland Australian practices while also following practices that the international community could approve. As Heather Douglas and Mark Finnane suggest:

> While the weight of historical debate about sovereignty has focused on land and property, it was when settler prosecutors and settler courts dealt with indigenous violence, especially that of indigenous assailants or Indigenous victims, that the exercise of sovereignty was truly tested.[31]

---

28 J. V. Barry, G. W. Paton and G. Sawer, *An Introduction to the Criminal Law in Australia* (London: McMillian and Co., 1948), 95.
29 'Women Sign Petition'; Editor, 'The Death Sentence'.
30 Nelson, 'The Swinging Index'.
31 Douglas and Finnane, *Indigenous Crime and Settler Law*, 2.

In meeting that test, Hasluck and his department wanted to use similar punitive practices for expatriates and Papua New Guineans.[32] Thus, mainland Australian thresholds for hanging guided the executive. Multiple murderers, such as Arnold Sodeman, the 'school-girl strangler' who confessed to four killings and was convicted and executed in Victoria in 1936, tended to be hanged in Australian jurisdictions. Since sentencing aims to be consistent in similar cases, this suggested that execution was the acceptable sentence for punishing a multiple murderer like Usamando.[33] Therefore, imposing such a penalty in a colonial setting was less likely to be contentious and draw condemnation from the Australian public and observers in the UNTC.

Papua New Guineans of Usamando's culture also felt that multiple killers should be executed. According to the former head of the PNG Crown Law Office, John Greenwell, most Papua New Guinean cultures believed in social consensus and harmony: those who disturbed the consensus, order and honour of others with killings were required to pay high compensation, or with their lives or the lives of their group members.[34] Having received a deputation from Usamando's village, Phillips had a clear idea about what locals thought about Usamando's punishment. Hasluck, too, was well aware that most Papua New Guineans favoured capital punishment for murder. Recalling his 1951 tour of PNG in his memoir, he wrote: 'A deputation of hundreds of people waited on me and with great eloquence asked that the prisoners be put to death' lest 'they would be back again, fat and boastful … They believed strongly in capital punishment.'[35] Yet meeting these expectations was not a simple obligation, as there were other interests in Australia and abroad to consider.

That Usamando's final two crimes were committed in prison highlighted both the need for prison reform and the role of execution in sending a message of deterrence to those already within the system. Intensifying the Executive Council's concern about prisons, another Papua New Guinean prisoner, Yerimbe, who was awaiting the outcome of his capital case review

---

32 Hasluck, *A Time for Building*, 176, 180; NAA: A452/1959/4611, item 533996; NAA: A518/A846/1/12, Item 107135.
33 See, for example, *Sodeman v. R. [1936] HCA 75; (1936) 55 CLR 192 (2 April 1936)*, Australian Legal Information Institute, University of Technology Sydney and University of New South Wales, www.austlii.edu.au/au/cases/cth/HCA/1936/75.html; George Marshall Irving, 'Sodeman, Arnold Karl (1899–1936)', *Australian Dictionary of Biography*, adb.anu.edu.au/biography/sodeman-arnold-karl-8574.
34 John Greenwell, *The Introduction of Western Law into Papua New Guinea*, unpublished manuscript given to author by John Greenwell, former first assistant secretary and director of Papua New Guinea Office Government and Legal Affairs Division, Department of External Territories, 1970–75.
35 Hasluck, *A Time for Building*, 179.

for murder at the same prison at which Usamando had murdered his last victim, committed suicide, an act that exposed the lack of effective prison management.[36] Usamando's crimes and sexual violence were indicative of the disorder in the prisons. As punishment theorist David Garland has observed, 'punishment, among other things, is a communicative and didactic institution'.[37] Officials in the Crown Law Office argued that an execution offered a temporary remedy to disorder within the prisons, as it would be a deterrent to disorder among the surviving prisoners.[38] However, it would not solve the problem; the process of reform would still be a long way from complete.

According to Finnane, one of the more compelling arguments against the abolition of capital punishment in Australian debates was that death was the only means of deterring and punishing desperate offenders who had been imprisoned for life.[39] Prison guards and other supporters of retaining capital punishment feared that prisoners incarcerated for life would act with impunity and violence, as they had nothing to lose. Mike Richards maintains that this argument was at its most potent in the case of the last man hanged in Australia, Ronald Ryan.[40] Such arguments were familiar in the public domain. Therefore, the execution of Usamando should be understood in the context of these concerns about prisons. As discussed below, officials raised these issues of protecting guards and remediating prison disorder in relation to Usamando's sentence.

'Our law provides for no further punishment in his case than death': PNG officials advise that Usamando should hang

PNG legal officials Chief Justice Phillips and Crown Law Officer Wally Watkins each told Minister for Territories Hasluck that Usamando should hang in separate submissions. In doing so, they framed their

---

36   Hasluck to Cleland, 23 November 1954.
37   David Garland, *Punishment and Modern Society: A Study in Social Theory* (Chicago: University of Chicago Press, 1990), 251.
38   Walter Watkins to administrator, 13 November 1954, 3–4, NAA: A4906, 205, item 4678943. See also 'Native Murderer Died Silently on the Scaffold', *South Pacific Post*, 16 December 1954, 5.
39   Mark Finnane, *Punishment in Australian Society* (Melbourne: Oxford University Press, 1997), 137–9.
40   Mike Richards, *The Hanged Man: The Life and Death of Ronald Ryan* (Melbourne: Scribe Publications, 2003), 255–6. Richards also highlights the argument that suggests Ryan was innocent of this crime.

recommendations around the concerns of the colonial administration. They engaged in debates on deterrence, generally, and discussed calibrating penalties to deter murder and the disorder of the prisons. Both men were concerned primarily about the number of Usamando's murders, the lack of provocation and his fundamental failure to reform and show remorse. They also wanted to deter the sort of homosexual conduct that had led to the final two murders, especially in prisons, which they regarded as depraved. Reinforcing this message of depravity, they argued that Usamando had also outraged the mores of his own people. Thus, he was condemned as immoral on several levels. Phillips and Watkins both concluded their submissions by arguing that discretionary justice gave the executive the freedom to choose a punishment that would protect the reputation of Australian justice in PNG.

The first step of the capital case review process was the judge's advice to the executive. In explaining his decision to pronounce a sentence of death, and to offer no alternative sentencing advice, Phillips observed that Usamando had not taken advantage of earlier chances to redeem himself: 'if his record of earlier killings were also taken into account, a recommendation by the court that he be shown mercy would still be less warranted'. Usamando, Phillips advised, 'is a confirmed "killer", and his own words confirm it'. The rapacious and violent nature of Usamando's sexual behaviour, which the judge considered separately from the number of murders, compounded his conviction that Usamando had little likelihood of reform. An attempted sexual encounter while in prison, or perhaps an attempted rape in prison with the threat of weapons, crossed a particular threshold in the judge's thinking. Phillips also reported that Usamando's community had spoken about their preferred punishment for him at the time of his murder of Lula in 1951:

> Madang natives called on me and stated that Usamando had killed a native at Modilon, Madang before he had killed the two women at Bogia: they forcibly expressed their opinion that Usamando should be executed forthwith and prophesied that, if Usamando were not executed, he would kill again.[41]

There was often anxiety in clemency discussions that the local people would not understand or support capital punishment, as was argued in the Telefomin case. That there was a clear direction from local people in favour of execution, in this case, seemed to circumvent the conventional argument

---

41   Phillips to administrator, 29 September 1954, 5–6.

for clemency—namely, that the offender's community was too non-Westernised or 'unsophisticated' for hanging to be just. Phillips's report on the local delegation reassured the executive that the offender's community would welcome a hanging and that they understood its purpose as both retribution and deterrence.

Phillips also recognised that the ultimate decision on clemency would be determined by wider political and social considerations, as is often the case with discretionary justice. Whether or not to hang Usamando was the Executive Council's decision, he reflected, as 'wide fields of inquiry are open to you that are not always open to a judge'.[42] Those wider considerations included international and domestic political questions and, particularly for the reputation of Australian colonialism, an awareness of the negative ramifications that might come from an execution, regardless, to some extent, of the sensitivities of the crime.

Before forwarding Phillips's recommendation to Canberra, Cleland commissioned Wally Watkins to report on the case. Cleland particularly wanted assurance on the fit between the law and the intricacies of managing the territories. Accordingly, Watkins methodically explored the nature of Usamando's offences as matters of law and also made reference to the implications for the PNG administration. Watkins is remembered as a 'legal eagle' among local officials and as someone whose 'justice was always tempered with mercy and understanding'.[43] Historian Donald Denoon, however, has described him as 'irascible' and 'abrasive' in his commitment to maintaining Australian colonial authority over a population he saw as unfit to rule itself.[44] This mix of traits is evident in his report.

Watkins emphasised the homosexual encounter that triggered Kago's 'unusually vicious' murder.[45] He established that it was the moral circumstances of an armed rape that made it particularly vicious, not the murder itself. Watkins also tested the proposition that Usamando was provoked into a rage by the sudden cessation of sexual access within an established relationship.[46] The Criminal Code held that murder might be

---

42 Ibid., 6.
43 PNG Association of Australia, 'Walter (Wally) Watkins (22 March 1984)', Vale, www.pngaa.net/Vale/vale_june84.htm#Watkins.
44 Donald Denoon, *A Trial Separation: Australia and the Decolonisation of Papua New Guinea* (Canberra: Pandanus Books, 2005), 52, 55.
45 Walter Watkins to administrator, 13 November 1954, 1, NAA: A4906, 205, item 4678943.
46 Ibid., 1–2.

reduced to manslaughter were a reasonable person to conclude that the offender was understandably in too passionate a state to make a rational decision due to a sudden and enraging circumstance, such as the sudden denial of usual sexual access.[47] Watkins rejected such a defence: he concluded that Usamando likely had raped Kago before, as shown by Kago's refusal to talk to him for a week. Further, Watkins argued that Usamando intended to do so again, as this explained why he had gone armed to the encounter. These assessments were informed by Usamando's past sexual behaviour: for example, he had transgressed by having sex with his sister-in-law without observing the customs of a bride price. There was also significant evidence of premeditation in each of Usamando's crimes. He had not only broken the rules of sexual conduct by Western standards, but also the sexual mores of his own people. Further, he had done so with a reasonable degree of familiarity with each. Usamando, as Watkins noted, had been under European influence all his life, having been born into a community under the supervision of the Germans and then worked for Australians. As a mature man who had experienced trials and gaol for four previous murders, he knew Australian law. In summary, Watkins wrote:

> Nothing in the circumstances of this case, or in what is known of his past history indicates a reason for extending clemency to Usamanda [*sic*]. His history shows that when frustrated in the gratification of his sexual passion, he resolves to kill and carries that resolve into effect in a most brutal way. Twice the death sentence has been commuted in his favour to one of imprisonment for life, and our law provides for no further punishment in his case than death.

Beyond Usamando's culpability for his crimes, Watkins reviewed the administrative implications of his punishment. The kinsman of Kago, he argued, must be prevented from engaging in payback killings by an execution that would satisfy their cravings for revenge. Within the prison system, Watkins argued, it was important also to maintain a clear standard of justice to protect and control prisoners. Thus, he reasoned, 'it is patent that a further commutation of the death sentence in favour of Usamanda [*sic*] must have a detrimental effect on all prisoners undergoing life sentence'. In other words, Watkins believed that executing Usamando would deter prisoners from violence, while not executing him would encourage disorder and endanger prisoners and guards.

---

47   New South Wales Law Reform Commission, *Provocation, Diminished Responsibility and Infanticide*, Discussion Paper 31 (Sydney: New South Wales Law Reform Commission, 1993), section 3.104.

Watkins also suggested that an execution would send a clear message to metropolitan and international observers:

> At any time a case may arise of a murder by a native of a European, or by a native of a European woman or girl, where the Executive would feel strongly that the sentence of death should be carried out. A commutation in Usamando's case would be a powerful precedent to the contrary, and if in the later cases the sentence were executed, it would be very hard to rebut the criticism that there is one law for the protection of the European and another for the native.

Indeed, this was his key point: he believed it was necessary to retain the death penalty in general so as to be able to punish the murder of an expatriate 'European woman or girl'. This seemed to be his greatest concern. Similarly, the *SPP* reported on 8 December 1954 that Justice Kelly of the Supreme Court, in sittings at Madang, had expressed the concern that recent punishments, such as clemency for Tunguan, were not effective in deterring crimes against Europeans.[48] Watkins, therefore, reflected expatriates' concerns about their personal safety and security from violence from Papua New Guineans and posited the old colonial solution—capital punishment as a form of deterrence.

Watkins had played a key role in managing the public reception of the trials of the Telefomin killers. Therefore, he was acutely aware of the problems Australia faced in defending its colonial presence in PNG from critiques in the UNTC and from the Australian electorate. He had been instrumental in persuading the parents of Harris and Szarka not to attend the trials of their sons' killers in PNG to minimise the negative publicity.[49] In drawing attention to the need to maintain the precedent for hanging just a few months later, he was well aware of the main audiences of concern: the UNTC and domestic Australian constituencies. As shown above, he argued that Usamando would have to hang for his murders of Papua New Guineans so that PNG authorities could appear to be just if they hanged a Papua New Guinean for killing an expatriate. Immersed as he was in the old colonial ideologies of justice and colonial management, he saw hanging the killers of Europeans as necessary for preserving the authority of Australian colonial officials and the integrity of the criminal justice system. Watkins wanted the

---

48 'Concern over Sex Cases', *South Pacific Post*, 11 August 1954, 8.
49 W. J. Hall to W. W. Watkins, Crown law officer, PNG, 31 May 1954, NAA: A4906, 4, item 209114.

law to appear even-handed to an international audience, and perhaps even be so, while also being able to protect whites from disorder and challenges to their power.

Cleland forwarded Phillips's and Watkins's reports to Hasluck with a covering letter endorsing their arguments. Contrary to his usual habit, Hasluck made no comment on the facts of the case and, while he presumably spoke in Cabinet and supported Phillips's and Watkins's arguments, his remarks are not recorded in the Cabinet notebooks.[50] The Cabinet upheld the pronounced sentence to hang Usamando.

The administration and federal government justify the executions

Cleland sought to minimise the publicity about the capital sentence prior to the execution; however, after it occurred and was reported on, officials made statements about it.[51] The statements, as reported in the press, as the public statement was not in the file, indicated an interest in deterring crime inside prisons and in the community and in finding a just outcome to the extreme crimes of Usamando.

The *SPP* focussed on the perceived local consequences that would flow from the execution. The themes Phillips, Watkins and Cleland raised in their submissions—about controlling prisons and wider questions of deterrence and community security—were highlighted by the paper in its report on Cleland's statement. On 16 December, the *SPP* recorded its appreciation of the administration's attempt to use punishment as a deterrent and inferred that the decision to execute would be of particular interest to those who had expressed concern about rising crime rates in the context of the Kita Tunguan trial. The paper justified the decision to execute by reminding readers that the execution had occurred because Usamando's case was extreme. Citing an unnamed authority, it reported the official explanation for choosing execution: 'The native, Usamando, in his 50 years, had killed five people including his wife and her sister.'[52] Further, the prisoner had been deemed sound of mind, so it was appropriate to hang him. Conversely,

---

50   Paul Hasluck, Confidential Minute for Cabinet, 21 November 1954, 1, NAA: A4906, 205, item 4678943.
51   J. C. Archer to secretary, 13 December 1954, 1, NAA: A4906, 205, item 4678943.
52   'Native Murderer Died Silently on the Scaffold'.

had he not been hanged, prisons in PNG would become more difficult to manage and 'there was no guarantee Usamando would not murder another prisoner'. The newspaper coverage reassured the expatriate community that the government was acting to improve the quality of prisons and also to protect the wider community.

Newspaper coverage in Australia and overseas largely accepted the punishment as reasonable given the extremity of the crimes. Removed from PNG, questions of community or prison safety were of less concern. Instead, Australian and international coverage focussed on the question of justice and the appropriate expiation for crime. Newspapers in Australia and London reported on the magnitude of Usamando's crimes and drew attention to the rarity of execution in PNG. The *Times* in London reported that:

> For the first time for 16 years the authorities today carried out a sentence of death when a native was hanged for murder … the condemned man had a record of four murders.[53]

The *Canberra Times*, the *West Australian,* the Adelaide *Advertiser*, the *Central Queensland Herald* and the *Townsville Daily Bulletin* all utilised the wording of the AAP-Reuters report on the execution:

> Police officials at Lae this morning hanged a New Guinea native, Usamando, who was found guilty on August 30 of having wilfully murdered a fellow prisoner, Kago, at Lae on June 22. Usamando had a record of four previous murders dating back to 1928. He was hanged for having killed Kago while he was a prisoner in the Lae Gaol. The last natives to be hanged in New Guinea were three on February 2, 1937, and a Papuan native hanged in 1938.[54]

Based on these reports, the administration seems to have been successful in controlling the public relations of the execution. None of the coverage was condemnatory and it largely repeated the official line: Usamando was a multiple murderer and execution was an extraordinary step for an extraordinary criminal. Legitimacy was built through the representation of

---

53 'Execution in New Guinea—News in Brief', *Times* (London), 17 December 1954, 7.
54 'Native Hanged in New Guinea', *Canberra Times*, 17 December 1954, 8; 'New Guinea Native Goes to Gallows', *West Australian* (Perth), 17 December 1954,15; 'First N.G. Hanging for 16 Years', *Advertiser* (Adelaide), 17 December 1954, 28; 'Native Hanged for Murder', *Central Queensland Herald* (Rockhampton) 23 December 1954, 17; 'Native Hanged', *Townsville Daily Bulletin* (Queensland), 17 December 1954, 1.

the administration as reasonable and just, as it used execution only in the most serious of cases. It would have been difficult for the many countries that retained the death penalty to argue that it was unjust.

Accounts of the actual hanging in PNG conformed to standard gallows narratives: a stoic acceptance of fate that further legitimised the power of the government in the eyes of the community.[55] The *SPP*'s report featured the sub-heading: 'Native Murderer Dies Silently on Lae Scaffold'.[56] The spectacle of cooperating with one's own execution indicated that even the executed approved of the sentence. This had the effect of alleviating discomfort with capital punishment, reinforcing the moral beliefs that underlay the law and legitimising the system that handed down the sentence. As Tim Castles has observed of such reporting in New South Wales:

> The execution reports, therefore, went beyond a mere account of what occurred in a factual sense. Instead they used those facts to create or share a sense of meaning about the use of violence by the state in inflicting death upon a subject, which was sanctioned by law and carried into effect by the Executive government.[57]

Thus, the *SPP*'s reporting acted to support and legitimise the decision to execute to the expatriate community. However, the press did not know that Usamando had been drugged to achieve the outcome of stoic silence. Cleland informed Canberra that Usamando had been given a 'heavy sedative dose of morphia', adding that those who witnessed the execution considered his conduct brave.[58] To the extent that Usamando entered the purview of the press, it was as a cipher, a representation of some other concern: he was a lesson to others, a symbol of justice done, a legitimisation of Australia's conduct.

---

55 See, for example, Karen Halttunen, *Murder Most Foul: The Killer and the American Gothic Imagination* (Cambridge: Harvard University Press, 1998); Daniel A. Cohen, *Pillars of Salt and Monuments of Grace* (Amherst and Boston: University of Massachusetts Press, 2006).
56 'Native Murderer Died Silently on the Scaffold'.
57 Tim Castle, 'Constructing Death: Newspaper Reports of Executions in Colonial New South Wales, 1826–1837', *Journal of Australian Colonial History* 9 (2007).
58 D. M. Cleland to secretary, Department of Territories, 17 December 1954, NAA: A518, CQ840/1/3 PART 1, item 3252669.

Conclusion

Usamando was a man between worlds whose entry into the historical record demonstrates fractures and tensions in the rapidly changing societies of PNG. He was seemingly uncomprehending of both his own society and colonial society and was condemned by both. His allocutus in the last two trials showed little awareness of the formal legal process, or his culpability, yet the system saw him as sophisticated enough to hang. Phillips, who was sensitive to Papua New Guinean culture and had been sympathetic to Usamando in the past, heard his cases. However, a fifth killing was a bridge too far for the chief justice.

Usamando's execution demonstrates the weaknesses of discretion in terms of maintaining a clear test for the condemned being sophisticated enough to hang. The primary purpose of executive review for PNG cases was to ensure that those who did not understand the system being imposed upon them did not hang. Usamando's confused and self-incriminating statements plainly showed that he did not understand. Yet, this, it seems, could be subsumed by the need for retribution and restitution when the crime was extreme, as in Usamando's case. The executive was able to use discretion to break its own rules in the interests of justice and community and prison safety. Yet, it was a prison, a poorly run colonial institution, that had failed Usamando by allowing him weapons.

Usamando seemed to both desire men and be shamed by sleeping with them, and he reacted with violent rape when refused his desires. Whether his Papua New Guinean community supported a diverse range of sexual practices, whether he was enmeshed in colonial proscriptions against sodomy or whether he was senile or mad, as Phillips seemed to suspect, is unknown. In this respect as well, he was a man between worlds, not understood by either and violating the rules of both.

From another part of the expatriate community, Watkins saw Usamando's pronounced sentence as an opportunity. The lawyer–administrator sought to protect the white expatriate community and the security of the administration by retaining the death penalty for use against killers of Europeans.

Usamando's tragic history also reveals the difficulties faced by the judiciary and discretionary justice in the 1950s in terms of ensuring accurate information, as his records were destroyed and the full extent of his crimes were only brought to the attention of the courts by his own testimony, which he should have been advised not to give. He was both failed by and a failure of the project to advance as it stood in 1954.

This case indicates that Papua New Guineans in the 1950s supported capital punishment for murderers, particularly in terms of deterrence. Significantly, it also shows that the documented views of Papua New Guineans could constitute a persuasive argument in terms of policy decisions. Phillips relayed the views of Usamando's community, including their strong view that he should have been hanged for his murders in 1951. It was unusual to have such certain data on local preferences and, with it, officials felt confident that an execution would be both welcomed and productive of social order and obedience to the law.

In many ways, the decision to execute Usamando was an easy one for the executive to make. All interests agreed that he should hang. An execution served several pressing needs: it would help to deter crime, restore order in the prisons and maintain the death penalty for future cases. The facts of the case were so different from the Telefomin killings and the Kita Tunguan case, and told a story of such apparent wickedness, that execution was justifiable on many grounds. Hanging Usamando allowed the courts to appear, and perhaps to actually be, even-handed in their use of punishment.

The colony wanted a particular kind of man to be produced by the new Australian institutions and Usamando was not that man. As this execution represented a dramatic departure from the generally merciful nature of the postwar administration, it sent a clear message about how the modern Papua New Guinean man should behave in prison and beyond. The prisoners of Lae Gaol knew the nature of Usamando's crimes and took heed of his execution. The message was clear: to kill in prison was to tempt the noose and to kill over sodomy was doubly dangerous.

5
'The Crown as the fount of justice': *R. v. Ako Ove, 1956* and *R. v. Sunambus, 1956*

Ako-Ove

Ako-Ove was born in Aurua near Port Romily in the Gulf District of Papua in around 1932. In 1948, he received one year's training as a medical assistant but left to take up a position as a house servant with the Australasian Petroleum Company until 1955. This was not unusual. The administration struggled to keep Papua New Guineans in education programs in the 1950s as people with some English were in great demand as servants, and such positions were desirable as they were quite well paid by Papua New Guinean standards. He then took a job with the Vanderiet family in Boroko, Port Moresby, in 1956. Both Mr Jan Vanderiet and Mrs Eugenie Vanderiet were employed by the administration. Eugenie was a clerk and Jan was registrar for the Department of Agriculture.[1]

Ako-Ove was thought to be 24 years old in 1956; he was married to Muruku-Ako and they lived in the servants' quarters of the Vanderiet home, a separate building on the grounds. Ako-Ove suspected Muruku-Ako of having an affair with a Kairuku man he had found in his quarters with his wife on two occasions. His shame and outraged honour drove him to search around town (such as pictured in Figure 5.1) for the offending

---
1 PNG Association of Australia, 'Jan Vanderiet', Vale, June 2011, www.pngaa.net/Vale/vale_june01.htm#Vanderiet.

man on his day off, 29 January 1956. He told all his *wantoks* (his friends from the same language group with whom he also shared kinship ties) that he was looking for the man and added that his wife was causing trouble.² From this testimony, it was implied that he was contemplating some sort of retributory violence.

Ako-Ove failed to find the man, so he returned home just before six in the evening. Muruku-Ako was in the house with Eugenie 'Gene' Vanderiet who reported that she seemed nervous or afraid. Ako-Ove then entered the house and spoke at length to his wife in their language. After that, he took Muruku-Ako by the arm and pulled her out of the house. Gene watched them from a window as he took her into their quarters about twenty metres across the garden.³

Figure 5.1: Native village, Port Moresby, 1955 or 1956.
Source: Tom Meigan, National Library of Australia, nla.gov.au/nla.obj-148185019.

---

2   R. T. Gore to administrator, 8 May 1956, NAA: A518, CQ840/1/3 PART 2, item 434881; PNG Association of Australia, 'Eugenie (Gene) Vanderiet (30 June 1997)', Vale, September 1997, www.pngaa.net/Vale/vale_sept97.htm#Gene.
3   Gore to administrator, 8 May 1956; R. T. Gore, handwritten transcription of *R. v. Ako-Ove*, Case Book, 'P.M. Criminal 1.5.56–18.6.56', Papers of Ralph Gore, 1930–1964, National Library of Australia (hereafter Gore Papers).

Ako-Ove testified that he threatened to call the police unless Muruku-Ako gave up the Kairuku man. Adultery was an offence under the ordinances controlling Papua New Guinean behaviour.[4] He claimed she told him that she had betrayed him eight times and that she wanted to leave him. Ako-Ove claimed that his 'head went no good' and he grabbed a knife and attempted to cut her throat. However, she fell over, and while she was down, he stabbed her repeatedly. He struck her in the head with the knife so hard that it broke, so he took up an iron bar and hit her in the head with that.[5]

Unaware of the bloody murder occurring metres from where she stood, Gene Vanderiet started to cook dinner. She testified that Ako-Ove came into the kitchen at about seven o'clock dressed only in his *rami* (sarong or skirt) and looking wild.[6] He dragged her into another room and attempted to rape her. She struggled free and ran to her next-door neighbour's house. Her neighbour, Mr E. Clough, grabbed his unloaded rifle and went outside. Ako-Ove's subsequent move towards Clough was interpreted as an attack and he struck Ako-Ove in the head with the rifle butt, a blow that fractured the Papua New Guinean's skull and broke the rifle. The police arrived shortly after and Ako-Ove was taken into custody.[7]

In contrast, Ako-Ove's testimony records that, after killing Muruku-Ako, he ran into the house to call the police. He was bleeding and upset and felt Mrs Vanderiet did not understand him and was scared and ran away. He followed her, at which point Clough struck him down. He recalled waking in custody. Allowing time for recovery, and after cautioning him that he could remain silent, the police interviewed him on 1 February.[8]

Ako-Ove was placed on trial in Port Moresby before Justice Gore on Tuesday 1 May 1956. The court-appointed defence lawyer attempted to plead insanity as Ako-Ove's defence. Based on the evidence of witnesses from Ako-Ove's past, the testimony of general practitioners and the presentation of medical textbooks, the lawyer argued that Ako-Ove suffered from a form of epilepsy and attacked his wife during a seizure. However, contrary medical evidence from textbooks in the possession of another general practitioner called to give evidence indicated that, in such a seizure, the sufferer would have no memory of actions committed during the episode. As Ako-Ove

---

4   *Native Regulation Ordinance, 1908–1930—Native Regulations, 1939* (Papua), section 84, Pacific Island Legal Information Institute, www.paclii.org/pg/legis/papua_annotated/nro19081930nr1939446/.
5   Gore to administrator, 8 May 1956; Gore, handwritten transcription of *R. v. Ako-Ove*.
6   *Ramis* were often incorporated into uniforms for workers.
7   'Amok Native Gets Death Sentence', *South Pacific Post*, 16 May 1956, 5.
8   Gore to administrator, 8 May 1956; Gore, handwritten transcription of *R. v. Ako-Ove*.

clearly remembered and described murdering his wife, this suggested that he did not murder his wife during a seizure. For Gore, the key fact was that Ako-Ove remembered his actions when the medical testimony tended to suggest that this would not be possible in the case of a seizure. Since the burden of proof in an insanity plea is on the defence, Justice Gore found the medical evidence insufficient to overcome the presumption of sanity and found Ako-Ove guilty of wilful murder. Ako-Ove had nothing to say when invited to respond to the verdict. Gore recorded a sentence of death, indicating an implicit recommendation for mercy, and subsequently made a recommendation for a term of ten years imprisonment.[9]

Sunambus

Sunambus was from the village of Puto on the less accessible western coast of Bougainville Island. This area was not subject to regular patrolling until 1955, though irregular patrols had occurred since 1946 and there had been some prior contact with Australians seeking contract labour for plantations.[10] Despite few patrols, there was a Christian mission ten miles from Puto, which indicated that some Westernisation had occurred in the area. There had been no serious cases heard in the Supreme Court from the Puto area prior to 1956.[11] However, a lack of trials does not necessarily mean a lack of violence. There was a belief among administration officials that, in such isolated areas, only cases the villagers could not resolve themselves made it to the attention of patrol officers. According to Dr Kenneth Read, an anthropology instructor at the Australian School of Pacific Administration (ASOPA) attended by patrol officer cadets, 'the respected village official in fact is the man who is successful in keeping cases from the courts'.[12]

On 15 November 1955, Sunambus came across two girls who were collecting firewood, Dabi and Ributeivi. Sunambus approached them, drew a frightened Ributeivi aside and raped her. Dabi stood by and then ran away when she saw what was happening. Fearful that Dabi would tell Ributeivi's relatives, Sunambus took a bush knife, like a machete, from the scattered belongings of the two girls and chased down Dabi and cut her throat.

9   Gore to administrator, 8 May 1956; Gore, handwritten transcription of *R. v. Ako-Ove*.
10 It was not clear from the source material if that actually meant blackbirding.
11 Gore to administrator, 27 April 1956, NAA: A518, CQ840/1/3 PART 2, item 434881.
12 Kenneth Read, 'Native Attitudes to European Law', Kenneth Read Papers Relating to Teaching Australian School of Pacific Administration (ASOPA) Courses, Australian National University Archives, ANUA444, box 1, folder 7, 1–4.

Sunambus boasted to his friends about the crime and officials were told about it, indicating perhaps that there were repercussions to the local social order that traditional systems of reconciliation could not accommodate without violence. Australian officials arrested Sunambus and detained him and witnesses and other parties to the case in the district's capital, Sohano, to appear at the Supreme Court when it was in session on 10 April 1956.[13] Holding the accused and witnesses for months in district capitals to await trial was a usual practice for offences committed in isolated places; it not only ensured their attendance at court but also helped to prevent inter-group violence and vendettas. However, the detention of witnesses and interested parties ran counter to the rule of law. Justice Gore found Sunambus guilty and recorded a sentence of death, with a recommended alternate sentence of eight years with hard labour.[14]

***

Ako-Ove of Arahavi and Sunambus of Puto were two very different men. Ako-Ove was employed as a servant in suburban Port Moresby. Sunambus lived traditionally in the mountains of Bougainville Island. Ako-Ove murdered his wife because he felt shamed by her perceived behaviour. Sunambus killed a witness to his crime of rape. Justice Gore heard both cases at different sittings. He found Ako-Ove's crimes to be more serious than Sunambus's and sentenced Ako-Ove to a longer term of imprisonment. Despite the lack of connection between the cases, the governor-general considered the capital case files on the same day and the question of just punishment for both became entwined.

Field Marshall Sir William Slim was the governor-general of Australia from 1953 to 1959. By 1956, he had considered quite a few clemency cases out of PNG and was not by temperament and experience prepared to act as a rubber stamp. While the Crown's prerogative of mercy in Papua and New Guinea was invested in the governor-general of Australia, by convention, this authority was exercised with advice from the minister for territories, the federal Cabinet and the presiding judge through the Federal Executive Council. Despite this convention, Slim's moral judgements and subsequent intervention led to the equalisation of punishments of Ako-Ove and Sunambus.

---

13   Low security detention cells. Detainees would also undertake maintenance on infrastructure and grounds of administration buildings.
14   Gore to administrator, 27 April 1956; Ralph Gore, *Justice versus Sorcery* (Brisbane: Jacaranda Press, 1964).

Typically in PNG cases, evidence in the form of records that show a governor-general's impact upon clemency considerations is limited in scope and detail, as discussions held with ministers were not minuted. These two case files provide an unusually dense paper trail of the governor-general's impact. Both the direct text and the conversations implied by those letters illuminate Governor-General Slim's role in imposing Australian law on Papua New Guineans. The cluster of evidence surrounding these two cases indicates the growing importance of the Executive Council and the governor-general in PNG capital case reviews once all capital cases were referred to Canberra after 1954.

Martin Wiener has concluded that colonial jurisdictions were invariably:

> all conditioned by the tug of war between judges, Governors and other officials on the spot (backed up in varying degrees by the colonial office) attempting for the most part to enforce empire-wide laws and principles, and local white populations pushing to expand their own autonomy.[15]

In these cases, the 'tug of war' was between distinct ideas of colonialism among old colonialists, the B4s, on one side, and the new liberal colonialists, progressive legal pluralists and the conservative colonialism of William Slim on the other. Justice Gore, an old colonial, pursued a punitive regime that considered the relative sophistication of the offender, the pressures of cultural conventions and the needs of colonial control. He took a very cautious approach to the reception of capital punishment in communities less habituated to Australian colonialism. As Heather Douglas and Mark Finnane note of Australian colonial justice, 'courts constantly adjusted their proceedings to circumstances before them—makeshift translation, forcible detention of witnesses, mitigation of sentences—were all characteristics of white justice as it proceeded against Indigenous offenders'.[16] Despite this tendency being evident in PNG, liberals such as Paul Hasluck, minister for territories, wanted the law to be enforced more equally, regardless of cultural background. He also wanted a more uniform implementation of legal standards across PNG and Australia. Slim's views were more in keeping with Hasluck's than Gore's. Slim and Hasluck shared a sense of right and wrong and a determined belief in the deterrent and retributive

---

15   Martin J. Wiener, *Empire on Trial: Race, Murder, and Justice under British Rule 1870–1935* (New York: Cambridge University Press, 2009), 230.
16   Heather Douglas and Mark Finnane, *Indigenous Crime and Settler Law: White Sovereignty and Empire* (Basingstoke: Palgrave Macmillan, 2012), 10.

effects of capital punishment, resulting in a greater desire for the uniformity of punishments, rather than Gore's highly particularised sentencing based on a set of assumptions about Papua New Guineans. Mistakes and scandals in the criminal justice system increased Hasluck's and Slim's concerns. Progressive legal pluralists had little or no presence in this debate, with all of the other groups pursuing the implementation of Australian law leavened by discretion rather than plurality.

These cases demonstrate the informal networks that shaped judicial decision-making in PNG. As sentencing, in part, served to expiate the outrage felt by the community and promote its security, the immersion of Justice Gore in his small community gave him informal insight into how that might be achieved.[17] Gore's decisions in these cases, reflected his personal knowledge, and that of his brother judges, of this small expatriate community.

In this chapter, after presenting the events of the cases, the first dimension to be considered will be the character and evolving role of the governor-general in the Executive Council. The chapter will then consider the nature of the legal scandals that affected Slim's and Hasluck's faith in advice from PNG and resulted in the minister's support for a more liberal, Australian legal process there. In light of these pressures, ultimately, the Executive Council determined punishment through a negotiation between the different levels of government and their competing liberal, conservative and old colonial understandings of how best to pursue the colonial project in PNG.

'1956 was about the time to make a change': Granting clemency in 1956

Sunambus and Ako-Ove committed their crimes at a time in which the Federal Executive Council, and particularly Governor-General Sir William Slim, wanted to change the direction of sentencing and punishment in PNG. The Executive Council's beliefs had formed over several years of supervising clemency in PNG. Their personalities and experiences beyond PNG also shaped their decision-making about these two Papua New Guinean murderers. In addition, after some errors and scandals in the

---

17   J. V. Barry, G. W. Paton and G. Sawer, *An Introduction to the Criminal Law in Australia* (London: McMillian and Co., 1948), 95.

law in PNG, Hasluck expressed his dissatisfaction with the legal culture in PNG by rejecting proposed reforms and appointing a new chief justice from outside of PNG, and that appointment was emblematic of the change in direction he wanted for PNG.

Field Marshall Sir William Slim was sworn in as the governor-general of Australia on 8 May 1953. He had fought in the First World War in the Middle East and then transferred to the Indian Army in which he progressed rapidly, commanding Indian forces in Africa against the Italians and in Burma against the Japanese. He was lauded in particular for maintaining the morale of soldiers in the retreat from Burma and by leading the defeat of the Japanese in its recapture. After the war, he commanded the Imperial Defence College, as well as visiting British commands in a range of colonial settings and military bases around the world. His tenure as governor-general was very successful in terms of gaining respect and popularity among Australians.[18] However, recently his reputation has been shadowed by allegations of sexual abuse of children.[19] In 1960, he was created viscount and styled Viscount Slim of Yarralumla and Bishopston, showing his sense of connection to his vice-regal role in Australia. Yarralumla is the official residence of the Australian governor-general in Canberra.

Paul Hasluck's and Slim's official secretary, Murray Tyrrell, remember Slim as having a great interest in Papua New Guinea. Hasluck wrote favourably of Slim, quoting a 1960 letter to himself from Slim in his memoir:

> I don't admire everyone in your Government and I don't admire everything your Government has done. In fact I think they've done some damn silly things and some of your colleagues have said even more silly things than they have done. But there is at least one thing that your Government has done well and perhaps it is their best job.
>
> I do admire you and I do admire what you have done in New Guinea. I know something about this. It is the sort of thing that I was trying to do during most of my life. Your young chaps in New Guinea have

---

18   Michael D. De B. Collins Persse, 'Slim, Sir William Joseph (1891–1970)', *Australian Dictionary of Biography*, adb.anu.edu.au/biography/slim-sir-william-joseph-11713/text20937.

19   Independent Investigation Child Sexual Abuse, ' Inquiry—Child Migration Programmes Case Study Public Hearing Transcript Day 7', 17 July 2018, 214, www.iicsa.org.uk/key-documents/5746/view/public-hearing-transcript-17-july-2018.pdf; Mick Gentleman, 'William Slim Drive Is Set to be Renamed Following a Review Into Place Names in the ACT', ACT Government, 06 June 2019, www.cmtedd.act.gov.au/open_government/inform/act_government_media_releases/gentleman/2019/place-names-to-meet-community-standards.

gone out where I would never have gone without a battalion and they have done on their own by sheer force of character what I could only do with troops. I don't think there's been anything like it in the modern world.[20]

Hasluck used this excerpt as the conclusion to his chapter on law and order, which both praised PNG officials and highlighted his own claims to success. He wrote:

> What moved me was his [Slim's] particular reference to our patrol officers. When every other word of criticism has been spoken and other defects in our administration have been discussed, I stand in amazement close to reverence at what was done, to my personal knowledge, in the ten years between approximately 1952 and 1962 by young Australian patrol officers and district officers in areas of first contact. There were a few mistakes and a few weak brothers, but the achievement, with the resources available, revealed a quality of character and manhood that should make our nation mightily proud that these fellows were Australians.[21]

The prominence Hasluck gave to Slim's praise suggests that he respected the governor-general and that they shared some ideas about law and order in PNG.

Slim had an interventionist approach to his position. The memoirs of administration officials such as Ian Downs and Rachel Cleland concur with an oral history recording of Tyrrell who recalled Slim as being actively engaged with his vice-regal responsibility to PNG; Slim was able to draw on his colonial experience in India and Burma and this gave him the confidence to speak out on issues of colonial administration.[22] During his tenure, he and his wife Aileen visited PNG in 1953, 1956 and 1957, and those experiences further bolstered his confidence in applying his own judgements on policy in PNG.

The memorialisation of the Second World War dominated Slim's early interactions with PNG. As a senior military officer, he was well briefed on the geopolitical significance of the territories to Australia as well as the

---

20   Paul Hasluck, *A Time for Building: Australian Administration in Papua and New Guinea 1951–1963* (Carlton: Melbourne University Press, 1976), 83.
21   Ibid.
22   Persse, 'Slim, Sir William Joseph (1891–1970)'.

challenges of their continued possession. Slim visited PNG to officially open the war cemeteries and monuments for those killed in the Second World War.[23] However, he was interested in more than PNG as a battlefield.

Slim was also interested in the mechanics of colonial administration, as evident in the speeches he gave at the opening of development projects in PNG in which he discussed tutelage and loyalty and pictured Australia controlling and educating a loyal ally. Newspapers throughout Australia reported positively on Slim's views. For example, the *Cairns Post*, quoting from one of Slim's speeches to Papua New Guineans, wrote:

> 'I have been struck by the way you natives, especially through your village councils, are taking an increasing share in the control of your own affairs', he said. He added, 'This is a house you cannot build too fast if it is to stand.'[24]

The *Cairns Post* went on to note Slim's interest in the work of colonial officials:

> Field Marshal Slim said he had gained an admiration for the devotion of the officers of the administration for the manner in which they undertook their duties. Aided by their wives, and often in remote areas, they played a major part in the progress.

In Tasmania, the Burnie *Advocate* quoted Slim's sentiments indicating the tutelary relationship he pictured for Papua New Guineans:

> Sir William told the native people (his speech was later translated into pidgin by a government official) that he represented the Queen and that when she came to Australia soon, he intended to tell her what loyal men and women they were.

Tyrrell recalled Slim's interest and influence on PNG policy:

> He took a keen interest in Papua-New Guinea and would return from visits to demand of Minsters (including the present Governor-General, then Minister for Territories) [Paul Hasluck], 'What are we doing about this ... or that.'[25]

---

23   'Governor-General to Visit New Guinea', *Canberra Times*, 11 September 1953, 2; 'Sir William Slim Visits New Guinea', *West Australian*, 19 October 1953, 20; 'New Guinea Unveiling', *Courier-Mail* (Brisbane) 23 October 1953, 3; 'First Victory was in New Guinea', *Canberra Times*, 20 October 1953, 2; 'New Guinea Greets Number One', *Advocate* (Burnie, Tasmania), 22 October 1953, 2.
24   'Governor-General Back from New Guinea', *Cairns Post* (Queensland), 26 October 1953, 1.
25   'Slim's Code Was Based on "Duty and Discipline"', *Canberra Times*, 15 December 1970, 2. The resemblance to the then closed oral history file on Slim by Tyrrell is substantial.

5. 'THE CROWN AS THE FOUNT OF JUSTICE'

Tyrell indicated that Slim's views were given great credence in the Executive Council. Slim's commanding style ensured, for example, that papers sent to the council were promptly delivered, that matters were well explained and that significant issues were discussed. Tyrrell recalled that:

> He [Slim] was very firm with the government, the Ministers. Nobody took liberties with him, not even Prime Minister Menzies. He was a Field Marshall and a leader, a natural leader, every inch of the way. He didn't mind telling Ministers at all if he thought what they were doing was wrong or he didn't approve, he said so.[26]

Slim's experiences in PNG (such as pictured in Figure 5.2) and Tyrell's observations are indicative of Slim's commanding role in the Executive Council, including during clemency case reviews.

Figure 5.2: 'His Excellency the Governor-General of Australia, Field Marshal Sir William Slim, inspects a guard of honour of the Pacific Islands Regiment at Port Moresby', 1956.
Source: NAA: A1200, L26884, item 11756539.

---

26   Murray Tyrell, interview by Mel Pratt for the Mel Pratt collection [sound recording], 1974, transcript, 43–6, 49, 60–3, National Library of Australia.

163

A similar increase in the influence of the role of a minister for territories was also indicated in both these cases and related decisions. In the first years of his ministry, Hasluck had been reluctant to interfere in the administration of justice until he felt he had learned more about the operation of the courts in PNG. For example, Hasluck wrote in response to a petition to intervene in a legal proceeding in 1951:

> I am extremely unwilling to intervene politically in the processes of justice, and in any case I have not yet had time to familiarise myself with the operations of the courts in the Territory, but from the present case and from three or four other matters that have come under my notice, I am beginning to think that the whole of the processes of justice in the Territory may need review. Will you let me know whether the Department has formulated any views on this matter … at present I have little knowledge, but a very uncomfortable feeling on the subject.[27]

By 1954, Hasluck was much less reluctant. He began to look more closely at legal issues as he became more familiar with his portfolio. After questioning the officials who had outraged the Telefomin, his annoyance at the failures revealed in both the Kita Tunguan clemency decision and the Usamando case prompted him to exert greater influence on deliberations at the executive level. He had a strong perception of inequity before the law and was mistrustful of the evidence and processes presented to him. Yet, he still tended to presume that judges would generally know better than politicians and that there should be some separation in those roles. There are several ways in which that greater intervention and the obvious tensions between trust in the rule of law and mistrust of a particular judicial culture played out.

In 1956, determined to both change and control the direction of the law in PNG, Hasluck rejected a PNG administration proposal to introduce native courts; although intended to blend indigenous and Australian legal practices and ideology, Hasluck concluded that they would give Australian officials too much power and violate principles of the rule of law.[28] Hasluck was

---

27 Paul Hasluck, minute to Cecil Lambert, 8 January 1952, cited in Hasluck, *A Time for Building*, 182–91.
28 John Greenwell, *The Introduction of Western Law into Papua New Guinea*, unpublished manuscript given to author by John Greenwell, former first assistant secretary and director of Papua New Guinea Office Government and Legal Affairs Division, Department of External Territories, 1970–75, 23; Hasluck, *A Time for Building*, 186, 435. Ian Downs, *The Australian Trusteeship Papua New Guinea 1945–75* (Canberra: AGPS, 1980), 149–50.

astonished at the proposed legislation, which represented a major change in policy, and one that he had never heard of before. In a damning critique, he criticised the process and practicalities of the proposal.[29] According to Ian Downs, Hasluck's opposition was implacable and based on his mistrust of the informal practices at work in PNG.[30] Hasluck was knowledgeable on colonial legal situations, having written a history of Western Australia's native policies, including a critique of its haphazard native court system, which, Douglas and Finnane note, drew on the PNG model, but did not translate it well.[31]

The injustices and idiosyncrasies of the Western Australian system have been critically examined by Kate Auty, Heather Douglas and Mark Finnane; their analyses suggest a certain wisdom in Hasluck's suspicions that the law in PNG was being distorted at the whims of *kiaps* (government field officers) and was inherently racist.[32] Hasluck told his officials that he favoured a traditional view of British law and he emphasised its fairness and objective rigour:

> Furthermore, I have an old fashioned regard for the crown as the fount of justice and old-fashioned respect for English law. In a dependent and primitive society such as that in Papua and New Guinea, I think the individual native would have a greater expectation of justice in the fullest sense of the term by arrangements that would make courts in the British tradition more accessible to him.[33]

According to Downs, Hasluck's comprehensive rejection of the native court's proposal was dispiriting and engendered much bitterness in the PNG public service.[34] There was a divergence in the thinking of the administration and the executive about the proper direction of legal policy.

This divergence was further manifest in the appointment of the new chief justice of the Supreme Court of PNG in 1956. When Chief Justice Monty Phillips announced his retirement, Hasluck rebuffed Cleland's attempt to advise him on a replacement. He noted in his memoir that he told Cleland

---

29   Hasluck, *A Time for Building*, 186–91.
30   Downs, *The Australian Trusteeship*, 149–50.
31   See Hasluck, *Black Australians: A Survey of Native Policy in Western Australia, 1829–1897* (Melbourne: Melbourne University Press, 1942); Douglas and Finnane, *Indigenous Crime and Settler Law*, 114–7.
32   Downs, *The Australian Trusteeship*, 149–50; Kate Auty, *Black Glass: Western Australian Courts of Native Affairs 1936–54* (Freemantle: Freemantle Arts Centre Press, 2005), 12–21; Douglas and Finnane, *Indigenous Crime and Settler Law*, 4.
33   Hasluck, *A Time for Building*, 186–91.
34   Downs, *The Australian Trusteeship*, 150; Hasluck, *A Time for Building*, 191.

that, as an administrator, it was none of his concern. Hasluck decided that, while Gore was the 'best of the old system ... 1956 was about the time to make a change'.[35] He appointed a Victorian QC, Alan Mann, as chief justice, rather than Gore, the next in seniority and Cleland's preferred candidate. By appointing as the senior judge a mere QC from a different jurisdiction, Hasluck demonstrated his extreme suspicion of the PNG bench's culture, systems and traditions. Gore, who was acting as chief justice, and others were completely surprised, offended and flummoxed, indicating the extent to which there was a divergence of expectations between the minister, the PNG administration and the legal fraternity in PNG.[36]

This divergence was also evident in Hasluck's dissatisfaction with what he saw as the differential treatment of people. Hasluck intended to remediate this with a greater separation of powers to prevent 'weak brothers' having too much control over the lives and possessions of people, such as in Telefomin.[37] Despite the PNG legal system's view of itself, Hasluck concluded that British legal traditions were not entirely in operation. For example, inquests were not routinely held into the deaths of Papua New Guineans prior to 1956. In Hasluck's mind, double standards such as this were another way in which the PNG system was failing to operate in an orderly, Australian way, making it incapable of supporting the advancement of the PNG people to independence.

Hasluck did not spare himself from criticism. He noted that as interest in his work in PNG increased among observers in Australia and abroad, his capacity to act as a 'benevolent autocrat' decreased.[38] He did not want observers to view a system dominated by mistakes and injustice, or a system that was autocratic; he wanted observers to see a system that was advancing PNG towards some sort of self-management. Thus, by 1956, there was less rubber-stamping of clemency recommendations; the views of the executive and the administration had diverged. Henceforth, the executive depended less on advice from within the territories and more on its own judgement.

---

35   Hasluck, *A Time for Building*, 344–5.
36   Rachel Cleland, *Pathways to Independence: Story of Official and Family Life in Papua New Guinea from 1951–1975* (Cottesloe: Singapore National Printer, 1985), 198–9.
37   Hasluck, *A Time for Building*, 185–91.
38   Ibid., 197; Allan M. Healy, 'Monocultural Administration in a Multicultural Environment: The Australians in Papua New Guinea', in *From Colony to Coloniser: Studies in Australian Administrative History*, ed. J. J. Eddy and J. R. Nethercote (Sydney: Hale and Iremonger, 1987), 224.

'What's this bloody rubbish; we'll hang the bastard': Determining clemency

Ako-Ove's and Sunambus's clemency reviews entered into this climate of divergent views and became a forum for the Executive Council to attempt to reorder the process and relationship between the parties of clemency decisions.

As usual, the documents for reviewing capital sentences arrived as a bundle of several cases to be considered together by the governor-general-in-council. Justice Gore had recorded sentences of death, but, as mentioned, he had also recommended that, in lieu of the death penalty, Sunambus receive eight years imprisonment with hard labour and Ako-Ove receive ten years imprisonment with hard labour. Douglas and Finnane suggest that the brutal killing of women in these cases drew the attention of white colonists, and drew Slim's attention to Sunambus in particular.[39]

In his submission to the administrator, and therefore to the Cabinet and the Executive Council, Justice Gore did not explain why he had judged a recorded sentence as most appropriate in Sunambus's case, nor why he had settled on eight years as a suitable alternative punishment. However, he provided details of the isolation of Sunambus's home village, suggesting that he believed that Sunambus had had little contact with, and therefore had acquired little knowledge of, Australian colonial governance and law—or, as it was phrased then, 'sophistication'.[40] Gore's uncharacteristically brief submission belied his belief that his recommendation was sufficient and that the case should follow the established precedent of commutation for persons with a low level of Westernisation.

By contrast, Gore explained his decision to recommend a ten-year sentence for Ako-Ove. He emphasised: 'I am considering the place where the murder was committed, the circumstances of the killing and the reason therefore.' Gore took into account that this was a murder by a relatively well-educated man of his possibly adulterous wife in suburban Port Moresby, which had subsequently risked the safety of expatriates. Such a crime struck at the heart of Australia's advancement project in PNG. If Ako-Ove could not resist the impulse to kill out of shame, with all his education and exposure to Australian practices, what hope could there be for the less Westernised,

---

39 Douglas and Finnane, *Indigenous Crime and Settler Law*, 3.
40 Gore to administrator, 27 April 1956.

unless they could be intimidated by penalties? Ten years was a long sentence for Gore, who was seemingly aware that the Port Moresby expatriate community required that their fears be expiated through strong punishment and deterrence.[41]

However, Gore did take into account the mitigating factor of Papua New Guinean cultural practices in relation to masculine honour and provocation. In recording a sentence of death for Ako-Ove, he considered the powerful effect that he thought shame and honour had upon the behaviour of Papua New Guinean men in relation to adultery.[42] The mitigating effect of cultural issues was only considered in commutation, as it did not meet the legislative requirements that might result in a reduction of sentencing to the manslaughter range, as the relevant sections of the Criminal Code on provocation defences were interpreted very strictly in PNG.[43] Nevertheless, and consistent with his decision in Ako-Ove, Gore theorised in his memoir that shame was often an overpowering impulse to action for Papua New Guinean men: 'Shame is a characteristic no doubt of most people, but among the dark races the force of it seems to be more intense and its reaction takes queerer forms.'[44] Gore discussed this particularly in relation to their sexual status if their wives became known as adulterers; inevitably, his racist perceptions of these issues were significant to his recommendations on sentencing.[45]

In Sunambus's case, the powerful impetus that drove Sunambus to protect himself from shame by killing the witness to his actions was relevant to Gore, as it indicated knowledge of his wrongdoing. PNG legal practice and Gore's socio-legal theorising indicate that provocation, as defined by the code, was difficult to translate to Papua New Guinean behaviour. The solution had been to leave such considerations to clemency pleas to deter the cultural practice of vendetta, as many of the murder cases related to questions of shame and sexual fidelity.

With Donald Cleland on leave, the acting administrator was Rupert Wilson, an experienced public servant in both state and federal services. Appointed during Hasluck's tenure, Wilson had considerably less experience in PNG than Gore and Cleland. He endorsed Gore's recommendations as 'might

---

41 See Table 6.1 for average sentencing.
42 Gore to administrator, 8 May 1956.
43 *Criminal Code (Queensland, Adopted) in Its Application to the Territory of Papua*, sections 268 and 304, Pacific Island Legal Information Institute, www.paclii.org/pg/legis/papua_annotated/cca254.pdf.
44 Gore, *Justice versus Sorcery*, 103.
45 Ibid., see also ch. 15 ('Shame'), ch. 32 ('A Wanton's Antics') and ch. 26 ('The Wives of the Beautiful Valleys').

be apt'.⁴⁶ This phrasing might indicate that Wilson had no view on the matter; alternatively, it could be read as indicative of the change to the more formal Australian bureaucratic culture that Hasluck wanted. As a career public servant, Wilson would have been familiar with the need to maintain a certain distance from legal matters.

Yet, Slim found Gore's and Wilson's lack of moral reasoning inadequate and disputed the justness of the sentencing. Of Slim's interventions in clemency, Tyrrell wrote:

> On one occasion I remember, years and years ago, there was a particularly bad murder in New Guinea and the culprit was duly sentenced to death by the Supreme Court of Papua New Guinea, the papers came to the Governor-General for consideration, with the advice of the then Minister for Territories, and the Minister advised in his wisdom that the penalty should be reduced to imprisonment for life and the death penalty shouldn't be carried out.

However, Slim found the lawlessness and self-interested cruelty of Sunambus's slaying of an innocent woman serious enough to warrant hanging. Tyrrell explained:

> Dear Bill Slim was so enraged about the facts of the case that he wouldn't listen to the Minister, simply refused to listen to him. He said, 'If I was in the Far East, Tyrrell, that man would have been hung long since.' I pointed out to him that he had the right to reduce the sentences, but that was all. If the judge and the minister in their wisdom recommended a reduction of sentence, he couldn't increase the sentence.

Slim was frustrated by the limits that convention placed upon his notional powers; in PNG, a recorded sentence was always commuted. Despite this not necessarily being the practice in other jurisdictions, Slim was specifically advised that he did not have the power to confirm or change the sentence.⁴⁷ Tyrell continued:

---

46   R. W. Wilson to secretary, Department of Territories, 22 May 1956, NAA: A518, CQ840/1/3 PART 2, item 434881.
47   Murray Tyrrell, interview by Mel Pratt for the Mel Pratt collection [sound recording], 1974, transcript, 45, National Library of Australia; Stacey Hynd, '"The Extreme Penalty of the Law": Mercy and the Death Penalty as Aspects of State Power on Colonial Nyasaland, c. 1903–47', *Journal of East African Studies* 4, no. 3 (2010): 542–59; Stacey Hynd, 'Murder and Mercy: Capital Punishment in Colonial Kenya, ca. 1909–1956', *International Journal of African Historical Studies* 45, no. 1 (2012): 81–101; Andrew Novak, 'Capital Sentencing Discretion in Southern Africa: A Human Rights Perspective on the Doctrine of Extenuating Circumstances in Death Penalty Cases', *African Human Rights Law Journal* 14, no. 1 (2014): 24–42; NAA: A432, 1958/3143, item 7801743.

> Well, he was adamant about this, so I got on to my old friend Professor Bailey, then Solicitor General and secretary to the Attorney-General's Department, and said 'You'd better come out and talk to the Governor General and tell him some law.' So Professor Bailey did come out and we finally convinced him that the man wasn't to be hung. That particular episode went on for two or three days, it wasn't just a flash in the pan job at all.[48]

Being thwarted in his desire to confirm the death sentence, Slim worked more circuitously and wrote a minute to the Executive Council expressing concern over the difference in punishment for Sunambus and Ako-Ove. Slim's moral judgement of Sunambus seems to have revolved around the fact that he had killed out of self-preservation and cold calculation whereas Ako-Ove had killed in a more agitated state and was a cuckold. Slim wrote to his officials in the Department of Territories:

> I realise—having had experience in such matters—that it is difficult to balance relative guilt when one has not been present at the trials but it does seem to me that the offence in Minute No. 131 [Sunambus] is palpably much greater than that in No. 132 [Ako-Ove].
>
> If the criminal in minute 131 is not to be hanged, I would suggest an increase in the sentence of hard labour, in his case, or a reduction in that of the murderer in minute 132, preferably the former.
>
> Before I sign these warrants may I invite you to give them further consideration?[49]

Slim was attempting to alter the established custom and practice of the governor-general or governor signing off on the decisions of the Executive Council. Seeking to increase the recommended punishments, he 'invited' a reconsideration of these matters. This invitation to reconsider the sentencing recommendations pre-empted any decision and therefore skirted around questions of procedure. It also placed pressure on judges to sentence more harshly. Tyrell remembers the field marshal saying: 'What's this bloody rubbish; we'll hang the bastard.'[50]

---

48 Tyrrell interview, 46.
49 Sir William Slim to Executive Council, 15 June 1956, NAA: A518, CQ840/1/3 PART 2, item 434881.
50 'Slim's Code Was Based on "Duty and Discipline"'.

Slim sought to influence the outcome, arguing in a letter to the Department of Territories that Sunambus had been very reasonably condemned to death, as he lived in a well-regulated area, received no provocation and showed no remorse in his boasting about his crime. Slim deplored what he saw as a trend towards commuting vicious murders of young women.[51] In contrast, it would seem he found the suspicion of adultery sufficient provocation to moderate the punishment from death to imprisonment in Ako-Ove's case.

This was the means by which Slim hoped to circumvent the limits placed on his authority and better reflect his experiences of prewar colonialism in Asia: he sought new recommendations from the judges. He also wanted the recommended sentences to be re-examined and, at the very least, justifications for the proposed punishments to be stated clearly, so that he could better understand the reasoning.

Hasluck confirmed the restriction on Slim's notional power to confirm the recorded death sentence, and responded to this request by writing to the secretary of the Department of Territories requesting a review of recommendations from Gore:

> I informed Mr Tyrell that I would be quite willing to give further consideration to the Warrants mentioned in Minutes 131 and 132 and that in cases affecting the prerogative of the Crown, I recognise the propriety of the Governor-General's action and appreciate the way in which the action has been taken.[52]

Hasluck's endorsement of Slim's request highlighted the increasing centralisation of capital case reviews, the diverging views of the Executive Council and PNG judges, and the movement towards the greater enforcement of Australian norms in PNG cases. Accordingly, Hasluck suggested, via Secretary Lambert, that Sunambus's punishment be increased to fifteen years imprisonment with hard labour, and invited Gore to justify his recommendations more fully if he wished them to stand. Secretary Lambert conveyed Hasluck's message to the administrator who conveyed it to Gore.[53]

---

51   Slim to Executive Council, 15 June 1956.
52   Paul Hasluck to secretary, Department of Territories, 28 June 1956, NAA: A518, CQ840/1/3 PART 2, item 434881.
53   C. M. Lambert to acting administrator, 2 July 1956, NAA: A518, CQ840/1/3 PART 2, item 434881.

Seemingly immune to vice-regal and ministerial pressure, Gore defended his original recommendation. He raised a series of points that differentiated between the two crimes on the basis of the offenders' acculturation and the limits to Papua New Guineans' comprehension of the exercise of colonial power and law. In doing so, he exposed his use of informal channels of information—channels similar to those Cleland had used in the Kita Tunguan case.

In justifying his recommendations, Gore addressed the key question of the relative acculturation of the perpetrators. He argued that Ako-Ove was more acculturated and therefore more culpable: by his immersion in the Westernised economy of Port Moresby, Ako-Ove had tacitly accepted colonial authority and understood its laws. According to Gore, at twenty-four years of age, Ako-Ove 'was a sophisticated Native who had some training at the Idubada Technical School and was a married man'. Moreover, his people had 'been under government control for fifty years'. By contrast, Sunambus was younger and 'had not been away from his village', and his people 'had not had a great amount of contact with the administration'. Gore determined that Ako-Ove was more culpable because he had been brought up with the Australian legal system. Conversely, Sunambus was little used to Australian ways and had killed Dabi 'owing to tribal customs'.[54] This formulation demonstrated Gore's awareness or assumption that there would be limits to Sunambus's and his community's acceptance of severe punishment due to their limited contact with Australians; following Hubert Murray's injunction to build confidence gradually in newly controlled groups, Gore believed that working within such boundaries was the key to successful colonialism. Employing the case law of the PNG bench, Gore offered the two most common mitigating factors for commutation, lack of 'sophistication' and the pressure of custom, both of which placed limits on culpability.

Gore's second point was that Ako-Ove's murder of Muruku-Ako was more painful, crueller and more brutal than Sunambus's relatively quick and clinical execution of Dabi. Gore asserted that Sunambus 'killed the girl with no evidence of brutality'. By contrast, Ako-Ove 'killed his wife in a very brutal manner. She was horribly mutilated.'[55] This seems to take account of the retributive function of sentencing. Gore was entering into

---

54 Gore to acting administrator, 6 July 1956, NAA: A518, CQ840/1/3 PART 2, item 434881.
55 Ibid.

the explanation of crimes in culturally mediated terms, with an eye to the acceptance of punishment within each community: in this view, cruelty required greater retribution on the part of society for justice to be restored.

The final reason in Gore's report was evidently the most significant to him, based on its development, volume and placement as the takeaway point at the end of his text. It referred to community reactions to the crimes and the need to deter crimes in towns, as they caused fear and dismay among expatriates. Gore contrasted the remote location of Sunambus's crime, a distant island, with Ako-Ove's suburban rampage. However, with limited coverage of the events in the *South Pacific Post*, it is likely that Gore gained his knowledge of community outrage and fear from conversations on the street, at parties and at the club; from his immersion in the small community; and from his own perceptions of the world. Expatriates did not like murder in their neighbourhood, so they wanted a severe punishment; Gore knew of their, and his own, preference in this regard.

Gore asserted that he would have given Ako-Ove a heavier penalty if not for the 'consideration which has been advanced by His Excellency' regarding the provocative nature of Muruku-Ako's adultery. He described Muruku-Ako as a 'bad woman' whose death would have been regretted more if her husband had not doubted her fidelity. Such a motivation was enough to mitigate the sentence, but not constitute a defence of provocation. This is consistent with the sort of gender ideology in which an offender's culpability for the murder of a woman was judged according to their victim's perceived sexual morality.

Finally, Gore discussed the meaning of time to a man like Sunambus. Here he adopted the Papuan judicial and administrative practice of 'thinking black' and taking anthropological advice in observing the behaviour of perpetrators.[56] 'Thinking black' was what the long-term lieutenant-governor Hubert Murray and some of his experienced officials had advised new officials to practise. Gore professed some suspicion of it, but, nevertheless, seemed content to practise it. He asserted the following, rather extraordinary, understanding of Papua New Guinean thinking:

---

56   Gore, *Justice versus Sorcery*, 28; Francis West, *Hubert Murray: The Australian Pro-Consul* (Melbourne: Oxford University Press, 1968), 211; Clive Moore, *New Guinea: Crossing Boundaries and History* (Honolulu: University of Hawaii Press, 2003), 185. Moore notes some acceptance and some rejection of the concept among officials.

> Whether the prisoner is given eight, ten, twelve or fifteen years' imprisonment, it is still to him just a long time. I do not believe an unsophisticated native has a clear conception of difference between, say eight, ten or twelve years. The paramount object of the punishment is the prevention of crime. If this object can be achieved by the awarding of a lesser term of imprisonment, then I think one is justified in imposing the lesser term.[57]

Gore's justification of his recommendations demonstrates the gulf that existed between his understanding and perception of administrative and cultural issues, and Hasluck's and Slim's assumptions of a more universal sense of proportion and retribution.

This divergence of views illustrates, in the PNG context, Matthew Hilton's argument about the old norms of colonialism continuing alongside postwar goals and movements towards change. Gore's ideas about differentiation and benevolence were challenged by Hasluck's determination to be equal, and both were challenged by Slim's determination to maintain order through deterrence.[58] While Gore accepted the differences, Hasluck wanted to change the differences with uniform development, using, if necessary, the force of criminal law.[59] Hasluck's position is consistent with Douglas and Finnane's observation of Australian colonial practice:

> Legal interventions variously thought of as a civilising influence in which savage or barbarous subjects would be transformed in governable one (nineteenth and early twentieth century), or more recently as a program of citizenship, rights and normalisation.[60]

Hasluck criticised the sort of attitude Gore displayed, describing it in his memoir as a barrier to the civilising process:

> But some of the native affairs officers spoke too confidently of their own wisdom and I was gradually confirmed in my own ideas about the need to ensure that the courts and the police and the prisons were not regarded simply as instruments to serve the ends of orderly administration.[61]

---

57   Gore to acting administrator, 6 July 1956.
58   Matthew Hilton, 'Ken Loach and the Save the Children Film: Humanitarianism, Imperialism, and the Changing Role of Charity in Postwar Britain', *Journal of Modern History* 87, no. 2 (2015): 357–94.
59   Frederick Cooper and Ann L. Stoler, 'Tensions of Empire: Colonial Control and Visions of Rule', *American Ethnologist* 16, no. 4 (1989): 616.
60   Douglas and Finnane, *Indigenous Crime and Settler Law*, 8.
61   Hasluck, *A Time for Building*, 176.

Hasluck wanted consistency and equal treatment across the territories. Gore presumed that Papua New Guineans needed different treatment. Yet, with the appointment of Mann as chief justice and the minister's cooperation with Slim on Sunambus's and Ako-Ove's sentences, Hasluck's rejection of differential treatment was made clear.

Changing the recommendations: Slim manipulates the capital case review

Amok Native Gets Death Sentence.[62]

Gore's reply to Slim's and Hasluck's criticisms—and, notably, his failure to take up their invitation to reconsider his recommendations—did not satisfy Slim and Hasluck. They disagreed with Gore's differentiation between the offenders, so they did not follow the judge's recommendation as was usual. Instead, the Executive Council, in an unusual piece of executive intervention, equalised the punishments at ten years, increasing Sunambus's punishment from eight to ten years with hard labour.

Hasluck explained his rejection of Gore's reasoning thus:

> The youth and lack of sophistication of the offender may be sufficient reason for commutation, but are insufficient reason for reducing his [Sunambus's] punishment below a sentence of ten years imprisonment.[63]

Further, Hasluck asserted that Gore had not addressed the governor-general's questions about the lack of provocation and the barbarity of Sunambus's crime. Hasluck found reasons to bend conventional arrangements that also enabled him to pursue his own convictions, which, in this case, aligned with the governor-general's. While Slim wanted greater severity, Hasluck wanted greater consistency. Hasluck believed that PNG judges placed too much weight on their own interpretations of Papua New Guinean culture in making decisions, which he saw as being out of step with a rule of law that could progress the society towards advancement and autonomy.

---

62 'Amok Native Gets Death Sentence'. Amok here means crazy as in 'run amok', rather than a Papua New Guinean name.
63 Paul Hasluck to acting administrator, 1 August 1956, NAA: A518, CQ840/1/3 PART 2, item 434881.

Hasluck thus proposed a compromise between Slim's severity and Gore's determination. He used his authority as minister for territories to advise the Executive Council that both men should receive ten years with hard labour.[64] Formally, the Executive Council made the decision to equalise punishment at ten years. The Executive Council was guided by Hasluck's advice, but Hasluck had also listened to the views of the governor-general in recommending sentences more acceptable to Slim's sense of justice. This level of negotiation was either unprecedented or previously undocumented.

The divergence between Canberra's and Port Moresby's perceptions of the crimes is possibly a product of their different experiences. To a metropolitan politician or public servant such as Lambert or Hasluck, the deadly pursuit of a witness to rape through the jungles of Bougainville likely would be thought more harrowing than murder in a suburban kitchen. One might assume, then, that to an expatriate colonial official, the jungle was less terrifying and the possibility of murderous events between Papua New Guineans was viewed more philosophically; after all, such officials had been quite forgiving of the Telefomin killers in allowing that they should live despite the conspiracy to kill their colleagues and friends. In fact, the harsher sentence for Ako-Ove shows that it was the white home they feared for: it was what Mrs Wyatt, Mrs Jewell and Gore feared for, as shown in Gore's relatively harsh sentences for Kita Tunguan and Ako-Ove. The expatriates' oasis from the jungle needed to be inviolate. Thus, they were inclined to demand harsher punishments for men like Ako-Ove who endangered the security of white families. However, not being entirely in keeping with the aims of postwar colonialism for advancement and uniform development, it was altered by Hasluck, but not with a hanging as Slim's brand of old colonialism preferred.

Nevertheless, the discussion and debate over these two cases resulted in a new understanding among Executive Council members about the limits of their role in regard to mercy. The Executive Council was empowered to review capital cases, but it was required by custom to depend upon the advice of the minister and the judge. As we have seen, in these cases, the governor-general sought to contrive a larger role for his own judgement, but his sense of suitable punishment was not based on the same ideas as Hasluck and nor was it consistent with Gore's use of the Murray system.

---

64 Ibid.

The question might be asked as to whether Slim's and Hasluck's intervention was inappropriate or at least contrary to the principles of discretionary justice. Legal scholarship of the time supported discussion and negotiation by those responsible for making decisions about clemency. This was juxtaposed against the practice of automatic commutation. In 1957, Peter Brett, an eminent and respected Anglo-Australian scholar at the University of Melbourne, wrote an article for *Modern Law Review* critiquing automatic commutation.[65] He argued in favour of active discretionary negotiation within the Executive Council rather than automatic clemency, which Brett felt was inappropriate and anti-democratic.[66] He analysed the history of Australian Labor Party prime ministers and premiers commuting death sentences, arguing that they did so as a matter of conscience and belief rather than after appropriate consideration of the particulars of each case.[67] He reasoned that if capital punishment was to end, it should be done legislatively and not through discretionary practice alone. He objected to the apparent subversion of the will of the citizenry as expressed through the existing legislation and the failure to properly consider the case of each condemned person. Brett recommended vigorous debate over an appropriate penalty, with deference to judicial decisions, rather than discretion being completely repressed by a misuse of the royal prerogative. The debate over Sunambus's and Ako-Ove's sentences, which was more extensive than usual, was certainly in keeping with Brett's ideas and suggests that the Executive Council's intervention was not inappropriate, but, rather, was robustly democratic. Nevertheless, it was unusual for PNG.

The divergence of views on both the relative severity of Sunambus's and Ako-Ove's crimes and the appropriate way to encompass Papua New Guinean cultural diversity in sentencing and punishment indicates a tension between old colonial and conservative/liberal interpretations of colonial law enforcement. The final punishments for Sunambus and Ako-Ove were the result of negotiations between these points of view within established conventions. Slim had conservative ideas about how colonies should be run, which involved hanging and deterrence.[68] His position was that 'bastards' like Sunambus should be hanged. He rejected the

---

65   Louis Waller, 'Brett, Peter (1918–1975), *Australian Dictionary of Biography*, adb.anu.edu.au/biography/brett-peter-9577.
66   Peter Brett, 'Conditional Pardons and the Commutation of Death Sentences', *Modern Law Review* 20, no. 2 (1957): 131–47.
67   Barry Jones, 'The Decline and Fall of the Death Penalty', in *The Penalty is Death: Capital Punishment in the Twentieth Century*, ed. Barry Jones (Melbourne: Sun Books, 1968).
68   Slim to Executive Council, 15 June 1956.

mitigating factors of cultural misapprehension, which were exactly the sort of mitigating factors PNG judicial culture encouraged judges to consider. Australia's policy of advancement and trusteeship, which Hasluck endorsed, called for liberality; however, in practice, treating people equally resulted in sterner punishments. In this case, then, Slim's prewar conservative colonialism and Hasluck's liberal desire for equal treatment resulted in Sunambus receiving a harsher punishment than he might otherwise have received. Sunambus could not be hanged, as, once the judge had recorded, rather than pronounced, a sentence of death, it could not be overridden. This convention was inflexible, irrespective of the governor-general's wishes.

Conclusion

Under Sir William Slim, the role of the governor-general in capital case reviews became more than a disinterested nod. His commanding nature led him to make firm judgements about the cases he was reviewing and, in some cases, to demand changes that suited his conservative view of law enforcement and justice. In learning to use the process, he found ways to change the advice he was given, which then allowed him to more agreeably enact the royal prerogative of mercy. He was able to express his more conservative approach to colonial control through harsher punishments for offenders, first with Sunambus and later with others.[69]

In this respect, Slim found a willing partner in Hasluck, who, while wishing to respect the role and expertise of judges, was increasingly uncertain about the quality and impartiality of the justice system in PNG. Hasluck found the exercise of justice too entangled with administration and wished for a more independent legal system exercised in a uniform manner across the territories. He wished for colourblind liberality, rather than permissiveness, idiosyncrasy and conversations between mates: jabber. As Frederick Cooper and Ann Stoler suggest of other postwar colonies, Hasluck wanted advancement and development and he wanted the legal system to pursue it.[70] In these two cases, these questions came into play in clemency considerations.

---

69   Sir William Slim to Paul Hasluck, 5 December 1957, NAA: M331, 8, item 511120.
70   Cooper and Stoler, 'Tensions of Empire'.

5. 'THE CROWN AS THE FOUNT OF JUSTICE'

The cases of Ako-Ove and Sunambus were watershed events in the history of PNG capital case reviews, with William Slim and Paul Hasluck demanding different outcomes from those proposed by the PNG Supreme Court. Hasluck felt that a liberal, egalitarian model of justice would be better for Australia's developmental goals and, therefore, for Australia's reputation, than an individualised system that depended on paternalistic and racist judgements about the nature of the colonised. As Wiener has argued of postwar colonialism, Hasluck had to walk the walk of the modern colonial power.[71] While previously the Department of Territories and the Executive Council had leaned heavily on advice from the colony, as they did in the Telefomin, Kita Tunguan and Usamando cases, in these two cases they showed a greater confidence in engaging with the substantive reasoning and exercise of sentencing discretion, and challenged the expert status of the colonial officials. In doing so, the Department of Territories and the Executive Council sought to impose their new direction for capital punishment and clemency on the B4s, including experienced old hands such as Ralph Gore.

---

71   Martin J. Wiener, *Empire on Trial: Race, Murder, and Justice under British Rule, 1870–1935* (New York: Cambridge University Press, 2009), 230.

6

'We do not think this is a sufficient deterrent': *R. v. Aro of Rupamanda, 1957*

Aro had lived all his life in the neighbourhood of Wabag in the Highlands village of Rupamanda.[1] A subdistrict headquarters, Wabag had a mission, a native hospital, a primary school, an airfield and *calaboose* (police gaol cells).[2] Although Aro was too old to have attended the school at the mission, his adult life had been spent under Australian law; like Usamando, he was poised between two worlds. As independence leader and politician Albert Maori Kiki put it, Papua New Guineans of Aro's and his age had experienced 'ten thousand years in a lifetime'.[3]

Due to a spear injury suffered in his youth, Aro was largely unemployed and lived off the labour of his two wives, Tipiwan and Ruai, as well as the sustenance derived from his family group. He had little property other than a hut in the 'garden', a small farm and a 'woman's house'—a separate house for women; a custom of his people. Evidently, his community regarded his claims of incapacity with some suspicion; the villagers saw him as indolent. Like Usamando, he was not successful by the terms of either local or Australian standards. In contrast, the big men of his village regarded his wives positively, as the *tultul* (deputy headman) Lipi told the court: 'He is

---

1   Unusually for this period, there is a full typed transcript of the trial available in addition to the usual summaries and judgement by the judge and other officials. Therefore, more specific references are possible.
2   D. M. Cleland to secretary, 17 September 1957, NAA: A4926, 882, item 4361268.
3   Albert Maori Kiki, *Kiki, Ten Thousand Years in a Lifetime: A New Guinea Autobiography* (Canberra: Cheshire Melbourne, 1968).

what we call a rubbish man … So far as I am aware Tipiwan and Ruai were hardworking women and faithful to the defendant.'[4] Tipiwan had borne a daughter in January 1957 and Ruai had two children by him, Preak, aged four and Pusi aged six.

According to court testimony, Aro was suspicious and litigious in regard to his wives. He suspected that the villagers and Tipiwan and Ruai and their families were all conspiring to cheat him. Aro had suspected Tipiwan of adultery early in their marriage. Adultery was an offence under the native ordinances.[5] Native ordinance cases were heard by the district officer, the leading Australian administrative official within districts, in the Court of Native Affairs, which dealt with issues pertaining to village life such as adultery, sorcery and theft.[6] Tipiwan had eventually allayed these suspicions and had worked hard in the garden and at child raising, but Aro's suspicions returned.[7] He took Ruai to court at the beginning of April 1957, accusing her of adultery. The action did not succeed, which made him angry.[8] He then attempted a reconciliation with Tipiwan by offering her a pig, but this upset Ruai who threatened him with court action for giving away her pig. He later testified that he was angry that they thought that, just because the Europeans were near, he could not hurt them. Thus, at the same time as rejecting the idea that Australian law could protect his wives, he tried to use it to protect his own honour and prerogatives. At the time of his capital case review, this selective use of Australian law made it unclear whether he was embracing only those aspects of Australian colonialism that he thought would benefit him, or whether he understood its fundamental principles to the extent required for execution instead of clemency. Regardless, the apparent hypocrisy evidently marked him as a man of poor character in the minds of his *tultul*, Lipi of Rupamanda, and Anglo-Saxon gentlemen like Governor-General Sir William Slim.

---

4   *Tultul*, deputy to the Australian-appointed leader of the village, the *luluai*. Testimony, Lipi of Rupamanda, trial transcript (second indictment, murder of Ruai), 10, NAA: A4926, 882, item 4361268.
5   *Native Regulation Ordinance, 1908–1930—Native Regulations 1939* (Papua), section 84, Pacific Island Legal Information Institute, www.paclii.org/pg/legis/papua_annotated/nro19081930nr1939446/.
6   John Greenwell, *The Introduction of Western Law into Papua New Guinea*, unpublished manuscript given to the author by John Greenwell, former first assistant secretary and director of Papua New Guinea Office Government and Legal Affairs Division, Department of External Territories, 1970–75, 20.
7   Statement of defendant, Aro of Rupamanda, 10 April 1957, NAA: A4926, 832, item 4361268; testimony of Aro, *The Queen v. Aro of Rupamanda*, trial transcript (second indictment, murder of Ruai), 7–8, NAA: A4926, 882, item 4361268.
8   Allocutus of Aro, *The Queen v. Aro of Rupamanda*, trial transcript (second indictment, murder of Ruai), 9–10. NAA: A4926, 882, item 4361268.

On 10 April 1957, Tipiwan, Ruai and Aro sat with their children in the garden hut. Ruai made up a little song about Aro always wanting to 'make Court' and suggested that his father had probably been the same. Tipiwan joined in the singing. The song caused Aro to become violent, probably as a reaction to the inference that Aro was the child of adultery, as accusations of adultery were taken to court. In his testimony, Aro said that he warned them: 'Are you trying to make me angry?' They continued to sing and Aro shouted: 'I didn't buy you so that should misbehave all the time. You two are humbugging. I will teach you not to.'[9] Aro then took up his axe and attacked his two wives while their children looked on. It took repeated blows about the head and abdomen with his axe to kill the women. Tipiwan's fingers were severed as she sought to protect herself. Ruai's abdomen was torn open by the blows.[10]

Aro then gathered up his children and took them to his relative, Piagon, who was employed at the local hospital. He told him: 'I have killed my wives.'[11] He asked his relative to care for the children and then hurried up the track to the subdistrict headquarters office and confessed. He was taken into the security of Australian custody, which made him safe from revenge attacks. To administration officials and the Executive Council, this action seemed to indicate two things: that Aro expected to survive under Australian justice, and that he knew he would not have survived a community-based vendetta. Aro was arraigned in the lower court where he again confessed to the murders.[12]

In the Supreme Court sitting at Wabag, the murders were heard as two separate indictments: Tipiwan's murder first and then Ruai's. Crown Prosecutor J. Greville Smith, later to become the PNG secretary for law, planned this separation to ensure at least one successful case.[13] In the court transcript, the prosecutor cited the Australian High Court judgement in *R. v. Packett, 1937*, probably because he feared that Aro's liability would be

---

9   Crown Prosecutor J. Smith, 'Prosecution Opening', *The Queen v. Aro of Rupamanda*, Wabag Criminal Sittings, 6 August 1957, trial transcript (first indictment, murder of Tipiwan), 1, NAA: A4926, 882, item 4361268.
10 Testimony, John William Jensen, senior medical assistant, *The Queen v. Aro of Rupamanda*, Wabag Criminal Sittings, 6 August 1957, trial transcript (first indictment, murder of Tipiwan), 6–8, NAA: A4926, 882, item 4361268.
11 Testimony, Piagon, *The Queen v. Aro of Rupamanda*, Wabag Criminal Sittings, 6 August 1957, trial transcript (first indictment, murder of Tipiwan), 2, NAA: A4926, 882, item 4361268.
12 E. B. Bignold to administrator, *The Queen v. Aro of Rupamanda*, 13 September 1957, NAA: A4926, 882, item 4361268.
13 Ibid.

mitigated to manslaughter on the basis of loss of control due to provocation in one or both counts; Greville Smith was adamant that the cases should be heard separately so that the facts of one did not contaminate the facts of the other.[14] Further, failures of due process had occurred in PNG courts in 1957 and this may well have made the prosecutor wary of procedural and technical disqualifications of the charges.[15] The prosecution was apparently intent on punishing a brutal crime.

Justice Esme Bignold, the presiding judge, agreed to two separate trials. He had a family background in colonial law. His grandfather had been a judge in Calcutta and his father, Harold Baron Bignold, had been a writer, lyricist, barrister, editor and legal scholar in New South Wales before and after the federation.[16] During the 1920s, Esme Bignold had practised as a barrister in New South Wales with his father. In 1930 he had moved to Papua to be a Crown law officer.[17] He enlisted in the Royal Australian Air Force in 1939 and served until 1948, then returned to the law in PNG.[18] Bignold had broad experience in PNG and was well-regarded by his fellow judges, although his poor health meant that he did not travel the circuit outside of the major towns very often.[19]

Pronouncing Aro guilty of the wilful murder of both women, Bignold stated: 'I am sorry to say that there seemed to me to be no mitigating circumstances.' He dismissed adultery as a mitigating provocation in the murders and instead cited Aro's long history of suspecting adultery as suggestive of premeditation. He also pointed out that Aro, having immediately reported his own crimes, appeared to show 'that he well knew that his acts were unlawful'.[20] Unusually for his sentencing record, Bignold, seeming to find the crimes more than usually abhorrent, pronounced a sentence of death on both indictments. Further, in his capital case review submission, he recommended that the sentences be carried out: clearly, Bignold saw the

---

14   *R. v. Packett [1937]* HCA 53; (1937) 58 CLR 190 (3 September 1937), High Court of Australia, *AUSTLII*, classic.austlii.edu.au/cgi-bin/sinodisp/au/cases/cth/HCA/1937/53.html?stem=0&synonyms =0&query=%20Packett,%201937; Justice Barry, 'The Defence of Provocation', *Res Judicata*, no. 35 (1950), www.austlii.edu.au/au/journals/ResJud/1950/35.pdf.
15   Those mistakes and problems of the justice system are laid out later in the chapter.
16   'Bignold, Hugh Baron (1870–1930)', *Australian Dictionary of Biography*, adb.anu.edu.au/biography/bignold-hugh-baron-5234.
17   Alfred James Kent, 'Bignold, Esme Baron', *NSW Law Almanac 1924* (Sydney: Government Printer, 1924); *NSW Law Almanac 1930* (Sydney: Government Printer, 1930), 75; *NSW Law Almanac 1944* (Sydney: Government Printer, 1944), 70.
18   NAA: A9300, Bignold E. B., item 5372360.
19   Ralph Gore, *Justice versus Sorcery* (Brisbane: Jacaranda Press, 1964), 203.
20   Bignold to administrator, 13 September 1957, NAA: A4926, 882, item 4361268.

crimes as inexcusable, wilful murder, and he was joined in this view by the local people, who also desired Aro's death. Unusually, Bignold made no alternate recommendation for a term of imprisonment, further underlining his pronounced sentence of death.

When the capital review process moved to Donald Cleland, administrator of PNG, he recommended clemency with the relatively severe sentence of twelve years with hard labour.[21] Cleland argued that, while Aro seemed to know what the law was, the people of the Wabag area were 'primitive' and the effect of a hanging could not be predicted. Indeed, he thought it might lead to the 'framing of those who [local] people wanted put out of the way'. He also 'found it difficult' to differentiate this crime from others of a similar type that had resulted in clemency, thus raising a justice question about the consistency of punishment. He was unconvinced that an execution would further the administrative project of modernising and folding people into a community policed by Australian law and thought imprisonment to be a better vehicle for acculturation.[22]

Minister for Territories Paul Hasluck recorded no recommendations under his own signature; instead, the notes for the Department of Territories Cabinet submission for this capital case review endorsed Cleland's recommendation. The department 'assumed that considerations of native policy other than fit punishment' motivated Cleland's recommendation.[23] While not exactly an enthusiastic endorsement, it emphasised to Slim the tendency of the administration to avoid heavier punishment, which the governor-general saw as risking the proper work of justice and deterrence.

Despite the recommendations of the administrator and the Department of Territories, the Executive Council ordered Aro's execution.[24] While the Executive Council usually followed the recommendation of Department of Territories officials, the precedent of Usamando, another 'rubbish man', and the failure to hang Ako-Ove and Sunambus, which had been the governor-general's preferred course of action, were seemingly influencing Aro's case. A more assertive position for the Executive Council was being normalised. Aro was hanged in Lae on 16 November 1957.[25]

---

21   On relative leniency, see Table 6.1 in this chapter.
22   Cleland to secretary, 17 September 1957.
23   'Notes of Submission No. 882', NAA: A4926, 882, item 4361268.
24   Cabinet minute, 'Decision No. 1035, Submission No. 882', 15 October 1957, NAA: A4926, 882, item 4361268.
25   'Death Penalty Carried Out on N.G. Native', *Canberra Times*, 18 November 1957, 7.

Administration officials local to Wabag and Rupamanda had advocated for a public hanging, or at least the public return of the body to Wabag and Rupamanda, as they claimed that the people would not believe that the hanging had occurred otherwise. Cleland did not take their advice, and one of the patrol officers who had advocated for a public hanging, Graham Hardy, wrote that some local people did not believe Aro was hanged, but instead said they saw him walking around.[26] Such anecdotes suggest that Slim failed in his purpose in terms of local deterrence. Without the deterrent effect of the hanging, it seemed to Hardy and his colleagues that even the supposed legitimation of Australian authority provided through clemency would have no impact on the local community. That expatriate officials believed that Papua New Guineans did not believe the hanging had occurred might go some way towards explaining why judges rarely resorted to that penalty. In contrast, favourable Australian and international newspaper coverage of the execution suggests that external legitimation of Australian colonialism was successful in this case.

Outlining the chapter

Governor-General Sir William Slim believed strongly in the educative and deterrent effect of the death sentence in the wider community and used Aro of Rupamanda's case to extend his views of justice to Aro's region. This was possible in 1957 because Slim and Hasluck had actively exercised their power in previous years. Hasluck, in particular, had become increasingly concerned about leniency stemming from racism—however benevolently intended—in the sentencing practices of the judges of the PNG Supreme Court. Thus, Slim and Hasluck welcomed Justice Bignold's response to the Executive Council's prompt for harsher sentences—that is, Bignold's pronounced death sentence, which allowed for Aro's execution.

In PNG, paternalism was a key part of liberal postwar colonialism, with its goal to 'advance' PNG through the UN Trusteeship and to inculcate Papua New Guineans, body, mind and soul, with Western modernity—with 'civilisation'. Martin Wiener's general observation of the nature of colonialism holds true of PNG:

---

26 Graham Hardy, 'Murder Trial of Aro of Rupamanda: Graham Hardy', *PNG Alumni Association Library*, www.pngaa.net/Library/Aro.htm.

Throughout the nineteenth and twentieth centuries, most officials saw most of the peoples they ruled over as simply less advanced in the universal march of civilization, a march led by themselves. Full 'civilization' was, in the view of most [of] them, attainable by virtually all subjects, in the fullness of time.[27]

Adding to Wiener's observations, Peter Gibbon argues that the paternalism inherent to trusteeship and colonialism was tolerable to liberals because it was temporary, even if the end date was unclear.[28]

The killing of wives, decried by Australian officials as not in keeping with people on a forward march into civilisation, was a particular justice issue that Slim and administration officials wanted to deter with strong penalties, which local people supported. Yet, even in pursuing this apparent good, a colonial power play was evident, for, in highlighting their work to prevent the killing of women, colonial officials employed a classic 'savagery' trope, which, as Regis Tove Stella argued, further justified the colonial presence.[29] Decrying Aro's killing of two innocent women facilitated a powerful and gendered representation of the savage 'other'—that is, killers of women who needed the colonial project to control them. in In Slim's mind, execution in this case would assist the community to advance morally and politically while also projecting the need for colonialism. As with Usamando, Aro was not the kind of man they wanted for the new country they claimed to be building; he did not embody the right kind of masculinity.

In 1957, the problem for Australian officials was determining at what point on the 'march' towards civilisation Papua New Guineans were; determining that placement was the meat of much discussion in the capital case review file for *R. v. Aro of Rupamanda, 1957*. What the clemency files usually called a lack of sophistication—a mitigating factor in granting mercy—had to be interpreted differently in this case, as it was seen to show Papua New Guineans using Australian justice selectively.[30] Many studies have shown that a synthesis of local systems and imported law was common in colonial settings; this case, unlike others in this book, provides clear evidence for the nature of Papua New Guineans' synthesis of Australian and their own

---

27   Martin J. Wiener, *Empire on Trial: Race, Murder, and Justice under British Rule, 1870–1935* (New York: Cambridge University Press, 2009), 231.
28   Peter Gibbon, Benoit Daviron and Stephanie Barral, 'Lineages of Paternalism: An Introduction', *Journal of Agrarian Change* 14, no. 2 (2014): 165–89.
29   See Regis Tove Stella, *Imagining the Other: Representation of the Papua New Guinean Subject* (Honolulu: University of Hawaii Press, 2007), 139.
30   Greenwell, *The Introduction of Western Law*.

practices in this region of PNG in 1957.[31] However, from the perspective of the Executive Council, the difficulties of interpreting Aro's idiosyncratic embrace of the rule of law led to different interpretations of the extent of Aro and his community's level of sophistication and embrace of Australian law. In the end, Slim and the Executive Council overruled Cleland's suspicion that the embrace of Western law in Wabag and Rupamanda was insubstantial. They preferred a strong deterrent message to make clear the limits of 'civilisation' and Australian justice for a community that had produced an individual who had tried to game the system.

This case also highlights Hasluck and his department's increasing mistrust of the Supreme Court and policing systems in 1957, suspicions that compounded their pre-existing concerns about the B4s and the old colonial Murray system. The reliability of other arrests and investigations undertaken in PNG came under question following a series of scandals that shook the institutions of law enforcement. Cleland recommended mercy for Aro because he was shaken and uncertain about policing and the courts. While Hasluck recognised that there were administrative problems in PNG and tended to favour mercy, in this case, Slim and the Executive Council rejected the advice to commute Aro's sentence of death, preferring instead to send a strong message of deterrence and racially blind justice.

Aro's case was the last hanging in colonial PNG. Subsequently, punishment standards moved away from the death penalty and mandatory death sentences were abolished in 1964.[32] As Aro was the last person hanged by Australian authorities, and, indeed, the last person hanged in PNG at all, this case provides a measure of the limits of colonial mercy. It sheds light on the message government intended to send by enforcing such punishment, and helps to describe the evolving moral imperative Australia felt in the context of the shifting policy demands of maintaining a legitimate, and strategic, hold on PNG across the period of this book.

---

31 See, for example, Manuela Lavinas Picq, 'Between the Dock and a Hard Place: Hazards and Opportunities of Legal Pluralism for Indigenous Women in Ecuador', *Latin American Politics and Society* 54, no. 2 (Summer, 2012): 6–7; Robert Cribb, 'Legal Pluralism and Criminal Law in the Dutch Colonial Order', *Indonesia*, no. 90 (October 2010): 47–66; Sally Engle Merry, 'Legal Pluralism', *Law & Society Review* 22, no. 5 (1988): 873.
32 The end of mandatory sentencing is analysed in the next chapter.

'The question has caused me considerable concern over the past two or three years'[33]

Australians in PNG in 1957 were concerned that Australian law was not successfully deterring crime. Alarm in the expatriate community over personal security was reported in the *South Pacific Post* (*SPP*), spurred by incidents of unusual attacks on women and several sensational and unsolved murders. The rhetorical use of women's security to demand greater colonial power, also evident in the *Kita Tunguan* decision in 1954, was an ongoing trope that heightened the call for harsher punishments and deterrence. In 1957, several scandals over the legality of police practice and the reliability of the courts compounded expatriates' and the federal government's distrust of PNG systems.

After the *SPP* reported two assaults on white women during January 1957, Cleland stated that he would investigate the prevalence of such attacks.[34] Subsequent attacks on women saw the paper report claims from an expatriate politician, E. A. James, that expatriates were leaving the colony out of a sense of insecurity and that something had to be done.[35] Such reports kept coming, heightening the paper's campaign for more severe punishment.[36] The Department of Territories and Hasluck monitored the *SPP*'s agitation; Cleland was well aware of its contents.

Vicious and unsolved murders in Rabaul in 1957 further contributed to the perception of insecurity. Carol Wright and Daniel Ng's bodies were found in dense bush on the outskirts of Rabaul. Wright was the child of a mixed-race relationship and Ng was a son of a well-off Chinese family. Local Tolai people felt so insecure and aggrieved at being suspected of the murders that they initiated a vigilante search in February to try to find the killer.[37] In October, just days before Aro was condemned by the Executive Council, the coroner returned a finding of 'murder by person or persons unknown'.[38] This prompted further calls for decisive action against crime among both Papua New Guineans and expatriates.

---

33 Paul Hasluck to governor-general of Australia, 18 December 1957, NAA: M331, 8, item 511120.
34 'Report Called for: Two More Women Attacked', *South Pacific Post*, 9 January 1957, 1.
35 'People Leaving the Territory', *South Pacific Post*, January 1957, 1.
36 Ibid.; 'Council Backs Judge on Native Attacks', *South Pacific Post*, 16 January 1957, 11; 'Two Servants Gaoled for Sex Offences', *South Pacific Post*, 24 April 1957, 5; 'Women Attacked in Port Moresby', *South Pacific Post*, 24 April 1957, 12; 'TAC Seeks Protection for Boroko Women', 29 May 1957, 13.
37 'Tolais Seek Murderer', *South Pacific Post*, 13 February 1957, 1.
38 'Coroner Ends Inquest on N.B. Murder', *South Pacific Post*, 2 October 1957, 3.

This lack of faith in the policing and security of the community was intensified by other news stories of 1957. At the same time as the Wright/Ng murder was captivating Rabaul, the 1956 conviction of Fredrick Smith for the murder of another Rabaul interracial couple, Adele Woo and Leo Wattemena, was overturned by the High Court of Australia on the basis of poor evidence, poor police methods and the nature of the confession extracted from Smith, a young, mixed-race man.[39] This censure of policing in well-staffed and Westernised Rabaul was a shock to all sections of the PNG expatriate community. The High Court essentially accused Rabaul police of victimising the 'half-caste' Smith.[40] The editor of the *SPP* wrote that this judgement 'must give Territory legal authorities and the police misgivings about how the course of justice runs in this country'.[41] Cleland was so unsettled by the incapacity of the police to prove their case to an Australian standard that he promised to use scarce funds to purchase scientific instruments and new equipment such as tape recorders and cameras to raise the standard of police investigations and evidence gathering.[42] The Port Moresby Town Advisory Council, an NGO group of expatriate residents, similarly called for a fingerprint expert to be hired by the PNG police.[43] The findings also raised concerns about the independence and capacity of Chief Justice Phillips who heard the case, but he had retired in January 1957.[44] While there were obvious concerns about the capacity of the police to conduct enquiries, there was also alarm at the unsolved murders. The *SPP* reported that Rabaul shops had completely sold out of guns, demonstrating disquiet in the community.[45]

Adding insult to expatriate disquiet and anxiety about racism to Canberra's concerns, a scandal broke involving Assistant District Officer Anderson, who was accused by a European medical assistant (junior doctor) of beating and torturing Papua New Guineans in the process of investigating crimes at his district headquarters. An investigation by the Crown Law Office led

---

39 'Smith Acquitted', *South Pacific Post*, 23 January 1957, 1.
40 'Smith Released', *South Pacific Post*, 30 January 1957, 1; *Smith v. R. [1957] HCA 3; (1957) 97 CLR 100 (21 January 1957)*, Australian Legal Information Institute, University of Technology Sydney and University of New South Wales, www5.austlii.edu.au/au/cases/cth/HCA/1957/3.html.
41 'Editorial: The High Court Judgement', *South Pacific Post*, 30 January 1957, 14.
42 'Scientific Equipment Promised to Police', *South Pacific Post*, 1 February 1957, 1.
43 'Finger-Print Expert Wanted', *South Pacific Post*, 20 March 1957, 5.
44 He died of cancer in May of 1957, indicating a probable reason for retirement rather than being dispirited at having his judgement so criticised. Paul J. Quinlivan, 'Phillips, Sir Frederick Beaumont (1890–1957)', *Australian Dictionary of Biography*, adb.anu.edu.au/biography/phillips-sir-frederick-beaumont-8034.
45 'The Drum', *South Pacific Post*, 30 January 1957, 1.

to a recommendation of reprimands and transfers for all involved; however, once publicity about the accusations reached Australia, the Department of Territories insisted on prosecution.[46] Anderson was charged; convicted; sentenced to twenty-one months imprisonment by Chief Justice Alan Mann in the PNG Supreme Court; and sent to Long Bay Gaol, Sydney, as the administration did not imprison European offenders with Papua New Guinean prisoners. The High Court, on appeal, found the sentence of twenty-one months for assault and unlawful custody too severe and reduced it considerably to time served, approximately eight weeks, and the rest on bail.[47] Anderson's case seemed to provide yet another instance of uncertainty, discord and distrust in the legal affairs of PNG. Rachel Cleland recalled that 'both Don [her husband] and the Minister [Hasluck] were [troubled by it] at the time'.[48] The simmering mistrust was further intensified by controversies over false translations by court translators who were seeking to manipulate the outcomes of trials.[49] These controversies struck at the heart of the reliability of judgements in the Supreme Court.

According to Rachel Cleland, whose memoir *Pathways to Independence* was, in many ways, a response to Hasluck's *Time for Building*, in that it challenged his positive representation of his work, such events:

> cast long shadows, seriously affecting the respect for the institutions [of the courts and police] … and undermining the confidence, both to the people of Papua New Guinea, and of those responsible for governing them.[50]

Many Native Affairs officers, including patrol officers, feared that their usual ways of managing Papua New Guineans would lead to prosecution. Indeed most expatriates felt that Anderson was prosecuted on poor evidence and only because Canberra politicians, in particular Hasluck, feared the public reaction to sensationalised reportage. Indicating expatriate rejection of the judgement of the metropolitan authorities, a large fund was raised among expatriates to support Anderson and his wife through the legal process and Anderson was welcomed back to PNG as a private businessman

---

46   Rachel Cleland, *Pathways to Independence: Story of Official and Family Life in Papua New Guinea from 1951–1975* (Cottesloe: Singapore National Printer, 1985), 202.
47   'Former Native Affairs Officer Wins Appeal', *Canberra Times*, 13 December 1957, 3; Cleland, *Pathways to Independence*, 204–5.
48   Cleland, *Pathways to Independence*, 205.
49   'Man Discharged: Interpreter Says He Would Falsify Evidence', *South Pacific Post*, 6 January 1957, 9.
50   Cleland, *Pathways to Independence*, 200–2.

after his release.⁵¹ To Hasluck, with his concerns about Raj-like colonialism in PNG, this signalled that racism was, in fact, a pervasive feature of the B4 and administration communities. To address these concerns, a commission of inquiry into PNG policing followed, and public service commissioners travelled around the territories investigating areas where the violent enforcement tactics allegedly used in Anderson's district were suspected of being employed. According to Rachel Cleland, 'a trail of humiliation, offence and gloominess followed behind it'. Describing 1957 as 'a "watershed year" in the mutual suspicions of Administration/Canberra relations', she reported stories of senior officials being escorted without notice back to head office where they were made to stand before commissioners and answer 'leading' and 'loaded' questions without representation.⁵² In district offices, wives, servants and staff were questioned in a similar manner. Equally unsettling, the findings of the inquiry were never communicated back to the staff. Donald Cleland was left unsure of his staff and their judgement.

On 2 October 1957, it was reported that an innocent man had served five years of a twelve-year gaol term because he had conspired with the village Big Man and the court interpreter to plead guilty to another man's murder.⁵³ It was only uncovered because the imprisoned man decided he had been imprisoned long enough. Hasluck related a similar story in his memoirs, describing it as a startling and bizarre event that hinted at such events having occurred before.⁵⁴ This was a shock to the expatriate community, further reducing their confidence in the administration.

Evidently, these problems of the process had an impact on Cleland's thinking about the administration, as, in his 1957 address to new recruits to the territory's public service, he pointedly took integrity and trust as his theme. He warned: 'There are … some within the Administration who have been false to the trust.'⁵⁵ This uncertainty was also reflected in Cleland's submission on clemency in Aro's case, as he carefully drew attention to possible errors in policing and court processes, noted the uncertain reception an execution might have in the area and chose clemency as a safer course.⁵⁶

---

51   Ibid., 205; *South Pacific Post*, 21 August 1957, 1.
52   Cleland, *Pathways to Independence*, 200–9.
53   'Big Man' is the term used in PNG to describe the influential men of the areas. 'Prison Inquiry: Native Says He Took Murder Rap', *South Pacific Post*, 2 October 1957, 1, 2.
54   Paul Hasluck, *A Time for Building: Australian Administration in Papua and New Guinea 1951–1963* (Carlton: Melbourne University Press, 1976), 178.
55   'Mr D. Cleland Addresses New Recruits', *South Pacific Post*, 13 February 1957, 10.
56   Cleland to secretary, 17 September 1957.

As we have seen, in 1952, Hasluck was 'extremely unwilling to intervene politically in the processes of justice'; however, by 1957, things had changed.[57] As Hank Nelson observed, to Hasluck, the Anderson case seemed like just another in a long line of administration mistakes.[58] The month before Aro's case came to Canberra, Hasluck had sent Cleland a damning indictment of all areas of his administration using phrases such as 'repeated inability to produce a satisfactory programme', 'continued inability', 'major imperfections', 'a falling off of promptness', 'a failure to correct' and 'a slowness in implementing policy'.[59] Hasluck's 'uncomfortable feelings' of 1952 had grown into dissatisfaction. In this context, the department's lukewarm endorsement of Cleland's recommendation becomes more explicable: the minister was not satisfied with the advice and information in general, and particularly with the administration's seeming inclination to use clemency as a default solution for uncertainty and poor policing. Clemency advice had become evidence of judges not knowing what they should know. Hasluck wanted just punishment rather than punishments that reflected guesswork.

Canberra wants greater severity in sentencing from the PNG Supreme Court

Even more pointedly, Canberra was at variance with the PNG Supreme Court's push to exercise even more discretion, and to have a more conclusive role, in determining sentencing. In 1956, the Department of Territories asked Chief Justice Phillips to prepare a report on a proposal from the PNG Supreme Court bench that judges in PNG no longer be constrained by a mandatory sentence of death when a person was found guilty of a capital offence. The bench proposed that judges should be free to sentence with greater discretion; specifically, they wanted to 'empower the Court to impose such penalty as, having regard to the circumstances of the case, appears to the Court to be just and proper' in sentencing Papua New Guineans.[60] This reform had been implemented in other colonies and jurisdictions within

---

57 Hasluck, *A Time for Building*, 182.
58 Hank Nelson, 'Papua and New Guinea', in *Paul Hasluck in Australian History: Civic Personality and Public Life*, ed. Tom Stannage, Kay Saunders and Richard Nile (St Lucia: University of Queensland Press, 1999), 154–5.
59 Ibid., 155.
60 J. Q. Evans, acting secretary, Attorney-General's Department, to secretary, Department of Territories, March 1957, NAA: A432, 1956/3371, 7801327.

the British tradition.⁶¹ The judges wanted greater control over sentencing so that they could deal with local conditions more precisely and speed up the judicial process, with hopes that the Australian processes would then be more comprehensible to local people.

The Attorney-General's Department reviewed these proposals. Subsequently, the acting solicitor-general wrote to the acting secretary of the Department of Territories, advising that: 'The proposals raise questions of policy rather than questions of law.' The acting solicitor-general was unsure of conditions in PNG: 'My own inclination would be to be much swayed by the considered views of the Chief Justice and the other judges in the matter.' However, exposing the worldview of the bench, he also argued that the amendment should apply to both Papua New Guineans and Europeans in PNG: 'it would be an undesirable departure at this stage of development of the territory to make the proposed distinction'.⁶²

Hasluck, seemingly, did not support the presumption that the PNG legal community knew best. His office withdrew the request for advice on this topic and the minister never officially saw the arguments, presumably because he did not like their conclusions.⁶³ This effective dismissal of advice that depended heavily on the wisdom and experience of PNG judges indicates that Hasluck did not trust their wisdom and experience.

Hasluck shared his concerns about the leniency and apparent racial disparities in the justice system with Slim. Correspondence between Hasluck and Slim refers to conversations in which those concerns were the meat of discussions over a period of time. For example, expressing his disquiet, Hasluck wrote to Slim following the capital case review that resulted in Aro's execution:

> Will you permit me to express my personal appreciation of your letter of 5th December discussing the problems of the commutation of sentences of death passed by the supreme court of the Territory of Papua and New Guinea? As you will be aware, the question has caused me considerable concern over the past two or three years. In general, I think that the tendency to commute all death sentences to a term of imprisonment—often a very short term—is lessening the deterrent effect of the penalty for murder.⁶⁴

---

61 Andrew Novak, 'Capital Sentencing Discretion in Southern Africa: A Human Rights Perspective on the Doctrine of Extenuating Circumstances in Death Penalty Cases', *African Human Rights Law Journal* 14, no. 1 (2014): 24–42.
62 Evans to secretary, March 1957.
63 Hasluck, *A Time for Building*, 343–5.
64 Hasluck to governor-general, 18 December 1957.

Hasluck was particularly thinking of discriminatory judgements based on judicial and administration perceptions of Papua New Guinean sophistication, and the apparent tolerance of cruel murders; the practice of judicial decisions taking too much account of administration policy and violating the separation of powers; and the use of clemency as a means of dealing with the suspicion that mistakes in policing and evidence had occurred. In the lead-up to December 1957, Hasluck and Slim had been discussing their preference that the courts deter crime by being more severe.

In early 1957, Hasluck asked the new chief justice, Alan Mann, whom he had appointed from the Victorian Bar, to place more emphasis on deterrence while also being humane. Mann had been appointed over the head of Ralph Gore because Hasluck 'thought 1956 was about time to make a change'.[65] In appointing Mann, then a mere barrister, rather than a PNG judge, despite Gore's and others' superior experience and knowledge of PNG jurisprudence, Hasluck demonstrated his intention to work towards a new legal culture that pursued deterrence and justice through tougher penalties.[66]

The combined impact of Hasluck's and Slim's requests to be more stringent and Mann's appointment had some immediate effect. Table 6.1, which shows the average sentencing for wilful murder handed down by Gore, Bignold, Kelly, Phillips and Mann, reveals that, in the wake of Mann's arrival and Hasluck and Slim's discussions, while there were fewer pronounced sentences of death and no executions, periods of incarceration after recording a sentence of death became longer by an average of 1.6 years.

Table 6.1: Tabulation of PNG Supreme Court judges' sentencing records, 1954–59.

	Gore	Bignold	Kelly	Phillips	Mann
Average sentence after a recorded sentence of death					
1954–57 (life sentences given a value of 25 years)	7.1 (+ 3 life sentences)	5.01	4.36	9.36 (+ 1 life sentence)	5
1958–59	5.76	9.67	7.25	Retired	8.87
Average sentence after a pronounced sentence of death	10 (1954) (+ 1 life sentence)				15 (1958)
Executions		1 (1957)		1 (1954)	

Sources: PNG Crown Law Office, 'Tabulation of Sentencing by Judge', 10 July 1959, Gore Papers, box 1, folder 8; 'Few Executed for Murder', *South Pacific Post*, 26 November 1957, 3.

---

65   Hasluck, *A Time for Building*, 343–5.
66   Ibid., 176–7.

Soon after Aro's execution, the *SPP* published an article entitled 'Few Executed for Murder', which indicated the sentencing statistics of the various judges and sought to emphasise how rare execution was in comparison to clemency.[67] This celebration of leniency and mercy so soon after the execution contrasted markedly with Slim's and Hasluck's concerns about leniency. Canberra's and Port Moresby's divergent views undermined the confidence of those who determined clemency.

R. v. Gaumbu, 1957 and the Executive Council's determination for longer sentences

As well as the appointment of Mann, *R. v. Gaumbu, 1957* reveals the manner in which Hasluck and Slim pressured the PNG bench to increase the severity of their sentencing, culminating in Aro's pronounced sentence of death and execution. Just prior to the Executive Council's deliberations on Aro, ministers had considered the case of *R. v. Gaumbu, 1957* heard by Justice Andrew Kelly.

In a hamlet close to Mt Hagen, PNG, Gaumbu had murdered a woman, Kongoba, who had fiercely resisted his attempts to rape her. He killed her with repeated axe blows to her head and abdomen as she attempted to flee through her doorway. As in the cases of Ako-Ove and Sunambus, Slim and the Executive Council were unhappy with the recommended sentence, which they felt bound to approve: six and a half years in gaol as an alternative to a recorded sentence of death. Instead, finding this killing of a woman during a rape particularly brutal and deserving of execution, they asked Administrator Cleland and Justice Andrew Kelly to reconsider their recommendations on sentencing.

Andrew Kelly had been a PNG judge since 1950; his sentencing philosophy, and his sentencing average for wilful murder of 4.36 years, typified Slim's and Hasluck's concerns. He was a B4, having been a solicitor and barrister in Rabaul before the Second World War.[68] In explaining his choice of sentence for Gaumbu, Kelly outlined his sentencing philosophy, which encapsulated the Murray system and valorised the very notions that Hasluck thought undermined justice:

---

67 'Few Executed for Murder', *South Pacific Post*, 26 November 1957, 3.
68 'Brisbane Man N. Guinea Judge', *Courier-Mail*, 12 January 1950, 5.

My personal approach to sentences on natives is that they should not be severe. Although natives are presumed to know our law, they do not fully understand the implications of our law. Therefore, generally, we should impose sentences as will be corrective rather than punitive. If we adopt the latter course, then I think we fail in achieving the objective of the administration—to convey to the natives that the administration desires to help them, but at the same time to mete out reasonable punishment when the occasion demands, rather than to impose sentences which, in the mind of the native, are excessive, whereon he convinces himself that the Administration is a hard taskmaster, ready to punish him severely when the opportunity arises, rather than educate him, with any necessary corrective punishment, to the stage of complete understanding of the Administrations/s aims and ideals. Perhaps your honour will appreciate my approach to sentences on natives—perhaps lenient—when I say that on very few occasions have I recommended, or imposed sentences over five years.[69]

In regards to *R. v. Gaumbu, 1957*, in particular, having noted that all his recommendations had been accepted in the past, Kelly wrote: 'Previously, I was under the honest belief that sentences recommended by me were deemed appropriate.'[70] Kelly's surprise suggests that neither fellow expatriates nor judges had ever challenged his ideas about the relationship between sentencing, administrative control and the Papua New Guinean people: his ideas and views represented the accepted wisdom, and, being unexceptional, can be generalised to his brother judges.

Nevertheless, Hasluck, Slim and Cleland sought to find a solution to Slim's and Hasluck's dissatisfaction with the sentence they were being asked to approve. Slim and Hasluck made several criticisms of the sentence, including that such a short sentence for the brutal killing of a woman was unjust and did not deter violence; that it did not consider the need to maintain a sentencing precedent for execution that would enable the administration to execute 'a native murderer of a white woman' that would not be, or appear to be, unjust; and that the failure to execute placed too little value on Papua New Guinean lives in actuality and in the eyes of the world.[71]

---

69 A. Kelly to administrator, 10 June 1957, NAA: A4926, 754, item 4361140.
70 Ibid.
71 Sir William Slim to minister for territories, 16 June 1957, NAA: A4926, 754, item 4361140; Paul Hasluck to secretary, 27 May 1957, NAA: A4926, 754, item 4361140; D. M. Cleland to secretary, Department of Territories, 11 July 1957, NAA: A4926, 754, item 4361140.

Despite such criticism, Cleland was wary of 'setting up outside of the judiciary a scale of punishments on an administrative level'. More in line with Kelly, he preferred a 'corrective punishment rather than a punitive one, unless the sentence recommended is manifestly wrong in all the circumstances of any particular case'.[72] Nevertheless, Cleland agreed with Slim and Hasluck that Gaumbu's crimes were similar to those of others recently condemned to ten years. Based on Cleland's new recommendation of ten years, which Slim and Hasluck wanted, the Executive Council commuted Gaumbu's recorded sentence of death to ten years with hard labour.

Slim sent a clear message to PNG judges via his demands in the Sunambus and Ako-Ove reviews and, most pointedly, during the review of Gaumbu's sentence, and his activism had resulted in more punitive sentencing. Subsequently, Kelly reoriented his sense of appropriate sentencing, as his philosophy of sentencing no longer seemed to be acceptable.[73] From 1958 to 1959, his sentencing average rose to 7.25 years. Bignold also increased his average sentencing from 5.1 to 9.67 years, and the chief justice established an average sentence of 8.87 years (see Table 6.1). However, Gore defied the trend; adhering to his Murray-era sentencing philosophy, he reduced his average sentence, which was inflated in the period 1954–57 by the mass sentencing of the Telefomin offenders. In 1957, there was a shift in favour of longer sentences, a more punitive system and what were intended to be deterrent messages.

'He well knew that his acts were unlawful': Deciding to execute Aro

Hanging Aro was unusual, as most wilful murderers received recorded sentences of death that resulted in commutations. However, in 1957, the Executive Council wanted to meet brutality with harsher punishments than had previously been the case. The written submissions to the executive from the Papua New Guinean leaders of Wabag, the judge, the administrator and the minister, when considered alongside the historical context outlined above, help to explain why Aro was the last man Australia hanged in PNG. Although the Cabinet notebooks for Aro's case are missing, insight into

---

72 Cleland to secretary, 11 July 1957.
73 Kelly to administrator, 10 July 1957, NAA: A4926, 754, item 4361140.

the decision to hang him can be gleaned by examining the documents put forward to the executive and by examining the public statements that were reported after the execution.

After sentencing Aro, Justice Bignold was approached by a delegation of eight *luluais* (headmen), Kibunki, Timun, Kerapim, Kifarin, Kunda, Lui, Neap and Mabasiun, from the Wabag area. Justice Bignold conveyed to Cleland the wishes of these *luluais* that Aro be hanged. The testimony of a community leader, Lipi of Rupamanda, the *tultul*, was also condemnatory. The *luluai* and *tultul* were the administration-appointed liaisons or spokespeople between the administration and the village. They 'wanted it known by the proper authority that they wished the hanging to be at Wabag'. Bignold asked them why this was their preference. In reply, the delegation, and Kerapim in particular, argued that:

> If the people see it, it will make then understand more fully that the killing [prevalence of murder] must stop; it will be a lesson to the local people … We have seen people receive a sentence of yours for killing and they come back, at its expiration, well fed and able to speak pidgin, and we do not think this is a sufficient deterrent. The people of Wabag wonder if these persons were ever in gaol, as they disappeared from Wabag and that was all the Wabag people knew about them, except they later returned fat and well.[74]

This desire to make an example of Aro indicates that the people of Wabag had clear ideas about the limits of mercy and that they believed that Australian justice was not a deterrent to crime. Aro was not respected in his community as he relied upon his relatives and members of his 'line' for subsistence. In his testimony, Lipi of Rupamanda labelled Aro a 'rubbish man'.[75] He was not the kind of man that was wanted by Papua New Guineans.

John Greenwell, former Crown law officer in PNG, has argued that, prior to the introduction of local government into all areas, *luluais* 'played a significant dispute settlement role as an adjunct to the District Officer' and as 'the channel of communication between [the] District Officer and indigenes'.[76] Taking note of the *luluais* complaints about Aro and their preference for more capital punishment, Bignold forwarded a summary to Cleland who relayed it to Hasluck and Cabinet. This signalled the

---

74 Kerapim, quoted in E. B. Bignold to administrator, 2 September 1957, NAA: A4926, 882, item 4361268.
75 Testimony, Lipi of Rupamanda, 10.
76 Greenwell, *The Introduction of Western Law*, 20.

administration's clear interest in calibrating punishment to community expectations and in building a relationship between the administration and the local people.

The 'rubbish man' epithet was repeated in all submissions in the clemency file, indicating not only a strong level of interest in local opinion but also the influence of idiomatic expressions and concepts. It was a potent image.[77] However, this local view did not necessarily assuage Cleland's concern that Aro's community might understand his execution as a form of vengeance.[78] Conversely, Bignold was confident that the local people would understand it as just punishment and a deterrent.

Justice Bignold recommended death for Aro by 'pronouncing' a sentence of death. In doing so, he employed the standard criteria for circumstances that could be used to commute death sentences. He analysed Aro's level of sophistication and noted that he had lived adjacent to the subdistrict headquarters for a considerable amount of time, which meant that the operation of Australian law and order was familiar to him. He also noted that Aro had given himself up to the law and confessed. Bignold concluded that these two elements indicated Aro's clear understanding of the law and his wrongdoing. He dismissed the defence of provocation due to adultery inducing uncontrolled rage because Aro had confessed that he had been thinking about the perceived adultery for some time.[79] Although somewhat concerned about Aro's strategic use of Australian justice, Bignold observed that that the accused 'well knew that his acts were unlawful, and … his long residence almost on the station precludes any other conclusion'.[80] Bignold read Aro's immediate confession as signalling his awareness of the danger he was in from the women's relatives. By contrast, Aro's lack of fear of Australian justice concerned him: Aro, it seemed, had sought shelter in the presumed leniency of colonial authority. That was just what Hasluck and Slim were afraid of: Aro had not been deterred by the consequences of Australian law in this premeditated crime.

Bignold pronounced the sentence of death, indicating that he thought Aro should be hanged. This was consistent with the punishment for multiple murderers, such as Usamando. The pronouncement was underlined when Bignold made no recommendation for an alternate punishment. This was

---

77 'Notes of Submission No. 882'.
78 Cleland to secretary, 17 September 1957.
79 Statement of defendant, Aro of Rupamanda, 10 April 1957; testimony of Aro, 7–8.
80 Bignold to administrator, 2 September 1957.

an unusually severe punishment for Bignold, who had not, in the period since 1954, pronounced a sentence of death, or even recommended a life sentence. However, the circumstances of the case, and Slim's communications with the administration and Justice Kelly, had apparently affected Bignold's sense of what was an appropriate expiation for the community in the face of such brutal murders. Certainly, from 1958 to 1959—that is, after the execution—Bignold increased the severity of his sentencing to an average of 9.67 years, but he never pronounced a sentence again.

Cleland disagreed with Bignold and recommended clemency with the relatively long sentence of twelve years in prison with hard labour. Cleland argued that there had been many cases of husbands killing wives due to suspicions of adultery and none of those killers had been hanged for their crime. Indeed, such killings were common and previously this 'provocation' and, more significantly, a lack of sophistication had been enough to result in a recorded sentence and then a commutation. The administrator found insufficient grounds to individualise punishment to the extent of requiring an execution for what amounted to common, domestic murders. Indeed, there are many such cases in the clemency files in the archives, though few involved multiple killings. Further, Cleland did not think that the community was sophisticated enough for a hanging:

> The Wabag people and those of the sub-district are still in a primitive state and a hanging could have just the opposite effect of leading to a framing of those people wanted put out of the way. If the murders had taken place in an area fully controlled and where there is a degree of sophistication and advancement, the significance of hanging would be appreciated and act as a deterrent.[81]

Cleland did not take the *luluai* at their word, as he did not think the local people would understand hanging as a deterrent as opposed to vengeance. He also seems to have had doubts about Aro's confession, referring to the danger of people being framed in his submission—a danger highlighted by recent scandals in the PNG legal system. For example, Cleland had recently discovered a case of a man confessing to murder and being imprisoned to protect the village 'Big Man'.[82] To Cleland, Aro's immediate confession was indicative of a need for caution. As a 'rubbish man', Aro would have been an ideal 'patsy'. With the legacy of the recent cases of legal malfeasance

---

81 Cleland to secretary, 17 September 1957.
82 *South Pacific Post*, 28 August 1957, 11; *South Pacific Post*, 2 October 1957, 1, 2.

weighing heavily on his mind, Cleland, seemingly, questioned whether Aro was the perpetrator at all and such doubts gave him sufficient reason to reject the finality of execution.

Despite contradicting Bignold on the matters of precedent and sophistication, Cleland still emphasised his uncertainty, repeating variations of the phrase: 'I find it very difficult to assess.'[83] Since the finality of capital punishment did not allow for possible errors in policing, translation and local conspiracies, Cleland thought clemency was more just and would bring more order to Wabag.

Hasluck, departing from his usually fulsome style of summation, did not provide specific recommendations to the Cabinet under his own name.[84] However, a set of notes introducing the submission and signed by the acting secretary for the Department of Territories record Hasluck's views in the third person.[85] These make it clear that the minister endorsed the administrator's views:

> We see no reason to disagree with the recommendation of the Administrator, and assume that considerations of native policy other than the fit punishment for the particular individual have been the reasons for his recommendation for commutation. There could be no grounds for commutation on extenuating circumstances.[86]

The usual extenuating circumstances would have been 'primitiveness' or some sort of cultural motivation. Despite noting that there were no 'extenuating circumstances', Hasluck endorsed Cleland's recommendation for mercy. The Department of Territories noted that there were recent precedents for commutations of similar cases, but it was far from a thorough endorsement. Given Hasluck's advocacy of greater severity and a more thorough separation of powers, his support of Cleland's views suggests a similar mistrust of judicial processes, such that he was willing to affirm Cleland's uncertainty. Indeed, the department explicitly stated that Cleland's reasoning was not about 'fit punishment'—in other words, that his reasons were 'administrative'. This effectively drew attention to the recent scandals in the administration of the law.

---

83 Cleland to secretary, 17 September 1957.
84 Paul Hasluck, confidential submission, NAA: A4926, 882, item 4361268.
85 Signature is illegible, but not Secretary Lambert's.
86 'Notes of Submission No. 882'.

With two influential officials recommending clemency, the decision to hang Aro is puzzling. It would seem that the governor-general and his Executive Council disagreed with Hasluck, as Aro was hanged despite the minister's recommendation. Thus, we must look to the governor-general to account for this outcome.

'I think this might be aided by the occasional enforcement of the death penalty': The governor-general's intervention

William Slim's determination to hang Sunambus of Puto had failed, yet he succeeded in gaining more severe sentences for Sunambus and Gaumbu, and, by his activism, longer sentences of imprisonment in general. For Slim, Aro's pronounced sentence of death conformed to this general pattern; it provided the first opportunity to enact his view that capital punishment was needed in PNG to both maintain law and order, and for justice to be done and be seen to be done. Slim's strengthening of the Executive Council's role in clemency can be seen in the fact that the administrator and the Department of Territories were overruled by the Executive Council's decision to hang Aro. However, as there are no minutes recording the Executive Council's discussion—as mentioned, that section of the Cabinet notebooks is missing—the reasons for its decision must be inferred. Seemingly, Slim used the opportunity offered by the unusual and clear statements by the Wabag leadership, which had been reported by Bignold, the judge's careful legal reasoning and Aro's clear confession as opportunities to argue for his preferred policy goals for justice and deterrence in PNG.

Slim had been looking for a case in which a hanging could take place to pursue just retribution for the victims, to deter crime and to protect the expatriate community, while also keeping an eye on the reputation of the colony for perceptions of racism. He argued that they needed to hang a Papua New Guinean for murdering a Papua New Guinean so that hanging a Papua New Guinean for murdering or raping a white woman would not look so unjust. This argument shows that he was aware of recent criticism. For example, his local paper, the *Canberra Times* (*CT*), had reported in 1956 on Australia being criticised by the Anti-Slavery Society in London for what it saw as the unjust imprisonment of the Telefomin killers for resisting administration officials, as well as regular criticisms of

Australia by the UN Trusteeship Council.[87] Despite Cleland's and Hasluck's thoughts on the matter, Bignold's pronounced death sentence gave Slim the chance to convince the Executive Council to confirm the sentence of death; significantly, a hanging would also provide for future colonial justice for white victims and minimise criticisms then being levelled at Australia in PNG.

Slim's opposition to clemency was largely focussed on crimes against women. His sense of justice was affected by his understanding of women as deserving of particular protection from the justice system and as being more vulnerable than men to crime. As such, he viewed crimes against women as particularly egregious and men who committed them as more wicked than men who murdered men. Regis Tove Stella has argued that such rhetoric in relation to PNG by Australian writers and politicians constructed Papua New Guinean men and their culture as being in need of guidance and, thus, colonisation.[88] Apparently, a society that could not protect its women was a society that needed Anglo-Australian governance and justice, provided it was conducted with suitable attention to the kind of penalties Slim thought such crimes deserved: death. In executing men for killing women, both white and black, Slim was seeking to justify Australian control of what seemed to him to be a culture in need of moral guidance.

Slim had engaged in frank discussions with Hasluck on the state of PNG and the state of justice in PNG. It is evident that Slim had listened to a range of standard objections to capital punishment since he had become engaged in reviewing sentences of death, such as those listed in Justice Kelly's rationale for lenient sentencing. After the Aro decision on 5 December 1957, Slim referred to discussions that had been held during the deliberations as to why the administration and the Department of Territories generally preferred clemency to capital punishment, 'such as the difficulty of obtaining accurate facts through unreliable interpreters and the prejudices and ignorance of the people themselves', and he rejected the notion that those problems should always preclude execution.[89] However, the clemency papers read by, and submitted to, Slim did not raise the issue of accurate facts, conspiracies and unreliable interpreters.[90] These reasons must, then, have been given during ministerial briefings with Hasluck and/or during Executive Council

---

87 'Anti-Slavery Body Told of Cruelty to Aborigines', *Canberra Times*, 13 July 1956. [Despite the title, the article is about PNG.)
88 Tove Stella, *Imagining the Other*, 139.
89 Sir William Slim to Paul Hasluck, 5 December 1957, NAA: M331, 8, item 511120.
90 Having read many of these files, this is my own conclusion.

deliberations, and, as such, they help to sketch the extent and the scope of the undocumented discussions Hasluck and Slim had on such matters. To justify his views, Slim also cited his own experience: 'after four years of studying such cases at the Executive Council', he believed he had a good idea of the mistaken direction of PNG justice and of what was an appropriate punishment.[91] It would seem, in this case, that he rejected the usual list of reasons for clemency in favour of capital punishment, as he believed it would make a definite statement about state retribution and deterrence. As mentioned, he also wanted to allow execution to remain in the state's arsenal to avenge the future murder of a white person.

The clear preference of the Wabag people also seems to have played a role in this decision. Indeed, the *luluais* indication that deterrence was failing was compatible with Slim's views that harsher sentences were required. Rather than paternalistic second-guessing of local demands for expiation in blood, the Executive Council, or at least William Slim, seems to have taken the *luluais* at their word. In accepting the *luluais* capacity to understand capital punishment, the Executive Council was accepting that the Wabag community was capable of comprehending Australian justice, indicating that they found the Wabag, the Rupamanda and, ultimately, Aro to be sophisticated enough to hang.

Executing Aro and others like him was a change in policy direction and that was exactly what Slim wanted. As he stated:

> The first step towards law and order in a country like New Guinea is the suppression of violent crimes. I think this might be aided by the occasional enforcement of the death penalty.[92]

Cleland had not argued strongly for a particular position but, rather, had emphasised the difficulty of reaching a particular position. In effect, this seems to have given the Executive Council space to make its own decision.[93] With Hasluck providing only qualified support for Cleland, the way was open for the Executive Council to determine the justice of hanging Aro of Rupamanda.

---

91 Slim to Hasluck, 5 December 1957.
92 Ibid.
93 Cleland to secretary, 17 September 1957; Cabinet minute, 15 October 1957.

In previous cases examined in this book, fear of international criticism was used to frame an argument for clemency. Slim turned that argument on its head when he argued that the precedent for execution must be maintained to allow for the avenging of white deaths, thereby extending Watkins's arguments regarding Usamando's execution and cultivating international legitimacy through equitable punishment, as opposed to mercy. Slim also argued that the pursuit of law and order would be productive of greater Australian influence and power in the area.[94] Cleland's uncertainty over the reception of capital punishment in Wabag might have held some sway against these arguments; however, in the end, his questioning approach proved no match against Slim's certain belief in deterrence and the requests of local people.

Building moral legitimacy: Representations of the execution

Representations of the execution of Aro can be analysed to indicate which ideas about the reasons for his execution resonated with the public sufficiently to extend into public discussions. The *CT* and the *SPP* reported in detail on the execution, including comments on the official statements.

The *SPP* led with the fact that a group of *luluais* had witnessed Aro's execution. Tim Castle, Daniel Cohen and Karen Halttunen have argued that this sort of representation of the witnessing of the ritual of execution signifies local participation and approval of the ideas and processes of execution, and, in doing so, confirms moral standards to the audience of the narrative. The telling of the story of the hanging then becomes a sort of morality tale for the community, the tragic outcome of which serves as a lesson about the wages of sin. The lesson's significance is underlined by the apparent support of those who come to watch it carried out.[95] Understanding the hanging and, more significantly, the reporting of the hanging in this way makes it clear that the *SPP* sought to demonstrate both

---

94 Slim to Hasluck, 5 December 1957.
95 Tim Castle, 'Constructing Death: Newspaper Reports of Executions in Colonial New South Wales, 1826–1837', *Journal of Australian Colonial History* 9 (2007); Karen Halttunen, *Murder Most Foul: The Killer and the American Gothic Imagination* (Cambridge: Harvard University Press, 1998); Daniel A. Cohen, *Pillars of Salt and Monuments of Grace* (Amherst and Boston: University of Massachusetts Press, 2006).

Papua New Guinean and expatriate acceptance of Australia's authority and rule of law to its readership. Witnessing suggests an acceptance of the moral correction of the community and Aro through hanging.

The *SPP* also reported on Cleland's explanation for why the unusual step of execution was taken. Paraphrasing the administrator, the paper explained that Aro was considered sophisticated because he had lived so long at the Wabag patrol station. Cleland, in emphasising the decisiveness and sternness of the administration, addressed the concerns expatriates had been expressing in the *SPP* in the wake of failures in policing and trial processes that year: 'this is the second hanging in the territory in the last two years'.[96] His stern tone addressed a community anxious about unsolved murders and violence against women. It would seem, then, that from the *SPP*'s perspective, the execution was a policy decision aimed primarily at Papua New Guinean and expatriate audiences to address their concerns about law and order.

By contrast, in Canberra, with its audience of public servants and diplomats, the execution was represented very differently. The *CT* did not discuss Aro's level of sophistication—his 'place on the march' towards civilisation— or any questions of PNG administration. It merely stated that Aro had murdered his two wives. It would seem, then, that for a Canberra audience, a double murder was justification enough for an execution. Indeed, in mainland Australia, sane, multiple murderers usually hanged.[97] The *CT* also noted that few executions had been carried out in PNG: 'Although many sentences of death have been passed on natives during the postwar period this is only the second occasion the sentence has been carried out.'[98] Thus, the *CT* article included content useful to defending the just character of Australian justice to a Canberran audience. The effect of citing the heinous crime and then citing the rarity of execution suggested to the reader that Australian justice was capable of reaching just verdicts appropriate to the situation; in other words, that it was working well.

---

96   Usamando had been hanged in 1955. 'Native Murderer Hanged at Lae', *South Pacific Post*, 20 November 1957, 1.
97   See, for example, *Sodeman v. R. [1936] HCA 75; (1936) 55 CLR 192 (2 April 1936)*, Australian Legal Information Institute, University of Technology Sydney and University of New South Wales, www.austlii.edu.au/au/cases/cth/HCA/1936/75.html; George Marshall Irving, 'Sodeman, Arnold Karl (1899–1936)', *Australian Dictionary of Biography*, adb.anu.edu.au/biography/sodeman-arnold-karl-8524.
98   'Death Penalty Carried out on N.G. Native', *Canberra Times*, 18 November 1957, 7.

Ultimately, both newspapers found the execution acceptable, but for different reasons. This suggests either that journalists in Port Moresby and Canberra selected material that seemed to them to be of interest to their respective audiences, or that journalists in those places were given differently worded statements. Regardless, it clearly indicates the differing demands being placed upon the discretionary process in PNG. The Department of Territories and the PNG administration were walking a narrow path between two different audiences and tailoring the representation of the same phenomena to be both tough on crime and legitimately just.

How the execution was represented to local people in Wabag is unclear. However, that the Wabag people's preference for execution played a role in the decision to execute is clear. This was evident in the administration's decision to bring all the *luluais* of the Wabag and Mount Hagen areas to Lae to witness the hanging, rather than just Aro's local *luluai* and the family members of the victims, as was more usual.

Despite this, it was suggested that the message of deterrence failed to reach its audience in Wabag. Graham Hardy, a patrol officer in the Wabag/Mt Hagen area at the time of the execution, later undertook research into Aro's hanging and its consequences around Wabag for the PNG Association of Australia's website. This website is devoted to sharing research and recollections and the sense of community among former and current expatriates in PNG. According to Hardy, local officials had wanted a public hanging in the district, or, at the very least, a public display of the body in Rupamanda and Wabag. His anecdotal evidence suggested that local people did not believe that the hanging had happened and, consequently, that wife murder had continued to occur because deterrence had failed due to disbelief.[99] This suggests two things: first, that expatriate officials saw hanging as an object and direct lesson in power to deter crime; and, second, that expatriate officials doubted the capacity of local people to believe in abstractions. Seemingly, Hardy doubted the sophistication of Aro's community. Nevertheless, his anecdotal evidence suggests that the administration had limited success in sending a message to the Papua New Guinean community.

Of course, public hanging had ended in Australia, and in most places worldwide, in the previous century, and it would have been morally courageous to say the least to bring it back in a colonial setting purporting to be advancing the local people to embrace a contemporary legal system.

---

99   Hardy, 'Murder Trial'.

Seemingly, the members of the Executive Council had their eyes on the wider international audience for this hanging, as, despite expert advice about how to communicate with locals, they maintained an international standard.[100] Slim's reference to the possibility of the future need to avenge a white death by an equitable use of punishment means that he was imagining a future audience in addition to the current Papua New Guinean, Australian and international one. A man had been hanged for killing a Papua New Guinean woman, so now there was a precedent for hanging a Papua New Guinean man for killing a white person. Thanks to Slim's intervention, were this to occur, colonial authorities would not be embarrassed by a perception of brutality. This demonstrates that discretionary justice could communicate different messages to different audiences.

The limits of severity: *R. v. Bok, 1958* and *R. v. Warira, 1958*

In August 1958, Chief Justice Alan Mann pronounced sentences of death in two cases that subsequently came to the attention of the minister for territories and Prime Minister Robert Menzies when the clemency files arrived together in Canberra. Due to the forthcoming federal election, the Cabinet was not meeting, so Hasluck and Menzies made the decision to overrule the judge's recommendations for execution and commute both sentences to fifteen years hard labour.[101] That these men escaped the escalating severity of the discretionary process indicates that there were limits to Slim's influence on punishment. These two cases suggest that these limits were reached in the face of determined opposition from Cleland and in the suggestion of misconduct in the chain of causation of the crimes. Hasluck and Menzies seem to have overruled any objections Slim may have made, as the warrant was signed by Slim.

Cleland's extensive exposition in these capital case review files saw him push back after losing the argument over Aro. Cleland asserted, quite strongly, that the men should not be hanged, as similar wife-killing cases had received sentences of between four and fifteen years in prison. He cited a range of similar cases in which the murderers' sentences were commuted and said

---

100 Ibid.
101 Allen Brown, secretary, Prime Minister's Department, to secretary, Department of Territories, 4 November 1958, NAA: A4926, 1442, item 4361818.

he saw little that was unusually severe or cruel about these cases that might differentiate them from other cases.[102] For example, he argued that, unlike Aro, each man had killed one person. His submission, which covered both murderers and was much more extensive and well-researched than usual, made an argument for sentencing consistency. This stood in marked contrast to his expressed uncertainty in discussing Aro's case. As Hasluck and Menzies took Cleland's advice, not the chief justice's, evidently it must have impressed them.

In Bok's case, Cleland pointed out that he was from a very 'primitive' area, an argument that had long been reason enough to commute sentences. Mann, having discussed the case with the local *luluai*, had tried to argue that Bok's actions were contrary to local custom and, therefore, that the question of primitiveness was beside the point, as Bok would have died under local notions of justice. According to Mann: 'The pattern of customs is clear enough and refutes any suggestion that the natives regarded the killing of a wife as a justifiable act.'[103] Rejecting that line of argument, Cleland focussed on Bok's level of comprehension of Australian laws and punishment, arguing that Bok 'is really a primitive native with no real contact of any appreciable extent with the administration and its laws'.[104] Discounting the *luluai's* reported attitude in favour of execution, Cleland argued that such a view could suggest either a limited acceptance of the execution of one of their own by foreigners or, given the level of fear experienced throughout the period, that the *luluai* saw execution as the fulfilment of a vendetta against his people. Under such circumstances, an execution would bring disorder to the barely controlled region by exposing officials to retaliatory killings. Hasluck pushed the idea that, in this particular situation, an execution would be misunderstood and would promote the continuation of cycles of violence and disorder.

In the case of Warira, who had been working for Australians and, thus, was well immersed in Australian PNG, Cleland acknowledged that lack of sophistication was not a consideration.[105] Yet, despite this, Cleland presented the precedents for imprisonments for such killings and repeated the generally accepted notion that Papua New Guineans, and Papua New

---

102 D. M. Cleland to secretary, Department of Territories, *The Queen v. Bok*, 9 September 1958, NAA: A4926, 1442, item 4361818; D. M. Cleland to secretary, Department of Territories, *The Queen v. Warira*, 9 September 1958, NAA: A4926, 1442, item 4361818.
103 Alan Mann to administrator, *The Queen v. Bok*, 26 August 1958, NAA: A4926, 1442, item 4361818.
104 Cleland to secretary (*Bok*), 9 September 1958; Cleland to secretary (*Warira*), 9 September 1958.
105 Cleland to secretary (*Warira*), 9 September 1958.

Guinean communities, did not really understand Western executions. Hasluck, despite agreeing with Slim that harsher punishments for actions 'repugnant to humanity' needed to be enacted, supported Cleland's recommendations for mercy.[106] There had also been disputes about local understandings of executions in Aro's case, yet Aro had been hanged. In this case, the difference was that Cleland gave certain, rather than qualified, advice; if nothing else, this indicates that Cleland was able to influence Hasluck when delivering definitive advice.

Perhaps the most telling reason for clemency in these two cases is that, as in the Telefomin case, there was evidence of misconduct and mistakes on the part of the administration. In Bok's case, the *kiap* (government field officer) had forced the victim, Bok's estranged wife, to return to her husband in spite of local custom and good sense, both of which would have let them part. Mann reflected that this mistake thrust the two into an unnecessarily charged situation.[107] In Warira's case, the murder was in revenge for the wife's adultery with a Papua New Guinean constable who broke the requirements of conduct under which he worked, as well as native affairs ordinances, in carrying out an adulterous affair.[108] In both cases, these errors contributed to the chain of causation that led to the murders. In light of the scandals described earlier in the chapter, it seems that Hasluck took the safer course of clemency, probably to avoid the suggestion of injustice. Likewise, it seems that Slim was either unable or unwilling to argue for execution under the shadow of possible misconduct and/or suspicion of unsound evidence.

The limits of severity were particularly marked in these two cases: Hasluck was unsure enough of the quality of PNG policing and judicial processes to confirm the sentences of death handed down by his own appointee, Mann, in case he had misjudged the evidence or had not accounted for official misconduct when he pronounced, rather than recorded, the sentences.

The limits of severity were further highlighted the following year when advice from the Solicitor-General's Office regarding the power of the governor-general in capital cases was seemingly rejected by the Department of Territories. The department received advice that the governor-general-in-council could, in fact, uphold a recorded sentence of death and have

---

106 On repugnance, see NAA: A432, 1961/2023, item 1172557; NAA: A518, BZ800/1/9, item 3235342.
107 Mann to administrator (*Bok*), 26 August 1958.
108 *Native Regulation Ordinance, 1908–1930—Native Regulations 1939* (Papua), section 84; NAA: A4926, 1442, item 4361818.

the offender executed. The file indicates that the advice was endorsed by the solicitor-general and conveyed orally and entered in the Opinion Book Index.[109] Given that the governor-general did not confirm any recorded sentences, despite his expressed preference for doing so, it appears that the advice was either not conveyed, not acted upon or rejected by the Department of Territories. As the advice directly contradicted advice given to the governor-general by the same solicitor-general, Kenneth Bailey, in 1956, it is unlikely that it was conveyed to Slim, who remained governor-general for another year. Despite Hasluck's apparent support for Slim's punishment goals, it seems that the minister was, in fact, unwilling to override the considered decisions of the judges of the Supreme Court in recording sentences of death, however much he might entertain suspicions of their conduct and leniency. This unwillingness placed a substantial limit on the possible severity of the PNG Supreme Court and the oversight of the Executive Council.

Finally, and speculatively, perhaps executing Papua New Guineans whose conduct might be the result of official mistakes was not the sort of issue to which the Liberal and Country Party wanted to draw attention in the midst of a federal election? Perhaps three executions in three years strained the qualities of just legitimacy being cultivated in PNG? Hasluck was conscious of the image of PNG that Australia projected domestically and internationally, and two executions so soon after Aro was not the image he would have wanted to project, particularly during a federal election.

Conclusion

The hand of Sir William Slim can be seen clearly in the execution of Aro of Rupamanda. After the legal difficulties of 1957 and what he felt was a mounting law and order problem, he advocated deterrence of crime through the judicious and pointed use of the death penalty. He wished an example to be made as soon as possible. Aro's case fell squarely within this determination to change policy direction. Aro, like Usamando, satisfied the standards of neither world. He was a 'rubbish man' and a man who attempted to bend the law to suit his own needs, yet he had not embraced the opportunities offered by colonialism and neither man was what was wanted by the policies of advancement.

---

109 NAA: A432, 1958/3143, item 7801743.

Indeed, the decision to execute Aro, a double murderer, would not have been exceptional in any of the jurisdictions in which capital punishment had been retained. In fact, the contrast between habitual clemency and the smiting of the truly wicked presented a legitimate face for Australian justice and colonial practice in the *CT*.

However, legal scandals had seemingly shaken the resolve of Administrator Cleland; his wife, Dame Rachel Cleland, reported that 1957 was a low point in morale for the administration. Justice Bignold responded to these scandals, and also to Slim's campaign for severity, with unusual harshness in his sentencing of Aro, whereas Cleland responded with uncertainty. Cleland was equivocal about whether to hang Aro. Thus, the Executive Council had more opportunity than usual to have an impact on the clemency deliberations and agreed with Bignold, rather than Cleland.

As the *CT* reported, this was a rare instance of capital punishment, but also a situation in which the diverse audiences to the execution found it acceptable to hang Aro. With the Wabag *luluais* seemingly in support, any fears of losing control of the area were set aside.

Yet the determination for greater severity also had limits and, with more dubious cases, such as Warira and Bok, Minister Hasluck was unwilling to execute more Papua New Guineans and expose Australia to accusations of brutality and incompetence. Reinforcing that impression, he was unwilling to accept the advice that would have given Slim free rein to confirm recorded sentences of death, indicating the limits of his demands for greater severity in punishment.

7

The end of mandatory sentencing

In 1965, the PNG House of Assembly, with the approval of the federal Cabinet, legislated to end the mandatory sentence of death for a finding of wilful murder. It was proposed that the governor-general would still retain the royal prerogative of mercy, but PNG judges could choose what sentences to impose on murderers, rather than being mandated to hand down a sentence of death. The legislation became operational in 1966. While capital punishment was not abolished, no further sentences of death were handed down. This chapter explains why the mandatory regime was ended and why the new punishment regime took the form that it did.

In June 1960, after a visit to the UK, Prime Minister Robert Menzies announced that Australia would go along with the British Prime Minister Harold McMillan's 'Wind of Change': Australia would move much more quickly towards independence for PNG.[1] As several historians have noted, Menzies's announcement surprised expatriates and colonialists in PNG and Australia. The subsequent acceleration of the devolution of Australia's power in the territory was accompanied by resistance, both to the plan itself

---

1 'Favours Early Independence', *Canberra Times*, 21 June 1960, 1; Ian Downs, *The Australian Trusteeship Papua New Guinea 1945–75* (Canberra: AGPS, 1980), 215–6; Christopher Waters, '"Against the Tide": Australian Government Attitudes to Decolonisation in the South Pacific, 1962–1972', *Journal of Pacific History* 48, no. 2 (2013): 194–208.

and to the pace of change.² The rationale for Australia's policy on managing capital punishment in PNG was caught up in this accelerated transition to independence. According to Brian Essai, a PNG bureaucrat, by 1960 Port Moresby's population comprised approximately 4,000 expatriates, 500 people of mixed European and Papua New Guinean descent, and 10,000–12,000 Papua New Guineans, some of whom came and went with seasonal labour.³

While some expatriates had thought it would take a century or so for PNG to gain independence—and/or that PNG would become a state within Australia—others had always supported a faster transition. According to Hank Nelson, 'criticism by the UN ... strengthened the hand of those officials who believed changes must come more quickly'.⁴ Placing PNG in a global context of decolonisation, Ian Downs pointed out that, between 1945 and 1960, fifteen African colonies became nations. Recognising this, Menzies stated in 1960: 'At one time it was thought better to move slowly towards independence, the school of thought now is that it is better to go sooner than later.'⁵ A more rapid schedule towards independence and the devolution of authority flowed from this statement, percolating into all areas of the PNG administration, including clemency and capital punishment; however, as Christopher Waters has shown, independence was still seen as a distant goal by many in the Australian and PNG administrations.⁶

This created certain ambiguities. For example, in 1965, the PNG House of Assembly legislated to end the mandatory sentence of death for wilful murder yet the governor-general of Australia retained the royal prerogative of mercy. While ending mandatory sentencing reduced the entanglement of the Australian federal Cabinet in the administration of justice in PNG,

---

2   Paul Hasluck, *A Time for Building: Australian Administration in Papua and New Guinea 1951–1963* (Carlton: Melbourne University Press, 1976), 215; Hank Nelson, *Taim Bilong Masta: The Australian Involvement with Papua New Guinea* (Sydney: Australian Broadcasting Commission, 1982), 209; 'Territory as 7th State "Impractical"', *South Pacific Post*, 2 May 1966, 1; John Dademo Waiko, *A Short History of Papua New Guinea*, 2nd ed. (Melbourne: Oxford University Press, 2007), 136; Murray Groves, 'The Reign of Mr. Hasluck', *Nation*, 5 May 1962, 7–9, cited in Downs, *The Australian Trusteeship*, 217; Donald Denoon, *A Trial Separation: Australia and the Decolonisation of Papua New Guinea* (Canberra: Pandanus Books, 2005), ch. 1; James Sinclair, *Middle Kingdom: A Colonial History of the Highlands of Papua and New Guinea* (Adelaide: Crawford House Publishing, 2016), 310; Waters, 'Against the Tide'.
3   Brian Essai, *Papua and New Guinea: A Contemporary Survey* (Melbourne: Oxford University Press, 1961), 84–5.
4   Nelson, *Taim Bilong Masta*, 209–14; Rachel Cleland, *Pathways to Independence: Story of Official and Family Life in Papua New Guinea from 1951–1975* (Cottesloe: Singapore National Printer, 1985); Hank Nelson, *Papua New Guinea: Black Unity or Black Chaos?* (Pelican Penguin, 1972), 127.
5   Downs, *The Australian Trusteeship*, 215–6.
6   Waters, 'Against the Tide', 170.

7. THE END OF MANDATORY SENTENCING

it still retained ultimate control through the governor-general. The legislation also introduced a new class of mitigation based on indigenous cultural impulses for indigenous offenders. A judge who determined that a Papua New Guinean had murdered due to ignorance of Australian law, fear of sorcery, cultural obligations or other issues pertaining to the local culture and notions of justice could hand down a sentence of imprisonment rather than death.[7] Although similar to powers that Supreme Court judges held in mainland jurisdictions that retained the death penalty, the cultural mitigation sections of this provision were distinctive. Thus, in principle, from this point onward, Canberra, with an eye to international criticisms, could point to a meaningful devolution of power while at the same time being able to prevent any potentially unjust, and embarrassing, executions from occurring. That PNG Supreme Court judges never again sentenced an offender to death made the royal prerogative moot. No more clemency appeals were forwarded to Canberra from PNG. To some extent, this reflected the general movement away from capital punishment in mainland Australian jurisdictions at this time; however, there were also distinct cultural dimensions at play.[8]

The Department of Territories, in its submission on the legislation, argued that this change would make sentencing more immediate, more culturally sensitive and more transparent—a vast improvement on the current situation, which was protracted, mysterious and suspicious to local people. The department hoped the certainty and clarity of the new process would deter crime; indeed, the public's fear of crime and the desire to deter crime was one reason why the death penalty was retained.

As well as accelerating the path to autonomy, a major reason for both the timing and form of the legislation was that, in 1963, a new minister for territories, Charles Barnes, a Country Party House of Representatives member, was appointed, replacing Paul Hasluck. A novice minister lacking in insight, Barnes was less capable of encompassing the vast detail of the portfolio, was less 'articulate', and was less interested in political and legal issues than Hasluck; consequently, he was much more inclined to allow

---

7 Territory of Papua and New Guinea, 'No. 69 of 1965, An Ordinance to Amend the Criminal Code (Queensland, Adopted) in its Application to the Territory of New Guinea, Assented to 7th December 1965', NAA: A432, 1964/2543, item 1184765.
8 Mark Finnane, *Punishment in Australian Society* (Melbourne: Oxford University Press, 1997); Barry Jones, ed., *The Penalty is Death: Capital Punishment in the Twentieth Century* (Melbourne: Sun Books, 1968); Jo Lennan and George Williams, 'The Death Penalty in Australian Law', *Sydney Law Review* 34 (2012): 659–94.

his secretary to take the lead. As well as lacking in capability and interest, Barnes, according to Allan Healy and Ian Downs, was uncertain about the desirability of the devolution of power in PNG; however, he felt the same pressure for decolonisation that Menzies and the administration felt.[9] Hank Nelson and Donald Denoon argued that Barnes was more interested in PNG's economic development, particularly mining, than its independence. In 1967, Barnes stated that 'the territory would not achieve independence for many years, if at all'.[10] Thus, while Barnes supervised some movement towards autonomy and independence in certain areas, he retained considerable control in other areas.

Revealing his lack of interest in legal matters, in 1964 Barnes and Attorney-General Billy Snedden made a submission to the Cabinet to change the law on mandatory sentencing in PNG that would devolve power away from Australia and the minister for territories. That submission will be the central source for assessing the reasoning behind the policy formation process discussed in this chapter, as it summarised the views of the federal government and PNG agencies on the justice and colonial policy issues that led to the change in the law.

Some Papua New Guineans who had benefited from an Australian or missionary education were beginning to push for change, questioning Australia's continued colonial policy and agitating for PNG independence.[11] They were beginning to take jobs in the public service and schools, run local councils and speak up in the PNG House of Assembly. This emerging group of people spoke strongly in favour of the continued use of capital punishment, creating additional pressure on Australian policymakers.

The devolution of power to Supreme Court judges suited the wider program of devolution demanded by the world decolonisation movement. Further, the new minister wanted to focus on economic rather than socio-legal issues, which were outside his area of expertise.[12] Yet, the new minister

---

9 Allan M. Healy, 'Monocultural Administration in a Multicultural Environment: The Australians in Papua New Guinea', in *From Colony to Coloniser: Studies in Australian Administrative History*, ed. J. J. Eddy and J. R. Nethercote (Sydney: Hale and Iremonger, 1987), 223; Downs, *The Australian Trusteeship*, ch. 10, p. 378; John Langmore, 'A Powerful, Formative Experience: 1963–1972', in *Australians in Papua New Guinea, 1960–1975*, ed. Ceridwen Spark et al. (St Lucia: University of Queensland Press, 2014), 122; Denoon, *A Trial Separation*, 40–5.
10 Denoon, *A Trial Separation*, 40; Nelson, *Papua New Guinea*, 110.
11 Waiko, *A Short History of Papua New Guinea*, 135–7; Nelson, *Papua New Guinea*, 124–6.
12 Charles Edward Barnes, interview by Pat Shaw, Parliament's Bicentenary Oral History Project, 19 November 1983, National Library of Australia, TRC 4900/13.

also believed that the deterrent effect of faster sentencing would help with lowering crime rates, and expatriates and Papua New Guineans supported that view. Ultimately, the legislation was acceptable to Canberra because, while it devolved some power, it maintained the governor-general's role as the ultimate arbiter of life and death, enabling the federal government to retain the ability to prevent potentially embarrassing executions.

Canberra and Port Moresby: Awareness of outside scrutiny and mutual suspicion

The first half of the 1960s saw steady and regular criticism of Australia's role in PNG from the Union of Soviet Socialist Republics (USSR), from India and from proponents of decolonisation in the UN Trusteeship Council (UNTC), as relayed in articles printed in the *Canberra Times* (*CT*) and *South Pacific Post* (*SPP*).[13] Indeed, a Soviet motion demanding immediate independence for New Guinea on 7 July 1961 at the UNTC was defeated by only one vote.[14] Yet, in 1964, apparently aware of such criticism, the PNG House of Assembly, with mostly Papua New Guinean members, passed a motion telling the UN to 'stop meddling'.[15] The process of the Dutch leaving West Papua in the early 1960s and its dubious re-colonisation by Indonesia drew attention to the colonial project in PNG.[16] Australia found itself vulnerable to repeated attacks targeting the slow pace of devolution, development and independence.

As mentioned, while the Menzies government responded with seeming alacrity to this pressure to decolonise, and devolved power in the legislation on capital punishment, it maintained ultimate power over life and death.

---

13 'Commission Likely On New Guinea Policy', *Canberra Times*, 15 August 1960, 2; 'Australia Proud of Papua Record', *Canberra Times*, 19 October 1960, 6; 'Calwell Criticises New Guinea Policy', *Canberra Times*, 29 January 1962, 3; 'Self-Rule Possible For Papua "in Decade"', *Canberra Times*, 30 May 1962, 3; 'U.N. Endorses Papua Policy', *Canberra Times*, 28 June 1963, 9; 'Discrimination Swept Away in New Guinea', *Canberra Times*, 14 December 1962, 3; 'Papua-N.G. Visits by Russians Advocated', *Canberra Times*, 25 July 1964, 3; 'Russia Renews Blistering Attack on Australia', *Canberra Times*,14 November 1964, 6; 'Discussion "Not over" in Papua', *Canberra Times*, 4 September 1964, 6; 'New Guinea Prisoners', *Tribune* (Sydney), 21 October 1964, 4. See also W. J. Hudson, *Australia and the Colonial Question at the United Nations* (Honolulu: East-West Centre Press, 1970), 175–6.
14 'Target for New Guinea Plans Soon', *Canberra Times*, 14 July 1961, 4.
15 'Papua-N.G. Tells U.N. to Stop "Meddling"', *Canberra Times*, 3 September 1964, 8.
16 'Dutch New Guinea Trusteeship', *Canberra Times*, 27 February 1961, 3; Letters to the editor, *Canberra Times*, 12 January 1962, 2; Christopher Waters, 'The Last of Australian Imperial Dreams for the Southwest Pacific: Paul Hasluck, the Department of Territories and a Greater Melanesia in 1960', *Journal of Pacific History* 51, no. 2 (2016): 169–85.

This suggests that the Cabinet was concerned that there could be poor judicial decisions due to the racially fraught situation that, arguably, was inherent to colonial situations; that the Department of Territories maintained its perception of a local administration and judiciary that was inclined to racism and paternalism; that the Executive Council saw capital punishment as a necessary last resort; and that Barnes was equivocal as to the desirability of devolving power.[17]

Australian colonialism in PNG in the 1960s was conducted in the context of outside scrutiny. As W. J. Hudson concluded:

> It seems that at this point Australia finally decided that less was to be gained from defying the Assembly than in going some way towards meeting its demands or at least appearing to.[18]

Figure 7.1: 'The valley floor—where once they were afraid to live (2) Wahgi Valley, Papua New Guinea, 1970'.
Source: Terence E.T. Spencer and Margaret Spencer, National Library of Australia, nla.gov.au/nla.obj-145573965.

---

17 Cabinet approved the recommendations in Cabinet Decision 1156 of 25 August 1965. Subsequently, an amendment to the law was made.
18 Hudson, *Australia and The Colonial Question*, 175–6.

During the 1950s and 1960s, one of Hasluck's responses to this scrutiny had been public diplomacy. Hasluck and his department's public diplomacy publications highlighted the successful economic and social development that accompanied Australian colonialism.[19] For example, in *The Territory of Papua and New Guinea*—a photographic essay distributed in New York and to those interested in PNG policy—the Department of Territories portrayed a prospering and developing new nation emerging from trusteeship.[20] For example, a page from the photographic essay, shows a prosperous, Westernised Papua New Guinean engaged in voting, thus demonstrating the successful approach to advancement Australia was taking in PNG.

Yet as seen in the title to Figure 7.1, colonial officials like Terrence Spenser believed Australian colonialism was beneficial and had brought peace to a land made desolate by warfare. There seemed to be a genuine belief among colonialists in the message purveyed to outsiders. Australians were among the critical audience commenting on the Australian government's policies in PNG and its poor treatment of Papua New Guineans. The *Tribune*, the official newspaper of the Communist Party of Australia (CPA), printed regular articles condemning Australia's continued presence in PNG.[21] The CPA was a small and politically insignificant group, yet its criticisms could bite internationally. On 8 May 1961, the Victorian Trades Hall Council (VTHC) and the Kilsyth and Sydney branches of the CPA sent a petition to the UN secretary general and Minister Hasluck protesting about colonial courts sentencing to death some Papua New Guineans from Tariga, Papua.[22] The petition was forwarded to members of the UNTC, some of whom, such as the USSR and India, were already opposed to Australian control of PNG and to colonialism by Western powers in general. Other members, such as Paraguay and Bolivia, were generally suspicious of colonialism, but less overtly critical of Australia. The petition became an agenda item for the next meeting of the UNTC, forcing Australian officials to coordinate a response and seek support from Australia's allies, such as the UK and US.[23]

---

19   Hasluck, *A Time for Building*, 284–5. Also see, Jane Landman, 'Visualising the Subject of Development: 1950s Government Film Making in the Territories of Papua and New Guinea', *Journal of Pacific History* 45, no. 1 (2010): 71–88.
20   Australia, Department of Territories, *The Territory of Papua and New Guinea* (Canberra: Australian Government Printer, 1961).
21   See, for example, 'New Manoeuvre on New Guinea', *Tribune*, 31 October 1962, 11; 'New Guinea Prisoners', *Tribune*, 21 October 1964, 4.
22   NAA: A452, 1961/4256, 3500477.
23   Ibid. Members of the UNTC for this meeting in 1961 were Australia, Belgium, Bolivia, Burma, China, France, India, New Zealand, Paraguay, USSR, UAE, UK and USA. See United Nations, *Index to Proceedings of the Trusteeship Council*, Eleventh Special Session.

That such a small gesture of protest from marginal groups was taken up by international diplomats highlights the vulnerability of Australia's role in PNG.

The VTHC and the CPA expressed concern about the punishment regime in PNG in an attempt to pressure Australia to minimise or prevent the punishment of the Tariga men, and, more generally, to hasten Australia's departure from PNG. The petitioners wrote that their concerns arose from press reports published in April 1961 in the major Sydney newspaper the *Daily Telegraph*, the widely read Melbourne *Herald*, as well as the much less prevalent and influential *Tribune*.[24] The petition called for different punishment for Westernised and non-Westernised Papua New Guineans, so that Papua New Guineans were not condemned under a system they neither understood nor wanted.

The petitioners demonstrated their own lack of understanding of the established mitigating factor of 'lack of sophistication', a reason that spared almost all Papua New Guinean offenders. Ironically, this call for differentiation of treatment amounted to a rejection of the liberal approach being taken under Hasluck to make Papua New Guinean law more colourblind and universal; indeed, it was more aligned with the old colonial view of justice. However, the VTHC, the CPA and Hasluck's administration all shared the same general idea that indigenous beliefs and practices needed to be considered when meting out punishment for non-Westernised Papua New Guineans. They differed over when this should happen, with PNG's existing system giving the power to the governor-general-in-council and the petitioners wanting local judges to make the determination at the point of sentencing. The very fact of the VTHC and CPA petitioning the UNTC shows that they were aware of the impact of international scrutiny on Australian policy. The petitioners were hoping to use international pressure to change Australian policy.

Soviet officials used the VTHC/CPA petition to criticise Australian colonialism at a UNTC meeting on 15 June 1961. Dudley McCarthy, a former patrol officer and PNG official, was the Australian representative at the UNTC at the time.[25] He accused the Soviets of making vexatious commentary:

---

24   'Nurse Writes on NG Agony', *Tribune*, 26 April 1961; Trades Hall to Hasluck, 4 May 1961, NAA: A452, 1961/4256, 3500477.
25   John Farquharson, 'McCarthy, Dudley (1911–1987)', *Australian Dictionary of Biography*, adb.anu.edu.au/biography/mccarthy-dudley-15053/text26251.

> Mr. Uberemko [the USSR representative] has also referred to reports of recent sentences in a certain area, which incidentally is a part of Papua. This reference is clearly tactical only, for he should know as well as I do myself—and I believe he does—that there is merely a legal form involved here; that in the whole post-war period in the territory, only two such sentences have been carried out. In this particular case, I am now able to report that in accordance with the standard procedure, the sentences have been reviewed and have now been commuted to terms of imprisonment of some three years in each case.[26]

Accusing the Soviets of being 'tactical only' indicates that McCarthy saw this as one move in an ongoing campaign to undermine Australia's presence in the territories. It further indicates that officials in the Department of External Affairs and the Department of Territories were aware of mounting opposition to trusteeship and colonialism in PNG, and that they were responding to it. Therefore, responses to the petition and wider policymaking should be considered in the context of such international scrutiny and awareness.

Australia did not persuade its allies to vote against hearing the matter, which it could have done as the murders in Tariga happened in Papua, not New Guinea, which meant that the UNTC had limited standing in the matter. That being so, the UN's jurisdiction over the non-trust colonial possessions of UN members was a matter of debate, and newly independent countries did not usually accept lack of jurisdiction as an argument against UN involvement.[27] In the 'spirit of openness', it was felt that removing the petition from the agenda would draw attention to the matter unnecessarily when the issue did not require hiding.[28] Indeed, the Department of External Affairs felt that openness, especially given Australia's blamelessness, was best.[29] Subsequently, the Department of Territories was asked to prepare a report for Australian diplomats to use in discussions with the UNTC. The task of preparing the report was delegated to Donald Cleland's administration.

---

26 'Extract from Concluding Statement by Special Representative Mr. McCarthy at Twenty Seventh Session of Trusteeship Council' (handwritten note), 15 June 1961, NAA: A452, 1961/4256, 3500477.
27 Hudson, *Australia and the Colonial Question*, 62–3.
28 Department of Law, PNG, to secretary, Department of External Affairs, 12 June 1962, NAA: A452, 1961/4256, 3500477.
29 Department of Law, PNG, to secretary, Department of Territories, 19 September 1961, NAA: A452, 1961/4256, 3500477.

Cleland set this task to Wally Watkins, who had been heavily involved in developing a political and policy response to the Telefomin killings and reporting on the legal issues arising from Usamando's murders. Watkins was an old colonial and enmeshed in the culture of the PNG administration and legal system.

Watkins emphasised that the judge in the case, Esme Bignold, had followed established jurisprudence in considering the murder typical of payback killings, had taken the murderers 'primitive condition and lack of contact with [Australian authorities]' into account and believed that justice in such cases was best achieved through clemency.[30] To substantiate the success of this system, Watkins cited both its very low levels of recidivism and Justice Gore's argument that a prisoner who had been granted clemency would return to their community after their imprisonment, taking their knowledge of Western culture and law back with them to educate and Westernise their community. As such, the Crown Law Office argued that it was in Australia's interest to imprison rather than execute Papua New Guinean offenders because it would better extend Westernisation, the rule of law and, ultimately, Australian authority.

Watkins provided a case study on the Telefomin killers to develop the themes raised in his report.[31] In the eighth year of their ten-year sentences,[32] the Telefomin killers, Watkins noted, had actually built Boram Prison (see Figure 7.2) and, in the process, some had become experienced and qualified brickmakers and layers. Watkins pointed out that they had learned Tok Pisin, had vastly improved their knowledge of Australian agricultural practices and had become familiar with Australian ways, except for two who died of old age. And, while a few had cooperated only minimally, all had worked in the gardens and supplied their own food. Significantly, none had committed any disciplinary offences while in prison. Indeed, three wished to be employed by the Department of Public Works on their release and had already been involved in training prisoners in other prisons in brickmaking and laying. However, most wished to return to the Telefomin region. Implicit in this recitation of the Telefomin killers' fine disciplinary record was that they had become accustomed to, and accepting of, Australian authority and

---

30   Department of Law, PNG, UN Petition 8/16 and 8/17, Tari Murders, 1–2, NAA: A452, 1961/4256, 3500477.
31   D. M. Cleland to secretary, Department of Territories, 16 March 1962, NAA: A452, 1961/4256, 3500477.
32   Crown Law Officer W. Watkins to secretary, Department of Territories, 28 February 1962, NAA: A452, 1961/4256, 3500477.

rules—they had been advanced on 'the march'. Watkins argued that such acculturation was what guided PNG sentencing policy and that it was the hoped-for outcome of imprisoning the 'primitive': that is, that they would be trained to understand and be in awe of Australian coercive power, as well as gaining knowledge and skills. This case study was relayed to New York to be presented as a measure of the success of Australia's system of sentencing and punishment because, it was believed, it showed how well Australian developmental colonialism was working.

Hasluck also replied officially to the UN representatives, and to the VTHC and Kilsyth CPA that had initiated the petitions, explaining the general principles of the sentencing process and how clemency was used to redress the particular situations of Papua New Guineans and ensure justice was done.[33] He noted the relatively lenient sentence of three years handed down to the Tariga men, and that prison in PNG was quite successful at education and rehabilitation, giving the example of the successful education of the Telefomin killers.[34] According to Hasluck's representation, Australia's approach was in keeping with the UN's advancement goals for places such as PNG. Reiterating a standard justification of the clemency process, he argued that it was successful; that it was rehabilitative; that it was educational, both to the prisoners and the community; and, perhaps most of all, that it was consistent and just.

Why, then, was the sentencing law changed in 1964? Frederick Cooper and Ann Stoler, and Martin Wiener have argued that, after the horrors of the Second World War, colonialism attempted to become something more acceptable to a world sickened by Nazi and Japanese imperialism, and, as such, that new types of imperialism began replacing older forms. Similarly, Michael Barnett has observed that the end of the Second World War marked a disjunction in the thinking about, and the practice of, colonialism, and that after the war colonialists used socio-economic and political development as a moral justification for continued colonial possession.[35] These analyses help to explain Australia's postwar engagement with colonialism. A politically active expatriate in PNG in the 1960s, Ian Downs reflected that:

---

33 'Observations of the Administering Authority on Petitions', NAA: A452, 1961/4256, 3500477; C. R. Lambert, secretary, Department of Territories, to secretary, Department of External Affairs, 6 June 1962, NAA: A452, 1961/4256, 3500477.
34 Ibid.
35 Frederick Cooper and Ann L. Stoler, 'Tensions of Empire: Colonial Control and Visions of Rule', *American Ethnologist* 16, no. 4 (1989): 609–21; Martin J. Wiener, *Empire on Trial: Race, Murder, and Justice under British Rule, 1870–1935* (New York: Cambridge University Press, 2009), 232–3; Michael Barnett, *Empire of Humanity: A History of Humanitarianism* (Ithaca: Cornell University Press, 2011), Table 1.

In 1962, the Australian Trusteeship was exposed by the ebb of the colonial tide. There was danger in seeming to be an anachronism in an age of colonial rejection. International support during trusteeship confrontations required Australia to have policies which her friends could support without embarrassment.[36]

While defending the system of mandatory sentencing and clemency, it is evident that Australian officials saw its deficiencies in 1961 when Watkins acknowledged to the administrator that the current system, which included recording or pronouncing sentences, would not make sense to anyone outside the system.[37] Due to events like the VCTU/CPA petition, Australia was conscious of international scrutiny. The 1964 legislation to end mandatory sentencing grew out of this context; its formulation becomes more comprehensible when viewed as a product of the changing language of colonial engagement and policy that emerged in the wake of such criticism.

'To abandon our responsibilities would be an almost criminal act'

PNG officials' awareness of the pressure of external judgement was enhanced by the regular visits of UNTC missions; such missions were made up of diplomats representing members of the council. In 1962, the UNTC visiting mission was led by the UK's Sir Hugh Foot, an eminent British diplomat. Former colonial secretary of Jamaica (1945–47), chief secretary for Nigeria (1947–50), captain-general and governor-in-chief of Jamaica (1951–57), and governor and commander-in-chief of Cyprus, Foot, when he wrote the report, was the current British ambassador and adviser for the UK Mission to the United Nations.[38] As such, he had been closely involved in both colonisation and the UK's moves towards decolonisation. According to Rachel Cleland, Foot told her husband Donald that he was there to put Australia 'into a gallop' in working towards PNG's independence.[39] Foot's and the UNTC's criticism of the pace of change was, according to Denoon, 'unusually effective'.[40] Australia was being pushed to devolve power faster. Yet, as Denoon also noted, Hasluck

---

36 Downs, *The Australian Trusteeship*, 240.
37 Watkins to secretary, 28 February 1962.
38 Peter B. Flint, 'Lord Caradon, Britain's Delegate to UN in 1960s, Is Dead at 82', *New York Times*, 7 September 1990, www.nytimes.com/1990/09/07/obituaries/lord-caradon-britain-s-delegate-to-un-in-1960-s-is-dead-at-82.html.
39 Cleland, *Pathways to Independence*, 253; Clive Moore, *New Guinea: Crossing Boundaries and History* (Honolulu: University of Hawaii Press, 2003), 197.
40 Denoon, *A Trial Separation*, 30.

told his department that he did not think scheduling independence without a full understanding of the facts on the ground was desirable, and that an appropriate 'eye-wash from time to time' should be supplied to satisfy the UN perceptions—an object fulfilled by the first World Bank study of PNG. Some of Foot's recommendations touched on policies already in train: for example, the establishment of the University of Papua New Guinea. Despite Hasluck's reservations, Foot was the UK's representative on the Trusteeship Council, and Australia depended on the support of its Western allies such as the UK to stave off the demands of newly independent and Eastern Bloc states that PNG's independence be imminent.[41] As such, when even the UK, with its own colonial issues to defend, spoke in favour of 'galloping' towards independence for PNG, Australia had to show that it was listening. Therefore, while some policies should be regarded as 'eye-wash', others represented a genuine attempt at hastened devolution.

Striking at the heart of Australian rhetoric around its place in PNG, the UN *Declaration on the Granting of Independence to Colonial Countries and Peoples* of December 1960 stated that: 'Inadequacy of political, economic, social or educational preparedness should never serve as a pretext for delaying independence.'[42] From Australia's perspective, the unpreparedness of PNG for independence was a primary justification for its continued presence there. Both Hasluck and Menzies had spoken publicly on how much the Papua New Guineans needed Australian assistance and how they would continue to do so for some years.[43] For example, in response to Soviet complaints, Menzies told the UN General Assembly that:

> Nobody who knows anything about these territories and their indigenous people could doubt for a moment that for us in Australia to abandon our responsibilities would be an almost criminal act.[44]

Similarly, Cleland, like most expatriates, imagined independence taking fifty or one hundred years. However, such views were starting to shift.

---

41 Hudson, *Australia and the Colonial Question*, 4–8.
42 United Nations General Assembly, 'Declaration on the Granting of Independence to Colonial Countries and Peoples', General Assembly Resolution 1514 (XV), 14 December 1960, www.ohchr.org/en/instruments-mechanisms/instruments/declaration-granting-independence-colonial-countries-and-peoples.
43 'No Hurry to Quit N.G., Says Minister', *Canberra Times*, 24 August 1960, 1; 'To Abandon N.G. Would Be Criminal', *Canberra Times*, 6 October 1960, 1; Waters, 'Against the Tide'.
44 'To Abandon N.G. Would Be Criminal'.

Figure 7.2: 'Detainees working on the Corrective Institution farm at Bomana near Port Moresby'.
Source: NAA: A1200, L27452, item 7572946.

Australian efforts to expand the number and type of democratic institutions in PNG, such as introducing local shire councils to replace direct administration by Port Moresby during Hasluck's tenure, increasing the number of directly elected Papua New Guineans in the PNG Legislative Council in 1961, and planning for a university to support such increased responsibility, were not enough according to UN officials who continued to pressure Australia to move even more quickly towards autonomy.[45] For example, Foot noted that:

> Taken as whole we feel that the effort made by Australia since its last war has been impressive in its range and most admirable in its drive. Its success makes it possible to be confident that further rapid advance is now possible … They [Papua New Guineans] must be given every opportunity to play full part.[46]

---

45 Waiko, *A Short History of Papua New Guinea*, 136; Nelson, *Papua New Guinea*, 127; Moore, *New Guinea*, 197.
46 *Report of the United Nations Visiting Mission to the Trust Territories of Nauru and New Guinea, 1962: Report on New Guinea* (New York: United Nations Trusteeship Council, 1962), digitallibrary.un.org/record/3935446?ln=en.

Australia was being pushed by the world community—both friends and enemies—and by the political left within Australia to speed up moves towards PNG's autonomy. Compounding the influence of external factors, Foot harnessed existing policy proposals, such as the establishment of a university in PNG, to gain the necessary funding to accelerate such development projects.[47] This pressure towards independence extended into all areas of the administration, including law and punishment.

New leadership and the shift in colonial policy

New leadership in 1963 led to changes in policy. Menzies made Charles 'Ceb' Barnes the new minister for territories in 1963 when Hasluck was promoted to the Department of Defence. As mentioned, Barnes was more interested in economics than legal issues, resulting in a noticeable shift in policy, including the decision to end mandatory sentencing. Historians have also clearly established that, under Barnes, the pressure to devolve power to PNG in preparation for independence competed with a new technocratic/bureaucratic culture in the Department of Territories that favoured centralisation in Canberra and matched Barnes's equivocal attitude towards PNG's eventual independence.[48] For example, according to Denoon, 'an elected house implied devolution, but Canberra's control tightened, partly through better communications but largely because of changes in personnel'—that is, Barnes and his staff.[49] As such, the policies that emerged during this time reveal both the stated intention to devolve Australian control and develop PNG institutions, and Canberra's continued insistence that it had the technical and bureaucratic capacity to provide those institutions with directions.

Later, Barnes reflected that, as Hasluck had done such 'tremendous' work on the social and political side, his contribution focussed more on economic and commercial development. For independence to occur, Barnes explained, 'we had to build the material side. Otherwise, you couldn't be independent if you had to have handouts from everyone about the place.' He thought that level of self-sufficiency was a long way off.[50] Nevertheless, Downs maintains

47 Cleland, *Pathways to Independence*, 264–5.
48 Healy, 'Monocultural Administration', 223.
49 Denoon, *A Trial Separation*, 40.
50 Barnes, interview, session 4, 10:43.

that 1960s Australia had abandoned the belief that it would be a trustee indefinitely; although some, as Waters has shown, thought that Australia would be involved in extended supervision of a Melanesian Federation.[51] Furthering the agenda to devolve power on legal issues, Barnes himself was less autocratic and controlling than Hasluck.[52]

In contrast to Barnes, the new departmental secretary, George Warwick Smith, was very interested in centralising decision-making in Canberra and controlling any decisions for which the minister was responsible.[53] Warwick Smith, a career bureaucrat, had begun his public service career in Queensland in the Department of Education before moving to the federal Department of Commerce. He rose to be deputy secretary at the Department of Trade, then moved across to the Department of Territories where he was deputy to Cecil Lambert. He became secretary of the Department of Territories when Lambert retired in 1964. According to his eulogist, he was remembered as being autocratic and uncompromising in his duties: 'by seeking to have all decisions run by his desk, [he] alienated people rather than got them on side'.[54] Downs argued that, despite the government's stated intention to devolve, Warwick Smith actually insisted on more communication and oversight from Canberra.[55] Attempts to balance this centralised and technocratic approach with the pressure to devolve are evident in the reworked clemency process, as, although control was supposed to be devolved, the ultimate power was retained in Canberra where officials from the Department of Territories could use their 'expertise' to control the fate of the condemned. In the end, this ultimate power was subverted by local judges who refrained from employing the death penalty.

Previously, Hasluck had refused a request for an end to mandatory sentencing; following a review of the situation in 1957, he had argued that the current checks and balances were desirable. In contrast, Barnes agreed with the judges that the system of Executive Council review for all wilful murder findings was too slow and confusing to local people.[56] The 1964 submission to end mandatory sentencing also proposed the establishment

---

51 Downs, *The Australian Trusteeship*, 273; Waters, 'The Last of Australian Imperial Dreams', 183–4.
52 Cleland, *Pathways to Independence*, 311; Denoon, *A Trial Separation*, 40–3.
53 Denoon, *A Trial Separation*, 40–5; Downs, *The Australian Trusteeship*, ch. 10.
54 John Farquharson, 'Warwick Smith, George Henry (1916–1999)', *Obituaries Australia*, oa.anu.edu.au/obituary/warwick-smith-george-henry-1003.
55 Downs, *The Australian Trusteeship*, 274–5.
56 NAA: A432, 1956/3371, item 7801327.

a PNG appellate court, before the High Court of Australia, and other changes to sentencing policy, to make PNG's courts more separate from Australian ones for the sake of independence.

Focussing on the question of sentencing reform, Barnes took the advice of judges in PNG and advocated for an end to mandatory sentencing. In conjunction with federal Attorney-General Billy Snedden, he submitted a proposal to the Australian Cabinet calling on the government members of the PNG House of Assembly to pass legislation to end the mandatory sentence of death for wilful murder. Barnes and Snedden acknowledged that local judges had requested more autonomy over sentencing before: 'Over an extended period the Chief Justice and the judges have put forward proposals for changes.' Judges in PNG had long complained that they had less authority than other Australian Supreme Court judges and that the practice of recording and pronouncing sentences followed by clemency was confusing to all concerned.[57] Given the circumstances, Barnes and Warwick Smith welcomed the proposal to devolve some power on legal matters to PNG-based judges.

Even Hasluck's appointment, Chief Justice Alan Mann, had apparently come around to the thinking of the judges of the Supreme Court that he had been sent to change. By 1964, Mann had been persuaded by the B4 view that the people on the ground were the best placed to make judgements about justice and colonial policy. The new sentencing laws were, perhaps, not that far removed from Hasluck's views on respecting judicial decisions; however, having already rejected them, it is clear that they were not what he had in mind when he appointed Mann to promote a bench more in keeping with Australian norms that was supervised by the Executive Council.

Issues of justice, compounded by the awareness of outside scrutiny, resulted in the maintenance of vice-regal oversight in the legislation to end mandatory sentencing. Judges might still sentence offenders to death, but the governor-general of Australia would review all such sentences under advice from the Federal Executive Council.[58] With the *CT* writing about colonial injustice and missteps on a regular basis, including the struggles of other colonial powers to devolve power in underdeveloped places such as Guiana and Kenya, Australian officials were certainly aware of the need for

---

57 B. M. Snedden and C. E. Barnes, 'Confidential for Cabinet Submission', 9 August 1965, 1, NAA: A432, 1964/2543, item 1184765.
58 Snedden and Barnes, 'Confidential for Cabinet Submission', 9 August 1965, 1.

care and due attention to international scrutiny.[59] Department of Territories officials such as Lambert and Warwick Smith were all too aware of the critical and unwanted attention a rogue judge ordering a racially charged execution could bring to Australian foreign policy.[60] Thus, while officials were swayed by arguments to devolve power to judges, they did not want to lose oversight entirely.

Consequently, the form of the legislation to end mandatory sentencing was mired in a space between devolution, centralisation and the desire to avoid international embarrassment. The reform left the problem of sentencing according to individual circumstances to the judges while providing a humanitarian and diplomatic safeguard.

Stepping into this space, Barnes and Snedden set out their primary rationale for the proposed amendments to the administration of justice—namely, that the proposed changes devolved power:

> Underlying the recommendation in this submission is the belief that the judicial system of the Territory should be appropriate to the emerging status of the Territory, and should therefore as far as practicable be self-contained and separate from the judicial system of the Commonwealth and be regulated by the Territory ordinances rather than by Commonwealth Acts.[61]

Prior to the 1960s, debates within and around capital case reviews were about putting the best face on colonialism, rather than ending it. In hanging Usamando and Aro, part of the consideration was that colonial authorities had to follow the precedent for hanging so that they could properly punish Papua New Guineans who might murder white officials in the future. The desire for colonialism to operate with equitable justice was present; however, also present was the idea that colonial justice would keep operating for some time, hence the need to protect white Australians in PNG. However, this legislative change suggests that, as the 1960s progressed, legal institutions were preparing for independence.

---

59 'Self-Rule Turns Sour for British Guiana', *Canberra Times*, 24 July 1963, 32; 'Kenya "Too Hot" for Governor', *Canberra Times*, 20 November 1962, 15; 'Crowds Cheer Mau Mau Chiefs', *Canberra Times*, 18 December 1963, 17.
60 See, for example, 'Soekarno Demands End of All Colonialism, Indonesians Show Might in Take-Over', *Canberra Times*, 2 May 1963, 1.
61 Snedden and Barnes, 'Confidential for Cabinet Submission', 9 August 1965, 1.

Hasluck was actively considering the autonomy of PNG's courts prior to Barnes's succession. He had ordered an inquiry into justice in PNG conducted by David P. Derham, professor of jurisprudence at the University of Melbourne. Derham made significant and, Downs argues, highly influential recommendations towards building the justice system that Australia intended for PNG's independence. Derham shared some of Hasluck's concerns about the ad hoc and fundamentally racist 'kiap courts'—the lowest level of courts for dealing with customary disputes, family law issues and petty crimes in PNG.[62] Kiaps, or patrol officers, were provided with training to run what was, officially, called the Court of Native Affairs; they had a broad remit for ordering resolutions, compensation and generally doing what seemed to them to be necessary to solve problems in line with the ordinances and local customs and ideas. This was generally done without the formalities of laws of evidence, procedures or depositions. Such courts were at the heart of old colonial legal affairs; they symbolised the practice of colonial officials using their expertise and judgement to do what they thought was best. Derham's report gave Hasluck the support he needed to begin to convert the native courts into something more comparable to Australian local courts to be run, eventually, by Papua New Guinean magistrates. However, according to Downs, Hasluck's changes, which were not imposed in the order or at the pace that Derham intended, resulted in a system that did not meet Melanesian notions of justice.[63] Hasluck's notion was that a system that depended on the fiat of colonial officials was unsustainable into the future, unlike the rule of law:

> Our present task, in following this tradition [of fair and impartial courts], is to build an implicit acceptance of the rule of law in Papua New Guinea on foundations that will outlast political change.[64]

The collision of old colonial and liberal notions of the law resulted in the latter becoming the basis of the local court system in PNG. However, by the time some of these policy proposals had to be delivered, Barnes was the responsible minister. Barnes and Snedden's proposal to end mandatory sentencing built on parts of Derham's report; for example, Derham recommended the establishment of an appellate division of the Supreme Court to be based in Port Moresby as a step before the High Court of

---

62 Downs, *The Australian Trusteeship*, 147–51.
63 Ibid., 147–55.
64 Paul Hasluck, speech, 24 October 1961, cited in Downs, *The Australian Trusteeship*, 147–55.

Australia to further build the independence of PNG's courts, and this was included in the suite of legislation that ended mandatory sentencing in 1965.[65]

Internal pressures reinforced the external pressures of decolonisation. Downs has described the pressure Arthur Calwell and his Australian Labor Party (ALP) placed on Barnes by openly criticising the slow pace of government policy on PNG, thereby bringing to an end the largely bipartisan approach that had previously characterised policy on PNG. Increasingly enmeshed in left-wing, anti-colonial movements, the ALP wanted more to be done for PNG, and sooner, to better prepare it for independence in the near future.[66] According to Downs, these changes in ALP policy posed significant new challenges for the Liberal government and hastened the movement towards setting a date for independence, making it 'sooner [rather] than later'.[67]

As well as concerns about building institutions for independence and maintaining control, the end to mandatory sentencing arose out of suggestions that clemency reviews in Canberra undermined the authority of PNG courts in the eyes of Papua New Guineans. This view was supported by Papua New Guineans, including PNG House of Assembly members who, in debating the reform, expressed the view that this disrespect was elevating crime rates. Thus, the proposal to end mandatory sentencing, with continuing vice-regal review, received wide support, as everyone agreed that punishment that was immediate and derived from the PNG court rather than distant Canberra would better deter crime.

Snedden and Barnes raised the same concerns about improving law and order that PNG judges had expressed in the 1957 and 1965 reviews— namely, that the authority of the PNG court was undermined by every wilful murder case going to Canberra.[68] While Hasluck, with his mistrust of the courts, had insisted on vice-regal review, Barnes was satisfied with the quality of the courts. The new minister was more concerned with the apparent reputational damage caused by the current system, as reported by judges and Papua New Guinean politicians:

---

65 Downs, *The Australian Trusteeship*, 151.
66 For Calwell's criticisms and other Labor criticisms, see 'Criticism of Menzies' Views on N.G.', *Canberra Times*, 22 June 1960, 1; 'More Effort to Bring New Guinea to Early Self-Rule Urged', *Canberra Times*, 27 June 1960, 3; 'Calwell Warns on Premature N.G. Self-Rule', *Canberra Times*, 1 July 1960, 1.
67 Downs, *The Australian Trusteeship*, 214; 'Favours Early Independence', *Canberra Times*, 21 June 1960, 1.
68 NAA: M331, 8, item 511120; Snedden and Barnes, 'Confidential Cabinet Submission', 9 August 1965.

> This procedure is damaging to the status of the court because the judge must explain that the real sentence is not a matter for him although he has heard the whole case. Equally important is that all the interested parties who are present do not hear the real sentence and much impact is lost especially when [later] rumours circulate that the convicted person has not been punished at all or has been given a lighter sentence than is the fact. The situation is not really comparable with that in a sophisticated country which has had prolonged experience of these matters, and which has the advantage of a wide press coverage and a literate community.[69]

PNG judges argued that an immediate sentence was needed to ensure that the wicked were seen to be punished completely and promptly. This was important, Barnes and Snedden argued, because the people of this 'unsophisticated country' might otherwise return to vendetta—a real concern to judges and the administration in every case examined in this book—to ensure that justice had been done. Bringing law and order and ending the system of vendetta was frequently cited as a particular success of Australian colonialism, and Barnes and Snedden were loath to endanger it.[70] This concern continued to be a preoccupation of judges as they debated ways to change Papua New Guineans into the kind of advanced person Australia intended to create.[71]

The problem of immediacy and deterrence was evidently of wide concern because officials in Canberra and elected members of the PNG House of Assembly spoke about it when supporting the sentencing reform.[72] Watkins, in reading the Bill in Port Moresby to abolish mandatory sentencing the second time, stated:

> Honourable Members will appreciate that the practice of recording [a] sentence of death has certain undesirable features. For one thing neither the accused not those present at the trial hear the final punishment awarded. For another, it detracts somewhat from the

---

69 Snedden and Barnes, 'Confidential Cabinet Submission', 9 August 1965.
70 Hasluck, *A Time for Building*, 84.
71 Bruce L. Ottley, and Jean G. Zorn, 'Criminal Law in Papua New Guinea: Code, Custom and the Courts in Conflict', *American Journal of Comparative Law* 31, no. 2 (1983): 251–300.
72 Official members were appointed by the administration to the House of Assembly whereas other members were popularly elected. This was intended to incrementally introduce parliamentary democracy in line with the evolution of democracy in colonial Australia. See Territory of Papua and New Guinea, *House of Assembly Debates*, Seventh Meeting of the First Session, 23 November – 29 November, 1965, vol. 1, no. 7, 1158–62.

status of the court that the judge does not carry the proceedings to a conclusion by pronouncing sentence, but has to explain that the matter of punishment be referred to another authority.[73]

Watkins, having been appointed an official member of the PNG House of Assembly by Cleland, was the mouthpiece of the administration in proposing this legislation and, as such, can be seen as representing the concerns of the Australian and PNG governments. The appearance and impact or conduct of justice were constantly raised in clemency deliberations. While a good deal of concern in Canberra was with the appearance of justice as much as with conduct—indeed, a court system must always be concerned with appearance if it is to work effectively—people in PNG were concerned with the actual conduct of justice.

Papua New Guinean politicians spoke in support of Watkins during the second reading of the Bill. Some spoke of the need for more stringency in punishments, indicating their own concerns and, perhaps, the concerns of their constituents. They wanted the legislation to give judges more control. Pita Lus (MHA Dreikikir) from East Sepik, who would go on to have a very successful career in PNG politics, reflected the views of other Papua New Guinean members when he asserted:

> I support the bill, but I reiterate that the penalties should be more severe in order that the people will be afraid of the law and thus not commit so many murders.[74]

As the debate progressed, the House was called to order due to members speaking too critically of judges and their so-called lenient punishments.[75] This criticism of judges indicates that concern over the courts losing authority had reached the emerging elite of Papua New Guinean society. Thus, part of the move to end mandatory sentencing was about making punishment more immediate to deter crime and restore the reputation of the Supreme Court of PNG.

An awareness that crime, particularly violent crime, was on the rise was a significant factor influencing the move away from mandatory sentencing. Judges, federal government ministers and members of the House of Assembly all felt pressure to exercise more visible and immediate justice as a

---

73   Ibid., 1158–9.
74   Ibid., 1160.
75   Ibid.; On Sir Pita Lus, see David Wall, 'Knights of the Realm in PNG', Stories by David Wall, 25 September 2013, deberigny.wordpress.com/category/sir-pita-lus/; Denoon, *A Trial Separation*, 48.

solution to the rise in crime. According to statistics reported to the UNTC and the Australian Parliament, violent crime had been trending gradually upward since the beginning of the 1960s.[76] Denoon suggests that this was the result of increasing urbanisation and associated social dislocations.[77] Whatever the cause, rising crime rates meant that Australian justice was encompassing more offences as more people were brought under actual, rather than nominal, Australian control.

It was in this context that Papua New Guinean members of the House of Assembly, including some who had not been especially critical of the government prior to 1964, expressed the hope that, in ending mandatory sentencing, more severe punishments could be handed down to deter people from committing crimes.[78] This is indicative of the high level of concern in the community about public safety and violence.[79] As Greenwell has observed, despite the use of clemency by Australian courts, Papua New Guineans continued to believe that, to achieve deterrence and retribution, murderers should die. This was based on the view that such deaths restored social harmony, which was the aim of the local conflict resolution systems that preceded and existed alongside Australian law.[80] Thus, Papua New Guineans' support for the legislation to end mandatory sentencing should be seen, at least in part, as their way of addressing these concerns; it signalled recognition that the existing system was no longer entirely satisfactory to the groups engaged with the processes of capital punishment.

Barnes and Snedden did not want to abolish capital punishment in PNG. Indeed, Barnes argued against this in his submission on ending mandatory sentencing, citing expatriate anxiety at high crime levels and the Papua New Guinean tendency to prefer capital punishment for offenders: 'In the present temper of the public opinion of the Territories it would not be practicable to deal with this situation by abolition of the Death Penalty.'[81] As shown in previous chapters, most people involved in the PNG justice

---

76 Australia, Department of Territories, *Territory of Papua: Annual Report for the Period [1949–1965]* (Canberra: Government Printer, [1949–66]). Note the shifting of reporting categories.
77 Denoon, *A Trial Separation*, 45.
78 Wally Watkins, 2nd Reading Speech, *House of Assembly Debates*, 3 June 1965, 1158–62.
79 Waiko, *A Short History of Papua New Guinea*, 136–7; Nelson, *Papua New Guinea*, 124–6; Denoon, *A Trial Separation*, 35–6.
80 John Greenwell, *The Introduction of Western Law into Papua New Guinea*, unpublished manuscript given to the author by John Greenwell, former first assistant secretary and director of Papua New Guinea Office Government and Legal Affairs Division, Department of External Territories, 1970–75, 11–14.
81 Snedden and Barnes, 'Confidential Cabinet Submission', 9 August 1965.

system believed in the deterrent effect of punishment, particularly capital punishment, and there was evidently pressure to produce a greater deterrent effect from punishment to meet the rise in crime.

Reflecting on his time in government, Barnes stated that he saw himself as having been very strict on law and order in response to rising crime in PNG; he felt that he pursued this policy in the face of opposition from Australian academics, in particular, who criticised him for his strictness.[82] Thus, the legislative change to end mandatory sentencing should also, in part, be seen as Barnes's and the Papua New Guinean legislators' attempt to increase law and order via deterrence, including the possibility of capital punishment.

The trend against the use of the death penalty in Australia and PNG

While the form of the 1964 legislation aimed to provide a solution to the tension between community expectations and judicial decisions, in fact, the judges defied expectations and no one was ever condemned to death again.[83] How can this be explained? The PNG Law Reform Commission attributed it to judges always finding extenuating circumstances to imprison rather than sentence offenders to death.[84] Another explanation is that the capacity to actually hand down death sentences and carry them out was limited by the shift in wider sentencing norms against the death penalty in PNG since 1954. The established nature of this practice of accommodating cultural clash and legal uncertainty through clemency between 1957 and 1964 was apparent in the process and the arguments around clemency, as well as the clear precedent that judges noted in their decisions.

There was a pervasive belief in PNG, stemming from the Murray system, that Papua New Guineans mostly did not understand Australian law or the intention of capital punishment as it was understood in Australia and like jurisdictions. In 1959 Justice Ralph Gore was still arguing that the PNG Criminal Code 'needed softening when applied to a primitive people ethically opposite'.[85] Up to 1957, capital punishment was reserved

---

82 Barnes, interview, session 4, 12:18.
83 Law Reform Commission of Papua New Guinea, 'Punishment for Wilful Murder', *Occasional Paper 1*, 1 July 1976.
84 Ibid.
85 Ralph Gore, untitled draft legal history of PNG, 2, Papers of Ralph Gore, 1930–1964, National Library of Australia (hereafter Gore Papers), box 1, folder 8.

7. THE END OF MANDATORY SENTENCING

for only the most extraordinary crimes committed by Westernised people such as Usamando and Aro. However, even this threshold seemed to be abandoned by the 1960s in favour of a more universal acceptance of Papua New Guineans' lack of understanding of Western law and punishment. The following analysis of *R. v. Endei, 1964* highlights the extent to which clemency was presumed in the 1960s; the case, which resulted in Endei's sentence being commuted, is useful because of its similarity to Aro of Rupamanda's, which resulted in execution.[86] Justice Ollerenshaw heard *R. v. Endei*. Ollerenshaw became a barrister in New South Wales in 1929 and later practised in Rabaul, where he also served as a member of the New Guinean Legislative Council from 1937. He served in the Australian Army during the Second World War. He acted briefly as a judge in PNG in 1954 to relieve a build-up of cases and was appointed on a permanent basis from the New South Wales bar by Hasluck on 12 September 1961.[87] He retired in 1970 to Buderim, Queensland.[88] In his obituary in 1972, Chief Justice Minogue noted his fine service, and, in particular, the importance of his judgements in relation to interpreting the defences of accident and provocation.[89] With this endorsement, the case of Endei takes on greater significance, as Ollerenshaw discussed the relevance of provocation in determining punishment.

Endei, a forty-one-year-old Papua New Guinean man who had some familiarity with the administration, a measure of Westernisation and, therefore, culpability, committed a double murder, killing both his stepdaughter and her friend. His crime, according to Ollerenshaw, was 'not induced by any traditional fear or belief [but instead was the] crime of a man who gave way to a viciousness'.[90] Ollerenshaw's sentencing commentary highlights the shift to the presumption of clemency that had developed in PNG at this time, for, despite his ringing condemnation of the accused, not to mention the complete absence of mitigating factors of local custom—such as honour, duty and shame—Ollerenshaw determined that it was best to record his sentence in order to protect the authority of the court.

Ollerenshaw's first argument rehearsed the usual reason for clemency—namely, that Papua New Guineans, neither the offender nor their community, could understand the death sentence and, in particular, the

---

86 See Chapter 6.
87 'Judge's Post in Territory', *Canberra Times*, 12 September 1961, 8.
88 'Judge Dies', *Post-Courier* (Port Moresby), 20 September 1972, 9.
89 'Praise for Dead Judge', *Post-Courier*, 21 September 1972, 13.
90 Ollerenshaw to administrator, 25 May 1964, 5, NAA: A452, 1964/3503, item 3541991.

distinction between pronounced and recorded sentences.[91] Refining this point, Ollerenshaw asserted that to pronounce a sentence only to have it overturned in Canberra would confuse the community, further reducing their confidence in the court.[92] Ollerenshaw was not alone in his belief that the mandatory sentencing and commutation process was undermining his authority in the eyes of the Papua New Guinean community, and other judges highlighted this argument in their campaign to end mandatory sentencing.[93]

In the recommendation of clemency he prepared for the governor-general, Ollerenshaw noted that he had been lobbied by local officials and local people about the case, so aghast were they at Endei's violation of both traditional and modern mores. Ollerenshaw explained that it was precisely because Papua New Guinean locals and expatriate officials had called for Endei to hang that he could not order it: 'A judge should not even appear to be influenced by particular local pressures.'[94] Had he sentenced Endei to death, it may have appeared that such lobbying was successful, thereby discrediting the independence of the court. To build confidence in his authority, Ollerenshaw argued that he needed to be seen as solely responsible for the sentence.

Further, Ollerenshaw questioned why Endei should pay paid price for earlier leniency and the current concern about law and order. This argument made it apparent that he thought the trend of clemency was so established that the act of hanging anyone to change that trend would be unjust 'scapegoating'.[95] Rather than a just outcome, Ollerenshaw made it clear in his clemency review submission that he thought 'scapegoating' Endei was unfair. This suggests that he was recording sentences because he thought that hanging was no longer supportable by the weight of sentencing precedents. At the same time, he believed that the practice of commutation was so entrenched that even if he pronounced the sentence, even with this particularly vicious crime, it would be commuted. Ollerenshaw was pointing out that sentencing standards had reached a point from which it was difficult to return. This case also indicates that, with the weight of precedents and sentencing norms, judges in PNG did not think capital punishment could be perceived as just,

---

91   Ibid., 1–2.
92   Ibid., 1–4.
93   Snedden and Barnes, 'Confidential Cabinet Submission', 9 August 1965.
94   Ollerenshaw to administrator, 25 May 1964, 5.
95   Ibid., 4–5.

neither in the service of the law nor for cultural purposes. His arguments highlighted a shift in the threshold of pronouncing a sentence—and in seeing a death sentence carried out.

My survey of clemency files shows that, after mandatory sentencing was abolished, the trend towards clemency continued, such that no one was sentenced to death, let alone executed, before independence. The PNG Law Reform Commission also noted that no one was sentenced to death between 1964 and 1976.[96]

'Prima facie, the sentence required by law should be death as now'

In 1964, the use of clemency to deal with cultural and evidentiary uncertainty, shown in cases such as the Telefomin killers and Sunambus of Puto, was no longer satisfactory to Papua New Guineans. Further, Ollerenshaw's commentary on Endei's sentencing shows that judges were also unhappy with reserving questions of cultural mitigation to the clemency process. They wanted a new solution. It was in this context that the legislation to end mandatory sentencing was extended to include mitigations drawn from Papua New Guinean cultural expectations, norms or obligations as a partial defence to a murder charge.

Barnes and Snedden argued that judges needed guidelines for interpreting violent crime that would allow them to understand what motivated Papua New Guineans, which, in turn, would allow them to develop laws that were suitable to the culture of the coming new nation. Thus, their 1964 submission proposed to allow judges to consider the cultural motivations of Papua New Guinean offenders as mitigating their culpability in a murder trial. Indeed, judges had long found that Papua New Guinean offenders were driven by impulses not encompassed by the elements of mitigation in Australian law. However, such matters were only discussed in capital case reviews or in the decision to record rather than pronounce sentences.[97] The advice from the PNG bench was to change those practices to build a more culturally independent Papua New Guinean legal system, rather than fixing it to Australian norms as Hasluck had intended: Barnes and Snedden agreed.

---

96 Law Reform Commission of Papua New Guinea, 'Punishment for Wilful Murder'.
97 Snedden and Barnes, 'Confidential Cabinet Submission', 9 August 1965.

The provisions of the legislation to end mandatory sentencing also indicated an interest in meaningful devolution and decolonisation of the notion of justice. In the case studies examined earlier, judges often recommended clemency on the basis of particular cultural circumstances, leaving Australian bureaucrats and politicians clamouring to understand the chain of causation—such as the shame and pride inherent to the motivations of Ako-Ove and the men of Telefomin. Indeed, in most cases across the period examined here, judges plainly would not have handed down a sentence of death were it not mandatory; yet politicians in Canberra were left to puzzle out why and if an execution was just.

Barnes and Snedden wanted to allow judges, rather than politicians, to match Papua New Guinean notions of provocation and duty to the outcomes of capital cases. Rather than trying to explain the culture of offenders to the less expert governor-general-in-council, They thought it more efficient and just for the judges to make the decision to imprison the offender, which they plainly wanted to make when they recorded, rather than pronounced, a sentence. Therefore, in their recommendation to the Cabinet, they argued that:

> After much thought and after consultation by the Attorney-General with the judges, we recommend that the trial Judge should have, in each case, the responsibility of deciding whether in all circumstances, imprisonment (for a term then and there decided by the judge) should be substituted for the death penalty. The criterion in deciding between death and imprisonment should be in the presence or absence of extenuating circumstances. Prima Facie, the sentence required by law should be death as now. If the judge finds that there are extenuating circumstances, he should be required by law to impose a term of imprisonment.[98]

In recommending that the exact extenuating circumstances not be iterated in the legislation, but be left to the discretion of the court, Barnes and Snedden signalled their recognition of the difficulties of writing specific legislation for the array of cultural impulses within the hundreds of PNG cultures. If the intention had been to maintain Australian norms, this aspect of the submission would not have been included.[99] It was not necessary to the process of ending capital punishment, as a purely Australian approach to mitigation could have been maintained. This indicates an interest in

---

98   Snedden and Barnes, 'Confidential Cabinet Submission', 9 August 1965.
99   *House of Assembly Debates,* 3 November 1968, 1158–62.

meaningful devolution and decolonisation. Effectively, it directed judges to return to the Murray system's dictum of 'thinking black', which Hasluck had resisted.[100] This policy direction under Barnes modified Hasluck's attempts to inculcate advanced Australian norms of punishment and justice and reform Papua New Guinean understandings of just punishment.

Further, this discretionary power reversed the direction of Hasluck's mistrust of PNG judges. The wording of the recommendations to the Cabinet, and the very similar terms in the second reading debate, gave great credence to the local knowledge of judges and lawyers in PNG.[101] Whereas previously, under Hasluck, judges and lawyers in PNG had been suspected of paternalism and discrimination, the new legislation would provide wide powers to interpret Papua New Guinean customs. Barnes and Snedden recommended that:

> Extenuating circumstances would not be defined, but that Judges would, in considering whether there are extenuating circumstances in a case, have regard to matters that presently lead the judge to record, rather than pronounce the death sentence. These include the shortness of the period of exposure to Administration influence, the strength of a native custom that has motivated the crime and the incapacity of the group of which the prisoner formed part to comprehend the gravity of the offence under our system of law.[102]

This modification under Barnes was a synthesis of the 'B4's'—or 'old colonialism's'—faith in PNG courts and the discretion of officials, and the views of progressives who wanted more emphasis placed on Papua New Guinean beliefs.[103] Under the new legislation, judges were expected to give weight to cultural factors that previously could only be considered in post-sentencing clemency processes, which could be highly political.

This change came less than ten years after Hasluck had rejected administration proposals for local courts that would have given some recognition to indigenous practices. The difference was that, under Barnes, Australia sought to meet the expectations of a world focussed on decolonisation and humanitarian development. As Emily Baughan and Bronwen Everill suggest:

---

100 Ralph Gore, *Justice versus Sorcery* (Brisbane: Jacaranda Press, 1964), 28; Francis West, *Hubert Murray: The Australian Pro-Consul* (Melbourne: Oxford University Press, 1968), 211.
101 *House of Assembly Debates*, 3 November 1968, 1158–62.
102 Snedden and Barnes, 'Confidential Cabinet Submission', 9 August 1965 (original emphasis).
103 On progressives' desire for more customary law see Healy, 'Monocultural Administration', 221–2.

> Humanitarian work was also revealed to be a site of active experimentation in the empire … and the relationship between the coloniser, the colonised and the imperial state were negotiated through the language of humanitarian reform.[104]

Australia was engaged in justifying its colonialism as a humanitarian project. According to Michael Barnett, in the postwar period, humanitarians who were engaged in the development of former colonies became more sensitive to infantilising language, processes and implications that cast the recipients of their endeavour as backward.[105] Including indigenous thoughts about justice in punishment decisions is consistent with Australia's claims to humanitarian colonialism, as self-determination, independence and sovereignty emerged as key concepts in development.[106] Sentencing measures that gave recognition to indigenous practices and beliefs fit with the tendency towards respect and self-determination. Thus, the rationale for ending mandatory sentencing and reconsidering mitigation, as steps towards independence, were consistent with the arc of change in postwar colonialism that placed more emphasis on autonomy and respect for non-Western cultural practices.

The new legislation not only acknowledged customary impulses as mitigation, but also the Papua New Guinean preference for capital punishment. Indeed, as was plain in Barnes's submission, the federal Cabinet intended the death penalty to remain in use.[107] The legislation passed the PNG House of Assembly in the midst of arguments mounted by Papua New Guinean members that offenders should be more severely punished—if necessary, by death.[108] The passage of the legislation shows that Papua New Guinean conceptualisations of what was just and right was being given more weight.

Yet, despite the clear arguments of Papua New Guineans for more capital punishment, Australians and Australian judges decided that clemency was more appropriate. In the 1970s, the PNG Law Reform Commission argued that Australian judges in the 1960s, guided by the doctrine of the unsophisticated perpetrator established by Justice Gore decades before, made

---

104 Emily Baughan and Bronwen Everill, 'Empire and Humanitarianism: A Preface', *Journal of Imperial and Commonwealth History* 40, no. 5 (December 2012): 727.
105 Barnett, *Empire of Humanity*, 105.
106 Ibid., 130.
107 Snedden and Barnes, 'Confidential Cabinet Submission', 9 August 1965.
108 *House of Assembly Debates*, 3 November 1968.

essentially colonialist and racist decisions in preserving life.[109] Australian judges were troubled by questions of justice relating to understandings of culture, sentencing norms and precedents, international and local status and reputation, and the ongoing problems of evidence. They were under pressure to implement a modern, Western legal system while also being sensitive to the shifts in thinking in world humanitarianism and developmental colonialism that held that indigenous cultures and rights should be respected. Giving judges space to consider local cultural imperatives went some way to respecting Papua New Guinean cultures while also allowing the legal system to function in a way that met evolving international standards that increasingly valued the views of colonised people. It allowed for uncertainty while also encouraging efficiency. It was hoped that the certainty in punishment, which would follow from judges being able to encompass cultural motivations immediately rather than waiting for decisions from Canberra, would also build respect for the judiciary. However, the intention that capital punishment would be employed regularly as a part of building that respect was not successful. It had been too long between hangings in a legal system moving away from execution, despite the stated wishes of the local people.

In 1964, the new, expanded House of Assembly replaced the Legislative Council in PNG; the first cohort of students graduated from the University of Papua New Guinea; and there were widespread protests following a wage decision that paid Papua New Guineans less than Australians for the same work. Papua New Guineans were starting to feel their power. However, their independence was still subject to boundaries set by Canberra, as Australians continued to justify their presence by the development they brought to the territories. Not everyone wanted change to occur quickly; for example, on 29 April 1966, an *SPP* editorial warned against hurrying independence. Some expatriates hoped that independence would never happen, to which view Cleland responded on 2 May 1966, publicly stating that PNG would never become a state of Australia.[110] Canberra and the world community insisted that power had to be gradually devolved to the territories; and institutions, such as the courts, in ending mandatory sentencing, began to reflect that change.

---

109 Law Reform Commission of Papua New Guinea, 'Punishment for Wilful Murder'.
110 'Canberra Begs the Issue—Editorial', *South Pacific Post*, 29 April 1966; 'Territory as 7th State "Impractical"'.

Notwithstanding the intention of the politicians who passed the legislation and the fact that vicious murders were committed that may have warranted its use, the death penalty was not used in PNG after mandatory sentencing was abolished. The courts resisted public pressure, both expatriate and Papua New Guinean, and did not execute murderers. In doing so, the courts brought about a de facto end to the death penalty.[111] This occurred alongside judges and colonial officials asking questions like those expressed during deliberations over clemency, as described throughout this book. How would the world see the vice-regal review? How would the local community react to a death sentence? How would expatriates react? How could justice be done in the unique circumstances of PNG? In 1965, under Barnes, and in the face of international pressure to devolve power, new solutions were needed. The previously standard practices of recording sentences and enacting clemency or pronouncing sentences and deferring the decision no longer sufficed. The responsibility for answering the questions posed by the colonial project was devolved to the local level rather than gathered into the hands of Canberra, as it had been under Hasluck. Papua New Guineans, judges, the administration and Barnes's ministry decided that problems had to be addressed in PNG, within structures and using concepts that would eventually allow Papua New Guineans to solve them for themselves.

Capital punishment for wilful murder was abolished by an independent PNG in 1976. However, the death penalty was reinstated as a prescribed punishment for treason and piracy in 1984. Later, it was also reinstated for wilful murder and aggravated rape and robbery with violence.[112] Yet, no one was executed due to a lack of enabling law or means to do so. Despite calls for sterner punishment in a time of high crime, the death penalty was abolished again in January 2022.[113] The government argued that it was ineffective and not consistent with Christian values or ethics.

---

111 'The Drum', *South Pacific Post*, 5 January 1966, 1.
112 *Criminal Code Act 1974* (PNG), sections 37, 81, 82, 299, Pacific Islands Legal Information Institute, www.paclii.org/pg/legis/consol_act/cca1974115/; *Criminal Code Act* (Independent State of Papua New Guinea), Pacific Island Legal Information Institute, www.paclii.org/pg/legis/PG-consol_act_1986/cca115/. Capital punishment was reintroduced due to concerns about crime in 1991. Section 299(2) amended by Act No. 2 of 1976; repealed and replaced by Act No. 25 of 1991. See 'Death Penalty Repealed', *National*, 21 January 2022, www.thenational.com.pg/death-penalty-repealed/.
113 Donald Nangoi, 'Death Penalty Act Repealed', *Post-Courier*, 21 January 2022, postcourier.com.pg/death-penalty-act-repealed/.

Conclusion

In this book, through the study of detailed and highly personalised capital case files, both the manner in which colonial officials conceptualised their duties and the lives of ordinary Papua New Guineans have become visible to the historical record. Each case has revealed debates about Australia's place in the territories as a self-appointed guide and guardian. Occasioned by the extremity of the crimes and penalties under discussion, the violence of which challenged colonial authority, the debates drew attention to the failure of Australia's colonialism to transform the legal culture of Papua New Guineans to an Australian rule of law. The capital case reviews provided an opportunity for Australian officials to strive for balance between self-interest and altruism. Each showed how the trusteeship was exercised on the bodies of offenders and in the experiences of their communities. The studies also shed light on a little-known aspect of PNG legal history in the colonial period.

The analysis of the case files with clusters of related sources has allowed for more than a recording of who was hanged or who was not. That said, discussing who was hanged contradicts commonly held views about the use of capital punishment in PNG, for it shows that Aro of Rupamanda was the last person hanged there in 1957. The work highlights the rationales under which decisions were made about Papua New Guineans, their culture and justice, and the role played by the shifting notions underpinning Australian colonialism in making decisions about punishment. It has also uncovered the effects of the engagement of decision-makers with multiple audiences—Papua New Guinean, expatriate, metropolitan and international.

This analysis has demonstrated that, in 1954, in an extremely diverse colonial setting, judges and bureaucrats in PNG were attempting to solve the ambiguities of evidence and the cultural complexities of implementing Australian law by making discretionary punishment decisions. They sought to bring peace and confidence through engineering social dynamics with clemency and relative leniency, and did so with limited oversight from Canberra. The exercise of mercy was calculated in terms that would serve Australia's need to maintain the legitimacy of its colonial presence by projecting an image of benevolence to appease critics inside and outside of PNG. Ostensibly, also through mercy, colonialists hoped to advance Papua New Guineans slowly towards a more peaceful approach to solving difficult breaches of communal trust, and thereby build confidence in the benignity of Australian control. The case studies show that these issues were debated at several levels when determining the fate of the accused in a process that was satisfactory to those involved until 1954.

By the mid-1950s, Minister for Territories Paul Hasluck had become more familiar with his role and had begun to bring his own emphases to it. He viewed the reliance on judicial discretion and leniency as racist and colonialist, based as it was on a presumption of Papua New Guinean incapacity. Moreover, he believed that such an approach would not be easily sold to a critical, anti-colonial—or, at least, Cold War–riven—world audience. Hasluck determined that the legitimacy of Australia's role in PNG, and the viability of its colonial project, required the inculcation of a consistent, Western rule of law that could assist in Australia guiding the transformation of PNG communities into an 'advanced society' as required by the UNTC. He moved against discretionary practices to alter the judicial culture to be more Australian by appointing an 'outsider' as chief justice. At the same time, he ensured more oversight in Canberra to ameliorate his reservations about PNG justice. Hasluck's changes rendered the governor-general, in particular, Sir William Slim, much more significant to the process than previous governors-general. Slim's prewar beliefs and perspectives on colonialism introduced a new level and set of parameters into the equation of determining justice and punishment. Yet, the evidence shows that Hasluck's changes were tempered by judges and officials negotiating to achieve the outcomes that they felt were best, resulting in some longer sentences, but not a trend towards more executions, despite Slim's preference. The PNG practice of never confirming recorded sentences of death was maintained in contrast to most other places in the world where such a distinction between recorded and pronounced sentences existed. Hasluck's brand of liberalism, which held that colonialism was only acceptable if it was egalitarian, altruistic and temporary, was in contrast to prewar paternalistic notions that Australians would decide what was best to advance and protect Papua New Guineans. This tension played out in debates over how to punish offenders and in Hasluck's attempt to fairly regularise and systemise a discretionary system.

By the early 1960s, as international scrutiny and, with it, demands for more substantial moves towards independence grew, another stage of reform devolved power to the judges and returned to depending on judicial discretion to interpret local cultures for decisions about punishment with less oversight from Canberra. At the same time, the effects of continuing difficulties of evidence and processes, and a general move away from capital punishment in Australian jurisdictions, reduced the possibility of using

7. THE END OF MANDATORY SENTENCING

capital punishment. The willingness of a less interested minister to devolve discretion to judges indicated the extent to which the exercise of this most extreme form of judicial power was fundamentally shaped by political considerations. In practice, by not sentencing people to death over the years, and by consistently using local cultural factors to mitigate culpability for murder, the judiciary in PNG brought about a de facto end to the use of capital punishment. That was not the result the Papua New Guinean legislators intended; they wanted more, not less, capital punishment, for reasons that were as much legal as they were political.

This book has explored why Australian judges in PNG, and officials at several levels, utilised clemency so much more often than executions in controlling, and communicating with, Papua New Guineans, decisions that were impacted by international, national and local changes in colonial authority following the Second World War. Compared to British colonies in Africa, PNG had high rates of commutation;[114] therefore, the case files discussed in this book provide a perspective on a distinctive technique employed by Australian colonialism, and also on the tensions, debates and transitions that occurred in the use of that technique.

This book is more than a history of law, governance and politics. The analysis in this book reveals something about the lives of ordinary people and their relationship to the colonial state. Their concerns with preserving law and order and preventing vendetta, their attempts to navigate the imposed legal system and their attempts to find justice can be excavated from court testimonies, the precis of testimonies, and the accounts of missionaries, bureaucrats and lawyers that were collected to make decisions about the fate of the condemned. In this detailed, but often selective and incomplete archive, we can see the lives of people who experienced Australian justice and how they engaged with attempts to 'advance' them through the criminal justice system. This book also shows that, while Australian officials were aware of the Papua New Guinean preference for responding to violent crime with capital punishment, Australia did not often see that method as meeting its social, political and diplomatic goals; consequently, the Australian judiciary and Executive Council used executions only twice after the war.

---

114 Stacey Hynd, '"The Extreme Penalty of the Law": Mercy and the Death Penalty as Aspects of State Power in Colonial Nyasaland, c. 1903–47', *Journal of East African Studies* 4, no. 3 (2010): 552–9; Stacey Hynd, 'Killing the Condemned. The Practice and Process of Capital Punishment in British Africa, 1900–1950s', *Journal of African History* 49, no. 3 (2008): 403–18; Stacey Hynd, 'Murder and Mercy: Capital Punishment in Colonial Kenya, ca. 1909–1956', *International Journal of African Historical Studies* 45, no. 1 (2012): 81–101.

The studies show how Papua New Guineans experienced a criminal justice system that was very different from local systems of community consensus and informal patronage. They show, too, the variable successes and failures of Australian justice that were embraced by some, rejected by others, and manipulated by others who sought to use it for their own political and personal objectives; the collision of ways of lives and how people negotiated a complex discretionary system; and the different ways societies yoked together in colonialism might 'jabber' their way to outcomes.

Through the lens of capital case reviews, we can see through the *Pandanas* curtain to the hopes, successes, failures and self-beliefs of Australia's colonial officials and expatriates, and how such beliefs changed over time. The capital case review files provide evidence to construct a narrative of the intersecting ideologies of Australian colonialism at its most profound, across questions of life, death, gender, race, justice and civilisation.

This book provides insight into a period in PNG history when it was unclear what the outcome of Australian colonialism would be; and evidence and argument that illuminates biographical, cultural, legal, diplomatic and political questions in Australian and PNG history. It deepens our understanding of PNG legal history during a period little studied by scholars; and explores a period of Australian history, and colonial practice, that has been neglected by Australian historians in recent decades. As such, it is an original and contemporary contribution to understanding PNG and Australian history and its colonial past.

This is also a legal history that connects with PNG's contemporary struggles to come to terms with capital punishment and its abolition. Even while it was possible to execute offenders in PNG, it did not happen. While the independent state's Criminal Code at first abolished capital punishment as a broken and redundant colonial relic, as mentioned, it was reintroduced for treason and piracy in 1984, for wilful murder in 1991 and for other violent offences in 2013. Yet, the means to actually end a life were never developed, until, finally, it was abolished again in 2022.[115] As during the colonial period, between 1984 and 2022, a judge sentencing someone to death did not do so in the expectation of the sentence being carried out, but, rather, in the hope of sending a clear message of deterrence.

---

115 Ibid.

7. THE END OF MANDATORY SENTENCING

The abolition of the death penalty in 2022 in PNG occurred despite a parliamentary committee recommending legislation to introduce either a firing squad, lethal injection or hanging. That advice was rejected and legislation converting death sentences to life imprisonment was introduced.[116] According to Prime Minister James Marape and Justice Minister Bryan Kramer, the death penalty was not in keeping with PNGs desire to be a just, modern and Christian country; it had been ineffective as a deterrent; and its abolition was welcomed by the United Nation Commissioner for Human Rights.[117] As in the 1950s and 1960s, capital punishment is still regarded as emblematic of the nature of a state. Finding a just punishment for awful offences that is acceptable to a range of disparate external and internal stakeholders and addresses the problem of pervasive violence is a continuing struggle.

Sean Dorney, in *The Embarrassed Colonialist*, noted the dearth of contemporary scholarship on the history of Australia's role in PNG and argued that:

> We need to acknowledge our colonial past as a starting point for deeper engagement with PNG today. And once and for all Australia needs to shed its embarrassment and embrace its relations with its nearest neighbour.[118]

This book offers a further step in that direction. It provides new perspectives on Australian colonialism through a study of the Australian officials who made decisions and judgements, and the Papua New Guineans who were subject to them. Finally, the rich archive from which this book is derived invites further study, providing untold opportunities to delve into the lived experiences, relationships and assumptions that shaped Papua New Guineans and Australians in their engagements with colonialism in the 1950s and 1960s.

---

116 APR editor, 'PNG's Death Penalty Law Repealed in Shake up over Criminal Justice', *Asia Pacific Report*, 21 January 2022, asiapacificreport.nz/2022/01/21/pngs-death-penalty-law-repealed-in-shake-up-over-criminal-justice/.
117 'The United Nations In Papua New Guinea Welcomes the Announcement of the Repeal of the Death Penalty', *Pacific Scoop*, 21 January 2022, pacific.scoop.co.nz/2022/01/the-united-nations-in-papua-new-guinea-welcomes-the-announcement-of-the-repeal-of-the-death-penalty/; Amrit Burman, 'Papua New Guinea Repeals Death Penalty 30 Years after Reintroducing It', *Republic World* (India), 21 January 2022, www.republicworld.com/world-news/rest-of-the-world-news/papua-new-guinea-repeals-death-penalty-30-years-after-reintroducing-it-articleshow.html; Moses Sakai, 'PNG and the Politics of the Death Penalty', *Interpreter*, Lowy Institute, 11 December 2020, online edition.
118 Sean Dorney, *The Embarrassed Colonialist* (Sydney: Lowy Institute Papers, 2016), Kindle edition, final paragraph of introduction.

Bibliography

Published sources

Acts of the Parliament of the United Kingdom/George IV. *Judgement of Death Act, 1823*. United Kingdom, 4 George IV, c.48.

Adler, Zsuzsanna. *Rape on Trial*. New York: Routledge and Kegan Paul, 1987.

Aldrich, Robert. *Colonialism and Homosexuality*. London: Routledge, 2003.

Anderson, David. *Histories of the Hanged: The Dirty War in Kenya and the End of Empire*. New York: W.W. Norton and Company, 2005.

Australia. Department of Territories. *Report to the General Assembly of the United Nations on the Administration of the Territory of New Guinea from 1st July, 1948, to 30th June, 1949*. Canberra: Government Printer, 1950.

Australia. Department of Territories. *Report to the General Assembly of the United Nations on the Administration of the Territory of New Guinea [1946–1966]*. Canberra: Commonwealth Government Printer [1947–1967].

Australia. Department of Territories. *Territory of Papua: Annual Report for the Period [1947–1965]*. Canberra: Government Printer, [1949–66].

Australia. Department of Territories. *The Territory of Papua and New Guinea*. Canberra: Australian Government Printer, 1961.

Auty, Kate. *Black Glass: Western Australian Courts of Native Affairs 1936–54*. Freemantle: Freemantle Arts Centre Press, 2005.

Barber, R. N. 'The Labour Party and the Abolition of Capital Punishment in Queensland 1899–1922'. *Queensland Heritage* 1 no. 9 (Nov. 1968): 3–12.

Barnett, Michael. *Empire of Humanity: A History of Humanitarianism*. Ithaca: Cornell University Press, 2011.

Barry, J. V., G. W. Paton and G. Sawer. *An Introduction to the Criminal Law in Australia*. London: McMillian and Co., 1948.

Baughan, Emily and Bronwen Everill. 'Empire and Humanitarianism: A Preface'. *Journal of Imperial and Commonwealth History* 40, no. 5 (December 2012). doi.org/10.1080/03086534.2012.730826.

Berger, Benjamin, Hamar Foster and A. R. Buck. 'Introduction: Does Law Matter? The New Colonial Legal History?' In *The Grand Experiment: Law and Legal Culture in British Settler Societies,* edited by Hamar Foster, Benjamin L. Berger and A. R. Buck, 1–11. Vancouver: University of British Columbia Press, 2008. doi.org/10.59962/9780774814935-004.

'Bignold, Hugh Baron'. *Australian Dictionary of Biography*. adb.anu.edu.au/biography/bignold-hugh-baron-5234. Published first in hardcopy 1979.

Bongiorno, Frank. *The Sex Lives of Australians: A History*. Collingwood: Black Inc., 2012.

Bourke, Joanna. *Rape: Sex, Violence, History*. Berkley: Counterpoint Press, 2007.

Brett, Peter. 'Conditional Pardons and the Commutation of Death Sentences'. *Modern Law Review*, 20, no. 2 (1957): 131–47. doi.org/10.1111/j.1468-2230.1957.tb00432.x.

Bridge, Carl. 'Diplomat'. In *Paul Hasluck in Australian History: Civic Personality and Public Life,* edited by Tom Stannage, Kay Saunders and Richard Nile, 133–50. St Lucia: University of Queensland Press, 1999.

Brown, Nicholas. *Governing Prosperity: Social Change and Social Analysis in Australia in the 1950s*. Melbourne: Cambridge University Press, 2009. doi.org/10.1086/ahr/102.5.1557.

Buchan, Bruce. *Empire of Political Thought: Indigenous Australians and the Language of Colonial Government*. London: Pickering and Chatto, 2008.

Bulbeck, Chilla. *Australian Women in Papua and New Guinea: Colonial Passages 1920–1960*. Melbourne: Cambridge University Press, 1992. doi.org/10.1017/cbo9780511518263.

Calavita, Kitty. 'Blue Jeans and the "De-Constitutive" Power of Law'. *Law and Society Review* 35, no. 1 (2001): 89–116. doi.org/10.2307/3185387.

Castle, Tim. 'Constructing Death: Newspaper Reports of Executions in Colonial New South Wales, 1826–1837'. *Journal of Australian Colonial History* 9 (2007).

Chalmers, Gloria. *Kundus, Cannibals and Cargo Cults: Papua New Guinea in the 1950s*. Watsons Bay: Books and Writers Network, 2006.

Cleland, Rachel. *Pathways to Independence: Story of Official and Family Life in Papua New Guinea from 1951–1975*. Cottesloe: Singapore National Printer, 1985.

Cohen, Daniel A. *Pillars of Salt and Monuments of Grace*. Amherst and Boston: University of Massachusetts Press, 2006.

Cooper, Frederick and Ann L. Stoler. 'Tensions of Empire: Colonial Control and Visions of Rule'. *American Ethnologist* 16, no. 4 (1989): 609–21. doi.org/10.1525/ae.1989.16.4.02a00010.

Craig, Barry. 'The Telefomin Murders: Whose Myth?' In *Oceania Monograph: Children of Afek: Tradition and Change among the Mountain-Ok of Central New Guinea*, edited by Barry Craig and David Hyndman, 141–5. Sydney: Oceania Press, University of Sydney, 1990.

Craig, Barry and David Hyndman, eds. *Oceania Monograph: Children of Afek: Tradition and Change among the Mountain-Ok of Central New Guinea*. Sydney: Oceania Press, 1990. doi.org/10.1525/aa.1992.94.2.02a00610.

Cribb, Robert. 'Legal Pluralism and Criminal Law in the Dutch Colonial Order'. *Indonesia*, no. 90 (October 2010): 47–66.

Crimes Act 1900 (NSW).

Criminal Code (Queensland, Adopted) in Its Application to the Territory of New Guinea. Pacific Islands Legal Information Institute. www.paclii.org/pg/legis/newguinea_annotated/cca254/.

Criminal Code (Queensland, Adopted) in Its Application to the Territory of Papua. Pacific Island Legal Information Institute. www.paclii.org/pg/legis/papua_annotated/cca254.pdf.

Criminal Code Act (Independent State of Papua New Guinea). Pacific Island Legal Information Institute. www.paclii.org/pg/legis/PG-consol_act_1986/cca115/.

Criminal Code Act 1974 (PNG). Pacific Islands Legal Information Institute. www.paclii.org/pg/legis/consol_act/cca1974115/.

Criminal Code Amendment Ordinance 1923–1939. Pacific Islands Legal Information Institute. www.paclii.org/pg/legis/newguinea_annotated/ccao19231939248.

Denoon, Donald. *A Trial Separation: Australia and the Decolonisation of Papua New Guinea*. Canberra: Pandanus Books, 2005. doi.org/10.26530/oapen_459759.

Denoon, Donald, Philippa Mein-Smith and Marivic Wyndham. *A History of Australia, New Zealand and the Pacific*. Oxford: Blackwell, 2000. doi.org/10.1080/03612759.2001.10525807.

Department of Foreign Affairs. *Historical Documents: Volume 26: Australia and Papua New Guinea, 1966–1969*. www.dfat.gov.au/about-us/publications/historical-documents/volume-26/Pages/345-letter-barnes-to-mcmahon.

Dinnen, Sinclair. 'Sentencing, Custom and the Rule of Law in Papua and New Guinea'. *Journal of Legal Pluralism* 20, no. 27 (1988): 19–54. doi.org/10.1080/07329113.1988.10756404.

Doran, Stuart. 'Toeing the Line: Australia's Abandonment of "Traditional" West New Guinea Policy'. *Journal of Pacific History* 36, no. 1 (2001): 5–18. doi.org/10.1080/00223340120049415.

Dorney, Sean. *The Embarrassed Colonialist*. Sydney: Lowy Institute Papers, 2016.

Douglas, Heather and Mark Finnane. *Indigenous Crime and Settler Law: White Sovereignty and Empire*. Basingstoke: Palgrave MacMillan Socio-Legal Studies, 2012. doi.org/10.1111/j.1467-6478.2013.00625.x.

Downs, Ian. *The Australian Trusteeship Papua New Guinea 1945–75*. Canberra: Australian Government Publishing Service, 1980.

Durnian, Lisa. 'Research Brief 21: Whipping as a Criminal Punishment'. *Prosecution Project*, 14 March 2016. prosecutionproject.griffith.edu.au/whipping-as-a-criminal-punishment.

Engle Merry, Sally. 'Legal Pluralism'. *Law & Society Review* 22, no. 5 (1988): 869–96. doi.org/10.2307/3053638.

Essai, Brian. *Papua and New Guinea: A Contemporary Survey*. Melbourne: Oxford University Press, 1961.

Estrich, Susan. *Real Rape*. Cambridge: Harvard University Press, 1987.

Farquharson, John. 'Warwick Smith, George Henry (1916–1999)'. *Obituaries Australia*. oa.anu.edu.au/obituary/warwick-smith-george-henry-1003.

Featherstone, Lisa and Amanda Kaladelfos. *Sex Crimes in the Fifties*. Carlton: Melbourne University Press, 2016. doi.org/10.1017/qre.2017.21.

Finnane, Mark. *Punishment in Australian Society*. Melbourne: Oxford University Press, 1997.

Fitzpatrick, Peter. *Law and State in Papua New Guinea*. London: Academic Press, 1980.

Flynn, Errol. *My Wicked, Wicked Ways*. Melbourne: Heinemann, 1959.

Foster, Hamar, Benjamin L. Berger and A. R. Buck. *The Grand Experiment: Law and Legal Culture in British Settler Societies.* Vancouver: University of British Columbia Press, 2008. doi.org/10.1017/s0829320100009972.

Gammage, Bill. *The Sky Travellers: Journeys in New Guinea 1938–39.* Carlton: Melbourne University Press, 1998.

Garland, David. *Punishment and Modern Society: A Study in Social Theory.* Chicago: University of Chicago Press, 1990. doi.org/10.1017/s0829320100001988.

Genty, Owen. *The Planter.* Wellington: Geebar Enterprises, 2006.

Gilmore, Robert J. and Denis Warner,, eds. *Near North: Australia and a Thousand Million Neighbours.* Sydney: Angus and Robertson, 1948.

Goava, Sinaka Vakai and Patrick Howley. *Crossroads to Justice: Colonial Justice and a Native Papuan.* Madang: Divine Word University Press, 2007.

Goldsworthy, David. *Losing the Blanket: Australia and the End of Britain's Empire.* Carlton: Melbourne University Press, 2002.

Gore, R. T. *Justice versus Sorcery.* Brisbane: Jacaranda Press, 1965.

Gosh, Durba. 'Gender and Colonialism: Expansion or Marginalisation?' *Historical Journal* 47, no. 3 (2004): 739–41. doi.org/10.1017/S0018246X04003930.

Griffiths, A. R. G. 'Capital Punishment in South Australia, 1836–1964'. *Australian and New Zealand Journal of Criminology* 3, no. 4 (1970): 214–22. doi.org/10.1177/000486587000300403.

Halttunen, Karen. *Murder Most Foul: The Killer and the American Gothic Imagination.* Cambridge: Harvard University Press, 1998. doi.org/10.1086/ahr/104.4.1289.

Hardy, Graham. 'Murder Trial of Aro of Rupamanda: Graham Hardy'. *PNG Alumni Association Library.* www.pngaa.net/Library/Aro.htm.

Hasluck, Paul. *A Time for Building: Australian Administration in Papua and New Guinea 1951–1963.* Carlton: Melbourne University Press, 1976.

Hasluck, Paul. *Black Australians: A Survey of Native Policy in Western Australia, 1829–1897.* Melbourne: Melbourne University Press, 1942.

Hay, Douglas, Peter Linebaugh, John G. Rule, E. P. Thompson and Cal Winslow. *Albion's Fatal Tree.* London: A. Lane, 1975.

Hay, Douglas. 'Property, Authority and the Criminal Law'. In *Albion's Fatal Tree*, edited by Douglas Hay, Peter Linebaugh, John G. Rule, E. P. Thompson and Cal Winslow, 17–63. London: A. Lane, 1975.

Healy, Allan M. 'Monocultural Administration in a Multicultural Environment: The Australians in Papua New Guinea'. In *From Colony to Coloniser: Studies in Australian Administrative History*, edited by J. J. Eddy and J. R. Nethercote, 207–24. Sydney: Hale and Iremonger, 1987.

Hemming, Andrew. 'Impermissibly Importing the Common Law into Criminal Codes: Pollock v The Queen'. *James Cook University Law Review* 18, no. 6 (2011): 113–43.

Hess, Michael. '"In the Long Run …" Australian Colonial Labour Policy in the Territory of Papua and New Guinea'. *Journal of Industrial Relations* 25, no. 1 (1983): 51–67. doi.org/10.1177/002218568302500104.

Hilton, Matthew. 'Ken Loach and the Save the Children Film: Humanitarianism, Imperialism, and the Changing Role of Charity in Post-war Britain'. *Journal of Modern History* 87, no. 2 (June 2015): 357–94. doi.org/10.1086/681133.

Howard Association Annual Report, October 1899. Queensland State Library: G 365189—1901, Prison System Reports.

Hudson, W. J. *Australia and the Colonial Question at the United Nations.* Honolulu: East-West Centre Press, 1970.

Hughes, Anuerin. *Billy Hughes: Prime Minister and the Controversial Founding Father of the Australian Labor Party.* Milton: John Wiley & Sons Australia, 2005.

Human Rights Watch. *This Alien Legacy: The Origins of Sodomy Laws in British Colonialism.* New York: Human Rights Watch, 2008.

Hynd, Stacey. '"The Extreme Penalty of the Law": Mercy and the Death Penalty as Aspects of State Power in Colonial Nyasaland, c. 1903–47'. *Journal of East African Studies* 4, no. 3 (2010): 552–9, doi.org/10.1080/17531055.2010.517422.

Hynd, Stacey. 'Killing the Condemned. The Practice and Process of Capital Punishment in British Africa, 1900–1950s'. *Journal of African History* 49, no. 3 (2008): 403–18. doi.org/10.1017/s0021853708003988.

Hynd, Stacey. 'Murder and Mercy: Capital Punishment in Colonial Kenya, ca. 1909–1956'. *International Journal of African Historical Studies* 45, no. 1 (2012): 81–101.

Iacovetta, Franca and Wendy Mitchinson, eds. *On the Case: Explorations in Social History.* Toronto: University of Toronto Press, 1998. doi.org/10.3138/9781442678071.

Independent Investigation Child Sexual Abuse. 'Inquiry—Child Migration Programmes Case Study Public Hearing Transcript Day 7'. 17 July 2018. www.iicsa.org.uk/key-documents/5746/view/public-hearing-transcript-17-july-2018.pdf.

Inglis, Amirah. *The White Women's Protection Ordinance: Sexual Anxiety and Politics in Papua*. London: Sussex University Press, 1975.

Irving, George Marshall. 'Sodeman, Arnold Karl (1899–1936)'. *Australian Dictionary of Biography*. adb.anu.edu.au/biography/sodeman-arnold-karl-8574. Published first in hardcopy 1990.

Jones, Barry, ed. *The Penalty Is Death: Capital Punishment in the Twentieth Century*. Melbourne: Sun Books, 1968.

Jones, Barry. 'The Decline and Fall of the Death Penalty'. In *The Penalty is Death: Capital Punishment in the Twentieth Century*, edited by Barry Jones, 257–71. Melbourne: Sun Books, 1968.

Jury Ordinance of 1907—Jury Ordinance Amendment Ordinance of 1909. Pacific Island Legal Information Institute. www.paclii.org/pg/legis/papua_annotated/joo1907joao01909480/.

Justice Barry. 'The Defence of Provocation'. *Res Judicatea*, no. 35 (1950). www.austlii.edu.au/au/journals/ResJud/1950/35.pdf.

Kent, Alfred James. 'Bignold, Esme Baron'. *NSW Law Almanac 1924*. Sydney: Government Printer, 1924.

Kerr, Martin D. *New Guinea Patrol*. London: Robert Hale, 1973.

Kiki, Albert Maori. *Kiki, Ten Thousand Years in a Lifetime: A New Guinea Autobiography*. Canberra: Cheshire Melbourne, 1968.

Kituai, August Ibrum. *My Gun, My Brother: The World of the Papua New Guinea Colonial Police, 1920–1960*. Honolulu: University of Hawaii Press, 1998. doi.org/10.1086/ahr/105.1.195.

Lal, Brij V. *The Defining Years: Pacific Islands, 1945–65*. Canberra: Division of Pacific and Asian History, The Australian National University, 2005.

Landman, Jane. 'Visualising the Subject of Development: 1950s Government Film Making in the Territories of Papua and New Guinea'. *Journal of Pacific History* 45, no. 1 (2010): 71–88. doi.org/10.1080/00223344.2010.484171.

Langmore, John. 'A Powerful, Formative Experience: 1963–1972'. In *Australians in Papua New Guinea, 1960–1975*, edited by Ceridwen Spark et al. St Lucia: University of Queensland Press, 2014.

Lanham, David, Bronwyn F. Bartal, Robert C. Evans and David Woods. *Criminal Laws in Australia*. Annandale: The Federation Press, 2006.

Lavinas Picq, Manuela. 'Between the Dock and a Hard Place: Hazards and Opportunities of Legal Pluralism for Indigenous Women in Ecuador'. *Latin American Politics and Society* 54, no. 2 (Summer 2012): 1–33. doi.org/10.1111/j.1548-2456.2012.00151.x.

Law Reform Commission of Papua New Guinea. 'Punishment for Wilful Murder'. *Occasional Paper 1*, 1 July 1976.

Lee, David. *Search for Security: The Political Economy of Australia's Post-war Foreign and Defence Policy*. St. Leonards: Allen and Unwin, 1995.

Lennan, Jo and George Williams. 'The Death Penalty in Australian Law'. *Sydney Law Review* 34 (2012): 659–94. www.austlii.edu.au/au/journals/UNSWLRS/2013/12.html.

Loo, Tina. 'Savage Mercy: Native Culture and Modification of Capital Punishment in Nineteenth Century British Columbia'. In *Qualities of Mercy: Justice Punishment and Discretion*, edited by Carolyn Strange, 104–29. Vancouver: University of British Columbia Press, 1996. doi.org/10.59962/9780774854757-007.

Lowe, David, ed. *Australia and the End of Empires: The Impact of Decolonisation in Australia's Near North, 1945–65*. Geelong: Deakin University Press, 1996.

Lowe, David. *Menzies and the 'Great World Struggle': Australia's Cold War, 1948–1954*. Sydney: UNSW Press, 1999.

MacWilliam, Scott. 'Papua New Guinea in the 1940s: Empire and Legend'. In *Australia and the End of Empires: The Impact of Decolonisation in Australia's Near North, 1945–65*, edited by David Lowe, 32–70. Geelong: Deakin University Press, 1996.

Mair, I. P. *Australia in New Guinea*. Carlton: Melbourne University Press, 1970.

Matthews, Jill Julius. *Good and Mad Women. The Historical Construction of Femininity in Twentieth Century Australia*. Sydney: Allen and Unwin, 1984.

McLean, David. 'Australia in the Cold War: A Historiographical Review'. *International History Review* 23, no. 2 (2001): 299–321. doi.org/10.1080/07075332.2001.9640932.

Michele, Foucault. *Discipline and Punish: The Birth of the Prison*. London: Allen Lane, 1977.

Mick Gentleman, 'William Slim Drive Is Set to be Renamed Following a Review Into Place Names in the ACT'. ACT Government. 6 June 2019. www.cmtedd.act.gov.au/open_government/inform/act_government_media_releases/gentleman/2019/place-names-to-meet-community-standards.

Millar, T. B. *Australia in Peace and War: External Relations since 1788*. 2nd ed. Canberra: Australian National University Press, 1991.

Moore, Clive. *New Guinea: Crossing Boundaries and History*. Honolulu: University of Hawaii Press, 2003. doi.org/10.2307/j.ctvsrfkh.

Moss, Tristan. *Guarding the Periphery: The Australian Army in Papua New Guinea, 1951–75*. Cambridge: Cambridge University Press, 2017. doi.org/10.1017/9781108182638.

Murray, J. K. 'The Provisional Administration of the Territory of Papua New Guinea: Its Policy and Problems' [1949]. In *Education and Colonial Control in Papua New Guinea: A Documentary History*, edited by Peter Smith, 161. Melbourne: Longman Cheshire, 1987.

Natives' Contracts Protection Ordinance 1921–1936. Pacific Islands Legal Information Institute. www.paclii.org/pg/legis/newguinea_annotated/ncpo19211936386/.

Native Labour Ordinance, 1911–1927. Pacific Islands Legal Information Institute. www.paclii.org/pg/legis/PG-papua_num_act/nlo19111927202/.

Native Regulation Ordinance, 1908–1930—Native Regulations 1939 (Papua). Pacific Island Legal Information Institute. www.paclii.org/pg/legis/papua_annotated/nro19081930nr1939446/.

Nelson, Hank. 'From Kanaka to Fuzzy Wuzzy Angel'. *Labour History*, no. 35 (1978): 172–88.

Nelson, H. N. 'Murray, Sir John Hubert Plunkett (1861–1940)'. *Australian Dictionary of Biography*. adb.anu.edu.au/biography/murray-sir-john-hubert-plunkett-7711. Published first in hardcopy 1986.

Nelson, Hank. 'Papua and New Guinea'. In *Paul Hasluck in Australian History: Civic Personality and Public Life*, edited by Tom Stannage, Kay Saunders and Richard Nile, 152–69. St Lucia: University of Queensland Press, 1999.

Nelson, Hank. *Papua New Guinea: Black Unity or Black Chaos?* Ringwood: Pelican Penguin, 1972.

Nelson, Hank. 'The Swinging Index: Capital Punishment and British and Australian Administration in Papua and New Guinea, 1888–1945'. *Journal of Pacific History* 13, no. 3 (1978): 130–52. doi.org/10.1080/00223347808572351.

Nelson, Hank. *Taim Bilong Masta: The Australian Involvement with Papua New Guinea*. Sydney: Australian Broadcasting Commission, 1982.

Nelson, Hank. 'The View from the Sub-district'. In *The Defining Years: Pacific Islands, 1945–65*, edited by Brij V. Lal, 34–5. Canberra: Division of Pacific and Asian History, The Australian National University, 2005.

New South Wales Law Reform Commission. *Provocation, Diminished Responsibility and Infanticide*. Discussion Paper 31. Sydney: New South Wales Law Reform Commission, 1993.

Newton, J. E. *Factors Affecting Sentencing Decision in Rape Cases*. Canberra: Australian Institute of Criminology, 1976.

Novak, Andrew. 'Capital Sentencing Discretion in Southern Africa: A Human Rights Perspective on the Doctrine of Extenuating Circumstances in Death Penalty Cases'. *African Human Rights Law Journal* 14, no. 1 (2014): 24–42.

NSW Law Almanac 1930. Sydney: Government Printer, 1930.

NSW Law Almanac 1944. Sydney: Government Printer, 1944.

Ottley, Bruce L. and Jean G. Zorn. 'Criminal Law in Papua New Guinea: Code, Custom and the Courts in Conflict'. *American Journal of Comparative Law* 31, no. 2 (1983): 251–300. doi.org/10.2307/839827.

Percival Wood, Sally. '"Chou Gags Critics in Bandoeng" or How the Media Framed Premier Zhou Enlai at the Bandung Conference, 1955'. *Modern Asian Studies* 44, no. 5 (2010). doi.org/10.1017/S0026749X09990382.

Persse, Michael D. De B. Collins. 'Slim, Sir William Joseph (1891–1970)'. *Australian Dictionary of Biography*. adb.anu.edu.au/biography/slim-sir-william-joseph-11713/text20937. Published first in hardcopy 2002.

Peter Gibbon, Benoit Daviron and Stephanie Barral. 'Lineages of Paternalism: An Introduction'. *Journal of Agrarian Change* 14, no. 2 (2014) 165–89. doi.org/10.1111/joac.12066.

PNG Association of Australia. 'Eugenie (Gene) Vanderiet (30 June 1997)'. Vale, September 1997. www.pngaa.net/Vale/vale_sept97.htm#Gene.

PNG Association of Australia. 'Jan Vanderiet'. Vale, June 2011. www.pngaa.net/Vale/vale_june01.htm#Vanderiet.

PNG Association of Australia. 'Walter (Wally) W Watkins (22 March 1984)'. Vale, June 1984. www.pngaa.net/Vale/vale_june84.htm#Watkins.

Quinlivan, Paul J. 'Phillips, Sir Frederick Beaumont (1890–1957)'. *Australian Dictionary of Biography*. adb.anu.edu.au/biography/phillips-sir-frederick-beaumont-8034. Published first in hardcopy 1988.

R. v. Packett, [1937] HCA 53; (1937) 58 CLR 190 (3 September 1937). High Court of Australia. *AUSTLII*. classic.austlii.edu.au/cgi-bin/sinodisp/au/cases/cth/HCA/1937/53.html?stem=0&synonyms=0&query=%20Packett,%201937.

Report of the United Nations Visiting Mission to the Trust Territories of Nauru and New Guinea, 1962: Report on New Guinea. New York: United Nations Trusteeship Council, 1962. digitallibrary.un.org/record/3935446?ln=en.

Richards, Mike. *The Hanged Man: The Life and Death of Ronald Ryan*. Melbourne: Scribe Publications, 2003.

Rowley, C. D. *The New Guinea Villager: A Retrospect from 1964*. Marrickville: F.W. Cheshire, 1967.

Sakai, Moses. 'PNG and the Politics of the Death Penalty'. *Interpreter*, Lowy Institute, 11 December 2020.

Sarre, Rick. 'Sentencing in Customary or Tribal Settings: An Australian Perspective'. *Federal Sentencing Reporter* 13, no. 2 (2000): 74–8. doi.org/10.2307/20640317.

Scaglion, Richard. 'Kiaps as Kings: Abelam Legal Change in Historical Perspective'. In *Customary Law in Papua New Guinea; A Melanesian View*. Port Moresby: The Law Reform Commission of Papua New Guinea, 1983.

Sinclair, James. *Middle Kingdom: A Colonial History of the Highlands of Papua New Guinea*. Adelaide: Crawford House Publishing, 2016.

Smith v. R. [1957] HCA 3; (1957) 97 CLR 100 (21 January 1957). Australian Legal Information Institute, University of Technology Sydney and University of New South Wales. www5.austlii.edu.au/au/cases/cth/HCA/1957/3.html.

Sodeman v. R. [1936] HCA 75; (1936) 55 CLR 192 (2 April 1936). Australian Legal Information Institute, University of Technology Sydney and University of New South Wales. www.austlii.edu.au/au/cases/cth/HCA/1936/75.html.

Spencer, Margaret. *Doctor's Wife in New Guinea*. Sydney: Angus and Robertson, 1959.

Stannage, Tom, Kay Saunders and Richard Nile, eds. *Paul Hasluck in Australian History: Civic Personality and Public Life*. St Lucia: University of Queensland Press Australian Studies, n.d.

Stewart, Christine. 'Men Behaving Badly: Sodomy Cases in the Colonial Courts of Papua New Guinea'. *Journal of Pacific History* 43, no. 1 (2008): 77–93. doi.org/10.1080/00223340802054693.

Stoler, Ann Laura. *Carnal Knowledge and Imperial Power: Race and the Intimate in Colonial Rule*. Berkley: University of California Press, 2002. doi.org/10.1017/s0165115300020726.

Strange, Carolyn. 'Discretionary Justice: Political Culture and Death Penalty in New South Wales and Ontario, 1890–1920'. In *Qualities of Mercy: Justice, Punishment and Discretion*, edited by Carolyn Strange, 130–65. Vancouver: University of British Columbia Press, 1996. doi.org/10.59962/9780774854757-008.

Summers, Anne. *Damned Whores and God's Police*. Ringwood: Penguin Books, 1994.

Territory of Papua and New Guinea. *House of Assembly Debates*. Seventh Meeting of the First Session, 23 November – 29 November 1965, vol. 1, no. 7, 1965.

Territory of Papua and New Guinea: An Information Folder Prepared by the Department of Territories. Canberra: Department of Territories, 1961.

The Versailles Treaty June 28, 1919: Part I. The Avalon Project: Documents in Law, History and Diplomacy. Yale University. avalon.law.yale.edu/imt/parti.asp.

Tipping, E. W. 'Australians in the Near North'. In *Near North*, edited by Robert J. Gilmore and Denis Warner, 1–54. Sydney: Angus and Robertson, 1948.

Tove Stella, Regis. *Imagining the Other: Representation of the Papua New Guinean Subject*. Honolulu: University of Hawaii Press, 2007. doi.org/10.1515/9780824862923.

United Nations. *Index to Proceedings of the Trusteeship Council*. Fourteenth Session 2 June to 16 July 1954. New York: United Nations Headquarters Library, 1955. library.un.org/sites/library.un.org/files/itp/t14_0.pdf.

United Nations. *Index to Proceedings of the Trusteeship Council*. Eleventh Special Session, 10 April 1961, Twenty-Seventh Session, 1 June to 19 July 1961. New York: United Nations Headquarters Library, 1961. library.un.org/sites/library.un.org/files/itp/t27_0.pdf.

United Nations. *United Nations Charter*. www.un.org/en/about-us/un-charter.

United Nations General Assembly. 'Declaration on the Granting of Independence to Colonial Countries and Peoples'. General Assembly Resolution 1514 (XV). 14 December 1960. www.ohchr.org/en/instruments-mechanisms/instruments/declaration-granting-independence-colonial-countries-and-peoples.

Valverde, Mariana, J. R. Miller, Doug Owram and Shirley Tillotson. 'On the Case: Explorations in Social History: A Roundtable Discussion'. *Canadian Historical Review* 8, no. 1 (2000): 266–92.

Waiko, John Dademo. *A Short History of Papua New Guinea*. 2nd ed. Melbourne: Oxford University Press, 2007.

Wall, David. 'Knights of the Realm in PNG'. Stories by David Wall. 25 September 2013. deberigny.wordpress.com/category/sir-pita-lus/.

Ward, R. Gerard. 'The 1950s and 1960s—An Information Age for the South Pacific Islands'. In *The Defining Years: Pacific Islands, 1945–65*, edited by Brij Lal, 1–17. Canberra: Pacific and Asian History, The Australian National University, 2005.

Waters, Christopher. '"Against the Tide": Australian Government Attitudes to Decolonisation in the South Pacific, 1962–1972'. *Journal of Pacific History* 48, no. 2 (2013): 194–208. doi.org/10.1080/00223344.2013.794576.

Waters, Christopher. 'The Last of Australian Imperial Dreams for the Southwest Pacific: Paul Hasluck, The Department of Territories and a Greater Melanesia in 1960'. *Journal of Pacific History* 51, no. 2 (2016): 169–85. doi.org/10.1080/00223344.2016.1195595.

West, Francis. *Hubert Murray: The Australian Pro-Consul*. Melbourne: Oxford University Press, 1968.

White Women's Protection Ordinance, 1926–1934. Pacific Island Legal Information Institute. www.paclii.org/pg/legis/papua_annotated/wwpo19261934342/.

Wiener, Martin J. *An Empire on Trial: Race, Murder and Justice under British Rule, 1870–1935*. Cambridge: Cambridge University Press, 2009. doi.org/10.3366/brs.2009.0020.

Wolfers, Edward P. *Race Relations and Colonial Rule in Papua and New Guinea*. Brookvale: Australian and New Zealand Book Company, 1975.

Wotherspoon, Garry. 'The Greatest Menace Facing Australia: Homosexuality and the State in NSW during the Cold War'. *Labour History*, no. 56 (May 1989): 15–28.

Wyatt, J. *Guide to Newcomers to Papua-New Guinea by a Port Moresby Housewife*. [Port Moresby]: Country Women's Association, 1957.

Yeates, Anthony. 'The Patrol Officers and Tom Kabu: Power and Prestige in the Purari Delta'. *Journal of Pacific History* 40, no. 1 (2005): 71–90. doi.org/10.1080/00223340500082335.

National Archives of Australia

NAA: A452/1959/4611, item 231528. Administration of Prisons—Policy Papua and New Guinea.

NAA: A452/1959/4611, item 533996. Administration of Prisons—Policy Papua and New Guinea.

NAA: A518, 280/3/2544, item 3309370. Application for Employment—Dr B. Parcen.

NAA: A518, BZ800/1/9, item 3235342. Application of Law and Justice to Home Island Malays—Cocos (Keeling) Islands.

NAA: A9300, Bignold E. B., item 5372360. BIGNOLD ESME BARON, Service Number—139813: Date of Birth—27 Apr 1900: Place of Birth—KIRRIBILLI NSW: Place of Enlistment—MELBOURNE: Next of Kin—BIGNOLD A.

NAA: M331, 8, item 511120. *Capital Punishment [Territory of Papua and New Guinea] 1957–58*.

NAA: A432, 1961/2023, item 1172557. Christmas Island—Administration of Justice.

NAA: A452, 1961/7632. Commutation of Death Sentence on New Guinea Native—Sakul, Commonwealth Department of Territories.

NAA: A452, 1964/3503, item 3541991. Commutation of Death Sentence on Papua and New Guinea Native—Endei.

NAA: A518, CQ840/1/3 PART 1, item 3252669. Commutation of Sentences on Natives in Papua and New Guinea.

NAA: A518, CQ840/1/3 PART 2, item 434881. Commutation of Sentences on Natives in Papua New Guinea.

NAA: A432, 1958/3143, item 7801743. Criminal Code Amendment Ordinance 1907 (Papua) Section 2—Criminal Code Amendment Ordinance 1923–39 (New Guinea) Section 8—Whether 'Recorded' Sentence of Death Can Be Enforced.

NAA: A1200, L27452, item 7572946. Detainees Working on the Corrective Institution Farm at Bomana Near Port Moresby [1958 photograph].

NAA: A4906, 4, item 209114. Fifth Menzies Ministry Second System Cabinet Submissions 91–115.

NAA: A1200, L26884, item 11756539. His Excellency the Governor-General of Australia, Field Marshal Sir William Slim Inspects a Guard of Honour of the Pacific Islands Regiment at Port Moresby in the Territory of Papua New Guinea [photograph].

NAA: K269, 8 MAY 1949 MOHAMMEDI, item 9245201. Incoming Passenger List to Fremantle 'Mohammedi' Arrived 8 May 1949.

NAA: A11099, 1/19, item 12105762. Cabinet Notebook, Notetaker A. S. Brown. Notes of Meetings 4 June 1954 – 27 October 1954.

NAA: A11099, 1/30, item 11584983. Notetaker E. J. Bunting—Notes of Meetings on 30/10/1952 (Cabinet); 7/11/1952 (Cabinet—Continuation of Notes for This Meeting by Notetaker A. S. Brown in item 1/16); 11/11/1952 (Cabinet); 12/11/1952 (Cabinet); 2/12/1952 (Cabinet); and 23/12/1952 (Cabinet).

NAA: A518, A846/6/45 PART 1, item 3272356. Ordinances—Papua New Guinea: Criminal Code Amendment (Papua) Ordinance.

NAA: A518, A846/6/21, item 3272255. Ordinances PNG Amalgamation of the Laws of Papua and New Guinea—The Criminal Code.

NAA: A432, 1964/2543, item 1184765. Papua and New Guinea Wilful Murder—Death Sentence.

NAA: A452, 1961/4256, item 3500477. Petition to United Nations from Kilsyth Communist Party and Others Re: Sentence of Death Passed on PNG Natives.

NAA: A518/A846/1/12, item 107135. Prisons Ordinance—New Guinea.

NAA: B6295, 3514M, item 30905872. Papua New Guinea [photograph].

NAA: A432, 1959/2208, item 7436109. R. v. R. J. Sear—Manslaughter of Male Native Papua New Guinea.

NAA: M332, 194, item 4027630. R. v. Sear Supreme Court of Papua and New Guinea.

NAA: A432, 1956/3371, item 7801327. Territory of Papua and New Guinea—General Question of Sentencing of Native Offenders Convicted of Wilful Murder—Pronounced or Recorded Sentence of Death.

NAA: A4926, 882, item 4361268. Territory of Papua and New Guinea—Sentence of Death on Native Aro, Decision 1035.

NAA: A4926, 754, item 4361140. Territory of Papua and New Guinea—Sentence of Death Recorded against the Native Gaumbu—Decision 889.

NAA: A4926, 1442, item 4361818. Territory of Papua and New Guinea—Sentence of Death on Natives Warira and Bok—No Decision.

NAA: A4906, 205, item 4678943. Territory of Papua and New Guinea—Sentence of Death on the Native Usamando—Decision 207.

Other archival sources

Papers of Ralph Gore, 1930–1964. National Library of Australia.

Greenwell, John. *The Introduction of Western Law into Papua New Guinea*. Unpublished manuscript, given to the author by John Greenwell, former first assistant secretary and director of Papua New Guinea Office Government and Legal Affairs Division, Department of External Territories, 1970–75.

Inglis, Amirah. 'The White Women's Protection Ordinance: A Study in the History of Papua New Guinea, 1926–1934'. MA thesis, The Australian National University, 1972.

Kenneth Read Papers Relating to Teaching Australian School of Pacific Administration (ASOPA) Courses. Australian National University Archives, ANUA444.

Oral history

Barnes, Charles Edward. Interview by Pat Shaw, Parliament's Bicentenary Oral History Project, 19 November 1983. National Library of Australia, TRC 4900/13.

Tyrrell, Murray. Interview by Mel Pratt for the Mel Pratt collection [sound recording], 1974. Transcript. National Library of Australia.

Newspapers

Advertiser (Adelaide, SA)
Advocate (Burnie, TAS)
Age (Melbourne, VIC)
Argus (Melbourne, VIC)
Asia Pacific Report (NZ)
Barrier Miner (Broken Hill, NSW)

British Pathé (London, UK)
Canberra Times (Canberra, ACT)
Cairns Post (Cairns, QLD)
Central Queensland Herald (Rockhampton, QLD)
Charleville Times (Charleville, QLD)
Courier-Mail (Brisbane, QLD)
Leader-Post (Regina Saskatchewan, CAN)
Malay Mail (Kuala Lumpur, MY)
Mercury (Hobart, TAS)
Morning Bulletin (Rockhampton, QLD)
National (Port Moresby, PNG)
New York Times (New York, US)
Papuan Courier (Port Moresby, PNG)
Pacific Islands Monthly (Sydney, NSW)
Pacific Scoop (NZ)
Post-Courier (Port Moresby, PNG)
Queenslander (Brisbane, QLD)
Republic World (Mumbai, IN)
Singleton Argus (Singleton, NSW)
South Pacific Post (Port Moresby, PNG)
St Joseph News-Press (Missouri, US)
Sunday Times (Perth, WA)
Sydney Morning Herald (Sydney, NSW)
Sun-Herald (Sydney, NSW)
Times (London, UK)
West Australian (Perth, WA)
Women's Weekly (AUS)

www.ingramcontent.com/pod-product-compliance
Lightning Source LLC
Chambersburg PA
CBHW051605230426
43668CB00013B/1994